Six Great Reasons to Buy This New Edition of *Short Takes*

If you're wondering why to buy this new edition, here are six good reasons!

1. **Shorter and more readable.** All explanations have been tightened and made clearer while the number of essays remains almost the same.

2. **Twenty-one new essays** (of 46) focus on engaging topical subjects ranging from popular culture and media to science and technology.

3. **Examples clarify distinctions** between revising, editing, and proofreading—and offer reasons for why writers make changes.

4. **Revised chapter introductions** focus more clearly on organization.

5. **Five new images—cartoons and comics**—comment on and enhance the essays, showing how the same analytical skills can be applied to other forms of expression.

6. **New selections reflect diverse perspectives,** including race, culture, technology, and gender.

PEARSON

Short Takes

MODEL ESSAYS FOR COMPOSITION

Eleventh Edition

Elizabeth Penfield
University of New Orleans

PEARSON

Boston Columbus Indianapolis New York San Francisco Upper Saddle River
Amsterdam Cape Town Dubai London Madrid Milan Munich Paris
Montréal Toronto Delhi Mexico City São Paulo Sydney
Hong Kong Seoul Singapore Taipei Tokyo

Senior Sponsoring Editor: Katharine Glynn
Senior Supplements Editor: Donna Campion
Senior Marketing Manager: Sandra McGuire
Production Manager: Ellen MacElree
Project Coordination, Text Design, and Electronic Page Makeup: Integra
Cover Designer/Manager: Wendy Ann Fredericks
Cover Photos: Clockwise from top left: © Jessica Cangiano/
Getty Images; © Andre Hoffman/Look Foto/Glow Images;
© Fotalia; © Dreamstime; and © iStockphoto
Senior Manufacturing Buyer: Roy L. Pickering, Jr.
Printer and Binder: Edwards Brothers, Inc.
Cover Printer: Lehigh Phoenix

Credits and acknowledgments borrowed from other sources and reproduced, with permission, in this textbook appear on pages 261–263.

Library of Congress Cataloging-in-Publication Data

Penfield, Elizabeth, 1939–
 Short takes : model essays for composition/Elizabeth Penfield.—11th ed.
  p. cm.
 ISBN-13: 978-0-205-17137-8
 ISBN-10: 0-205-17137-0
 1. College readers. 2. English language—Composition and exercises.
3. English language—Rhetoric—Problems, exercises, etc. 4. Report writing—
Problems, exercises, etc. I. Title.
PE1417.P43 2012
808'.0427—dc23

                                                2012017749

10 9 8 7 6 5 4 3—EDW—15 14 13

ISBN 13: 978-0-205-17137-8
ISBN 10:   0-205-17137-0

CONTENTS

3   Define   84

4 Compare and Contrast   **109**

5 Divide and Classify   **132**

THEMATIC GUIDE

Science and Technology

Language and Education

Popular Culture and the Media

PREFACE

When the first edition was only an idea, I was teaching freshman English in a structured program that emphasized rhetorical modes and final product. My dilemma then was one many teachers still face: how to incorporate the modes with the tangle of the writing process. But once I focused on the aims of discourse, the modes fell into place as means, not ends, and as patterns of organization used in combination, not just singly. There remained the problem of the textbooks: many contained essays of imposing length and complexity that intimidated and overwhelmed students. Any short essay was apt to be an excerpt. *Short Takes* was my solution. This eleventh edition still reflects the rhetorical framework of the first one, but it is flexible. You can ignore it and use the thematic table of contents, but if you find the modes useful you'll see them here.

This edition remains a collection of short, readable, interesting essays written by professionals and students, and the commentary continues to focus on reading and writing as interrelated activities. Much, however, is new:

- revised and shortened "Freeze Frame," the opening section that introduces students to critical reading and the writing process, including explanations of how to get started, revise, edit, and proofread
- increased emphasis in "Freeze Frame" illustrate how to read critically and how to revise
- completely revised and shortened chapter introductions that highlight the most important points and are therefore more accessible to students
- fresh topics and 21 new essays that engage students by analyzing subjects as varied as the effects of technology and the hazards of genetic testing
- emphasis on subordinate modes so students can more clearly understand how various modes are used singly and together
- five new drawings—cartoons and comic strips, seven in all—that comment on or add to several of the essays
- revised chapter on argument (Chapter 8) that includes both individual and paired essays

- two sets of three essays each that present differing perspectives on timely subjects—such as a sense of place—so students can respond with their own analytical essays
- many writing assignments that include the use of the Internet, a ready resource for most students

At the same time, features that teachers particularly liked are still here:

- chapter introductions directed to students that emphasize the writing process (as well as the kinds of choices and decisions all writers face)
- short, engaging, accessible essays and helpful introductions to each rhetorical pattern
- complete essays, not excerpts
- information about the author, context for the essay, and the essay's notable stylistic features
- questions on organization, ideas, technique, and style that engage students to think critically about the readings
- a large number of topics for writing journal entries and essays
- a variety of authors, styles, and subjects
- emphasis on how the rhetorical modes interact with invention and the entire writing process
- an alternate thematic table of contents
- an *Instructor's Manual* that includes: key words and phrases for each essay; suggestions for group work; writing prompts keyed to the thematic table of contents; and additional suggestions for each rhetorical mode and for comparing two or more of the selections

Chapters 1–7 build on previous ones and lead to the one that follows, culminating in argument—but argument with a difference. The chapter on argument is a basic introduction, an extension of the kind of emphasis on thesis and evidence that exists throughout the text. All the supplementary information—the chapter introductions, background information, notes on style, questions on the essays, and suggestions for writing—balance process and product, working on the premise that they are so closely interrelated that one cannot be considered without the other.

As always, I welcome responses from students and teachers, along with suggestions for the future. You can e-mail me at epenfiel@uno.edu or care of Longman's English Editor at Pearson, 51 Madison Avenue, New York, NY 10010.

The Essays

Because most of the papers assigned in composition courses fall into the 400- to 1000-word range, most of the essays are short—about 1000 words or so—and therefore lend themselves to scrutiny and emulation. A few are longer and rely on the kind of research that students may be asked to carry out. Most illustrate the kind of prose expected from college students—analyzing and incorporating sources. And a few illustrate the problem–solution organization often found in argumentative pieces. All of the essays are complete pieces, not excerpts.

To write is to choose among alternatives, to select the most appropriate organization, persona, diction, and techniques for a given audience and purpose. Each of the essays included in this edition was chosen because it exemplifies each author's choices, and the apparatus emphasizes those choices and alternatives. The essays, therefore, serve as illustrative models of organization and stylistic techniques available to the writer. The essays were also chosen because their authors represent different genders, ages, and cultures. As a result, the subjects of the essays are accessible and their perspectives are lively, qualities that also allow them to serve as sources of invention, as jumping-off places for students to develop their own ideas in their own styles.

Rhetorical Modes and the Aims of Discourse

Anyone who has used a reader with essays arranged by mode has probably run into two problems: first, few essays are pure examples of a single mode; second, most collections of essays treat argument—an aim of writing—as though it were the equivalent of description, comparison/contrast, and so on. *Short Takes* addresses these inconsistencies by emphasizing the difference between mode—how an essay is organized—and purpose—how an essay is intended to affect the reader—and by pointing out how writing frequently blends two or more modes.

The essays here are grouped according to the *primary* rhetorical pattern that guides their organization; the questions that follow each essay point out the subordinate modes. As for the aims of discourse, the essays represent the various purposes for writing. The writers' self-expressive, informative, and persuasive purposes are underscored in the discussion questions. In addition, the apparatus connects academic writing and the kind of writing found outside the classroom.

Apparatus for Reading and Writing

Chapters 1 through 8 begin with a brief introduction that depicts the mode or purpose under discussion, showing how it can be used in formal essays and in practical, everyday writing tasks. The introductions point out how the modes can be shaped by considerations of audience, purpose, particular strategies, thesis, and organization, ending with advice on finding a subject, exploring a topic, and drafting a paper. This division of the writing process approximates the classic one of invention, arrangement, and style but is not intended to imply that these are separate stages.

To emphasize both what a text says and how it says it, each essay in Chapters 1 through 8 is preceded by background information on the author and the text and a brief discussion of a stylistic strategy. Two sets of questions—"Organization and Ideas" and "Technique and Style"—follow each essay, along with ideas for journal entries and essays. Throughout, process and product, as well as reading and writing, are interrelated, emphasizing the recursive nature of the act of writing.

"Suggestions for Writing" follow each essay and contain options for both journal entries and essays, all related by theme, organization, or ideas to the work that has just been read. The assignments allow a good deal of flexibility: Some lend themselves to general information or personal experience, some to research papers, many to group work (outlined in the *Instructor's Manual*), some to the classic technique of imitation.

Whether working alone or in groups, once students select their subjects, they will find flipping back to the chapter introductions helpful. There, "Exploring the Topic" shapes questions so that no matter what type of paper they are writing, students can generate information. "Drafting the Paper" then helps organize the material and points out some of the pitfalls and advantages inherent in a particular mode or aim.

The index includes key terms as well as author names and essay titles, but the text is essentially a reader, not a handbook. That's a conscious decision. Discussions of usage and documentation are best left, I think, to the individual teacher.

The Instructor's Manual

An *Instructor's Manual* (ISBN 978-0-205-18455-2) includes additional writing assignments, key words and phrases, responses to the questions, and teaching suggestions for both the questions and the longer writing assignments. The manual also contains additional writing prompts at the end of each chapter for the mode or aim under discussion as well as for comparing and evaluating the essays. You'll also see an appendix that has writing prompts for the text's Thematic Guide.

Acknowledgments

I have many to thank for their help in bringing this book to publication: Katharine Glynn, Rebecca Gilpin, Cheryl Wilson, Jenny Bevington, Teresa Ward, Hope Rajala, Leslie Taggart, Karen Helfrich, Liza Rudneva, and Lynn Huddon, for their able assistance with past editions; the students and their teachers for their contributions to this edition; and Theodora Hill for her sound recommendations, patience, and help with the more mundane aspects of preparing a manuscript. The following reviewers all provided guidance and advice that improved the manuscript: Marie Eckstrom, Rio Hondo College; Marion G. Heyn, Los Angeles Valley College; Brain Hill, Columbia College-Lake of the Ozarks Campus; Theodore Johnston, El Paso Community College; Peggy Redmond, Piedmont Virginia Community College.

ELIZABETH PENFIELD

Freeze Frame
Reading and Writing

In filmmaking, a "short take" is a brief scene filmed without interruption. Similarly, short essays, articles, and editorials—even cartoons and ads—quickly make their points. Those are the kinds of texts you will find in this book, short pieces that explain, argue, express the writer's opinions, or simply entertain.

Just as the examples collected here are short takes, this essay is a freeze-frame, as though you had stopped the film on one shot to get a better look. So, too, this essay will stop and take a close-up look at what goes on when you read and write.

Reading Critically

A skilled reader interacts with the words on the page: reshaping, evaluating, selecting, analyzing. After all, you have your own world—everything you have experienced, from your first memory to your most recent thought—all of which you bring to what you read.

An essay analyzing why people like beaches may remind you of beaches you know and pleasurable associations. As you begin to read the essay, you discover that the writer's associations are also pleasant ones that reinforce yours. You read on, constantly reassessing your ideas about the essay as you add more and more information to your first impression. Now and then, you may hit a sentence that at first doesn't make much sense, so you stop, perhaps to look up an unfamiliar word, perhaps to go back and review a previous statement, then read on, again reevaluating your ideas about what the author is saying and what you think of it.

The result is analytical, critical reading—not critical in the sense of judging harshly but critical in the sense of questioning, weighing

1

evidence, evaluating, comparing your world to the one the writer has created on the page.

While you read, you should:

- scribble
- underline
- question
- challenge
- analyze .
- evaluate

Reading critically with pen or pencil in hand will give you a fuller appreciation of what you read and a better understanding of the techniques the writer used to create the essay.

Reading Oliver Sacks' "When Music Heals Body and Soul"   To illustrate critical reading, here's an annotated example from the introduction to the essay that appears on page 188. There it's preceded by information about the author and publication, so you'd know Oliver Sacks is a physician and neurologist and that his essay appeared in *Parade*, a Sunday newspaper insert aimed at a general audience. Even so, you might suspect you'll encounter some difficulty because Sacks' experience differs from yours. His title gives you a general idea about his subject and suggests a causal relationship. You might think, "How can music heal the body? Soul, maybe, but body?" Then as you start to read the essay, you might make marginal notes similar to the following ones. The result would be an analysis of Sacks's introduction to the essay, giving you a good sense of direction for what follows.

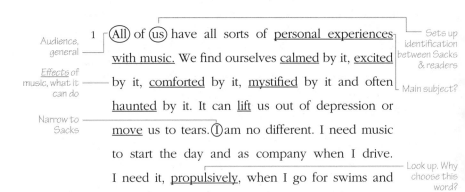

runs. I need it, finally, to still my thoughts when I retire, to <u>usher</u> me into the world of dreams.

Good verb

Move to narrative, explaining what happened — 2   But it was only when I became a patient myself that I experienced a <u>physical need for music.</u>

Narrows subject

Cause —— A <u>bad fall</u> while climbing a mountain in Norway had left me incapacitated by damage to the nerves

Effects —— and muscles of one leg. After surgery to repair the torn tendons in my leg, I settled down to await some return of function in the torn nerves.

3   With the leg effectively paralyzed, I <u>lost all</u> —— *Effects*
<u>sense of its existence</u>—indeed, I seemed to <u>lose the very</u> <u>idea</u> <u>of moving it.</u> The leg stayed nonfunctional for the longest 15 days of my life.

Effects of paralysis & no music —— These days were made longer and grimmer because there was <u>no music</u> in the hospital. —— *Back to music*
Radio reception was bad. Finally, a friend brought me a tape recorder along with a tape

Classical —— of one of my favorite pieces: the <u>Mendelssohn</u> _ *Sacks is losing me here—don't know music*
<u>*Violin Concerto.*</u>

Effects of Concerto — 4   Playing this over and over <u>gave me great plea-sure</u> and a <u>general sense of being alive</u> and <u>well.</u> But the nerves in my damaged leg were still healing. Two weeks later, I began to get small twitches

Look up —— in the previously <u>flaccid</u> muscle and larger sudden, involuntary movements.

5   Strangely, however, I had no impulse to walk. I could barely remember how one would go about walking—until, unexpectedly, a day or two later, *Cause. Music in mind (soul)*
the <u>Violin Concerto played itself in my mind.</u> —— *heals body.*

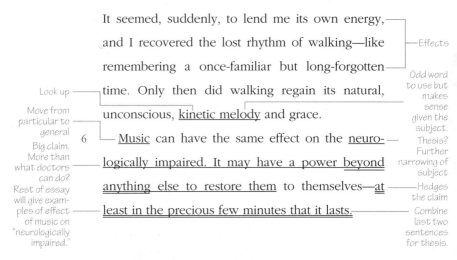

Identifying the Purpose   Whether business letter, lab report, journal entry, news story, poem, or essay, all focus on a subject, address a reader, and have a point. All, too, have a purpose and a style; they are written for specific reasons and in a certain way. You can explore how the writer uses these elements by using the familiar journalistic *who? what? where? when? how? why?*, questions perhaps more familiar when used to spark ideas for writing. Yet these questions can be equally useful for reading, and thinking about them will help you analyze what you read.

If you were to apply those questions to Oliver Sacks' opening paragraphs, here is how the journalistic questions might apply:

- **To whom is an essay addressed?** Sacks' "all of us" suggests a general audience.
- **What is the writer's main point?** "I experienced a physical need for music."
- **Where and when does the action take place?** "When I became a patient"
- **How is the piece organized?** It moves from "I" (Sacks) to the general statement "Music can have the same effect on the neurologically impaired."
- **Why is it structured that way?** The organization allows Sacks to place his unique experience into a larger context that his readers can identify with—the power of music.

Many, many more inquiries can be spun off these seemingly simple questions, and they are useful tools for exploring an essay.

Looking for the Point   In much of the reading we do, we are looking for information. The election coverage reported in the newspaper, the syllabus for a course, and a set of directions all exemplify this kind of reading, but reading for information and reading for comprehension are as different as a vitamin pill and a five-course dinner.

The title of an essay is a good place to start because a title can:

*   **Announce a subject:** As in Sacks' "When Music Heals Body and Soul"
*   **Imply the subject:** The healing power of music
*   **Set the tone:** The writer's attitude toward the subject, a serious one that suits the subject
*   **State or imply the thesis:** The assertion the author is making about the subject

As for other essays, you don't need to turn to an essay titled "Why English Professors Love Country Music" to figure out its subject and what it has to say about it. Some titles focus clearly on their topic, as in "Living on Tokyo Time." Still others tip you off to the author's tone—"Have Fun" suggests a humorous narrative.

Knowing or at least having a hint about the subject is the first step to discovering the thesis. The first paragraph or set of paragraphs that acts as an introduction will also help you deduce a tentative version. Sometimes the writer places the thesis in the first paragraph or introduction or even in the last paragraph, but sometimes a bare-bones version appears in the title: "Vote for X," "Join the Marines," or "Spay Pets." If you don't spot a thesis in the title or first few paragraphs, you should still write down a tentative version of what it may be so that you focus on what follows, an idea against which you can test other ideas.

If the thesis isn't readily identifiable, you can find it by marking key sentences and then mentally composing a statement that covers those ideas. Even then, you may well find that someone else who reads the essay comes up with a different thesis statement. And you both may be right.

What's happening here? If you think about how slippery words are and the different experiences that different readers bring to an essay, you can begin to see why there's more than one "correct" thesis. If you were to give the same essay to ten critical readers, you would find that their versions of the thesis differ but overlap. But sometimes writers unwittingly set snares, making it easy to mistake a fact for a thesis. Keep in mind that a thesis is both a sentence and an assertion—a value judgment—so you can avoid these traps. "The average American watches a lot of TV" states a fact; "Television rots the minds of its viewers" takes a stand.

Recognizing Patterns of Development   Once you've nailed down a thesis, go a step further to examine how that thesis is developed. Writers depend on various patterns of thought or modes of thinking that are almost innate.

- To tell a joke is to narrate.
- To convey what friendships are like is to define, describe, and use examples.
- To decide which among many courses to take is to divide and classify.
- To figure out which car is better is to compare and contrast.
- To analyze the steps involved in researching a topic is to use process analysis.
- To analyze a baseball team's successful season is to weigh cause and effect.

Narration, description, example, division and classification, comparison and contrast, process, cause and effect, and definition are the natural modes of thinking on which writers rely.

These patterns of thought provide the structure of an essay. A piece on the ethics of using prisoners to test new medicines might open with a brief narrative that sets the scene, go on to define what kinds of medicines are involved, and then explain the effects of such experiments on the prisoners, the development of new drugs, and society's concept of ethics. As you read, you should note each type of mode the writer uses so you can more fully understand how the thesis is developed and how the essay is organized. Though you may find an essay uses many types of modes, it's likely that one predominates.

From Reading to Writing

What you see on the printed page resembles the writer's efforts about as much as a portrait resembles the real person. You don't see all the beginnings and stops, the crumpled paper, the false starts, the notes, the discarded ideas, or the changed words. Instead, you have a finished piece—the result of the writer's choices. Yet the process most writers go through to produce their essays resembles your own.

Stated concisely, this book reinforces a basic assumption: Reading and writing are highly individual processes that are active, powerful, and interrelated ways to discover meaning. To write, then, is to create and structure a world; to read is to become part of someone else's. And just as reading makes a better writer, writing makes a better reader.

The Rough Draft: Getting Started

Whether you're working on an assigned topic or one of your own, a blank sheet of paper or an empty computer screen can be a terrifying thing, so how should you begin? Generating ideas isn't as hard as it may seem. You can try

> using ideas from your journal
> creating clusters of ideas
> writing whatever comes to mind
> asking questions
> working with a list
> discussing ideas with your classmates

Journal   A journal provides a good place to comment on what you read or discuss in class. An essay that argues the minimum wage should be raised might make you think about your own experience and the jobs you've had in the past and now. But you need to go beyond your own experience; jot down some questions that put your experience into a larger context so that you don't focus only on yourself. Flesh out answers to the questions, and you will have the makings of an essay.

Clusters   On a blank sheet of paper, start by putting your topic in the middle, for example "Raising the Minimum Wage." Then, scattered around the page, write what you need to know and your ideas. The initial result may look like this:

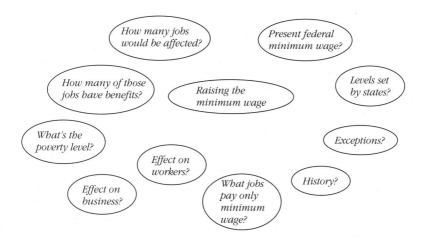

Analyzing what's on paper by linking like items, you find that many questions can be grouped under "facts" and a few under "speculation." Now you need to do research. You can go to the Internet to gather answers from sites such as the U.S. Department of Labor's www.dol.gov/esa/minwage/america.htm. Armed with answers, you are in a position to draw a tentative conclusion. Then you can come up with a working thesis and more questions to research.

Writing   Without stopping to think analytically, start writing about your subject. Some people find it helpful to set a timer for, say, five minutes. After that time, stop, read what you have written, and then in one sentence sum it up. Take that sentence as the lead for your next timed writing, and again, stop and sum up. Within an hour or so, you will have written your way into a working thesis and probably some topic sentences for paragraphs.

Asking Questions   Explore and develop your topic by using the standard journalistic questions: *who? what? where? when? how? why?*

> *Who* am I writing this for? *Who* is my audience?
> *What* is my main idea? *What* is my point?
> *Where* is the evidence for my point?
> *When* is that evidence sufficient?
> *How* is my thesis relevant?
> *Why* is what I say believable?

Or use the various patterns of development as strategies for expanding and generating ideas.

> How can minimum wage jobs be *described?* How many businesses or workers fit the category?
> What *examples* work well?
> What are the key terms that need to be *defined?* How *minimum* is minimum?
> What kind of jobs are involved? How can they be *classified?*
> What would be the *effects* of raising the wage? On businesses? On workers? On the economy?
> How does the present minimum wage *compare* to those in the past in terms of buying power?
> What short *narrative* would work as an introduction?

These strategies provide notes to help work out a thesis as well as come up with ideas that can be turned into lead sentences for paragraphs.

Listing Experienced writers sometimes work from a list of their ideas, reworking it by numbering each one to organize and rank its importance. No list is sacred, however, and often what was first most important may later give way to a more powerful point. Outlining is a variation of this strategy but some reject it as too restricting or too inflexible.

Discussing This method is the most obvious, but it works best if some written record of the discussion is kept. If your class uses peer groups, then you can take turns keeping notes. Then with notes in hand, you can clarify ideas and add to them.

At this beginning stage, you're brainstorming, coming up with ideas and bouncing them off each other so that you can figure out what you are trying to say. Figuring out how you want your reader to respond, shaping your ideas, organizing, and then polishing them can come later. Now you just want ideas to organize into a rough draft.

Revising, Editing, and Proofreading

Revising, editing, and proofreading are three different stages of the writing process, but they don't necessarily occur as a sequence. If you had a rough draft for an essay arguing for a federal speed limit, you would be revising if you moved paragraphs around or added examples or narrowed your thesis—all major changes. If your writing group suggested shifts or substitutions, that would be editing. And when your essay is ready to be turned in, then you would check it carefully for spelling and punctuation—proofreading. The process appears to be linear, but it's fluid: while revising, you might correct a misspelled word; while proofreading, you might add another example or change a sentence.

Major revision is often so messy that it's hard to reproduce as an example, but here's how a previous draft of paragraph 4 on page 5 was revised:

1 *Original:* Knowing or at least having a hint

2 about the subject is the first step to discovering

3 an essay's thesis. The first paragraph or set of

4 paragraphs that acts as an introduction will also

deduce ────── *version*

5 help you form a tentative thesis. Sometimes the

6 writer places the thesis in the first paragraph or

or even in the last ¶ ─
7   introduction, but sometimes a bare-bones version

8   ~~of the thesis~~ appears in the title. If ~~you see it,~~

add examples

that's where it is, ─
9   ~~you should~~ mark it. If you don't spot a thesis,

in the title or first few ¶s

what it may be on ─
10   you should still write down a ~~tentative version~~ of

working idea

11   ~~your own~~ so that you ~~have a~~ focus ~~for~~ what ~~is to~~

on

12   follow, an idea against which you can test other

13   ideas.

Lines 3, 5, 6, 8, 9, 10, and 11: unnecessary words cut
Line 5: more precise word substituted; wording changed to avoid repeating *thesis*
Line 7: idea of where thesis placed expanded, examples added, wording made more precise
Line 10: changed for greater clarity; "working idea" to avoid repetition
Line 11: emphasizes tentative version of thesis may change; noun replaced by verb for emphasis

If you are like most writers, your first draft won't look much like the finished work, so don't be afraid to be messy. Double space so you leave lots of room for scribbles. When you revise you're focusing on

Thesis
Ideas
Audience
Organization

Reread your draft, marking the main ideas and checking them to make sure they are related to and support your initial thesis. Then as you refine your thesis, check the main ideas again.

When you shift to proofreading, hone in on clarity, style, and matters of usage and punctuation. Read the paper out loud to check for repetition and sentence variety, and watch out for overusing *I*. Make sure you check your spelling and reexamine your punctuation. You don't want your credibility as a writer questioned because of a misspelling or vagrant semicolon.

The Writing Process

Far from following a recipe, you will find that writing is like driving a car while at the same time trying to impress the passengers, talk on the cell phone, read a road map, recognize occasional familiar landmarks, follow scrawled and muttered directions, and watch for and listen to all the quirks of the car and other drivers. You know vaguely where you are going and how you want to get there, but the rest is risk and adventure. With work and a number of dry runs, you can smooth out the trip so that the passengers fully appreciate the pleasure of the drive and the satisfaction of reaching the destination. That is the challenge the writer faces, a challenge that demands critical reading as well as effective writing.

POINTERS FOR READING

1. **Settle in.** Together with a dictionary and pen or pencil, find a comfortable place to read.
2. **Think about the title.** What sort of expectations do you have about what will follow? Can you identify the subject? A thesis?
3. **Look for a specific focus.** What may be the essay's thesis? At what point does the introduction end and the body of the essay begin? What questions do you have about the essay so far?
4. **Think about the intended reader or readers.** How would you describe the intended audience?
5. **Look for a predominant pattern of organization.** What patterns or modes does the writer use to develop important ideas?
6. **Identify the conclusion.** Where does the conclusion begin? How does it end the essay? How does it affect you?
7. **Evaluate the essay.** Did the essay answer the questions you had about it? How effective was the support for the main ideas? Did the writer's choice of words fit the audience? Why did the essay affect you as it did?

Pointers for Writing and Revising

1. **Settle in.** Start by jotting down words that represent a general idea of your subject. As words cross your mind, write them down so that at this point you have a vague focus.

2. **Focus.** Generate ideas by using your journal, clusters, timed writing, questions, strategies, listing, discussing—whatever works for you. Review your ideas and come up with a working thesis.

3. **Reread.** Go over what you've written, looking for sentences that state an opinion. Mark them in some way (a highlighter is useful). These sentences can become topic sentences that lead paragraphs and therefore help organize the ideas. Work up those sentences and your tentative thesis into a rough draft.

4. **Organize what's there.** Go through the draft asking questions: What would make a good introduction? A good conclusion? What order best suits what's in between? What examples can you find? Where would they work best?

5. **Think about purpose.** As you reread, think about the kind of effect the paper should have on readers. Does it explain something to them? Argue a cause? Entertain? Some combination of purposes?

6. **Think about the readers.** What do they know about the subject? The answer to this question may help cut out some information; and what they don't know can be a guide to what needs to be included. Do they have a bias for or against the thesis? The answer will reveal whether those biases need to be accounted for and suggest how to do that.

7. **Revise.** You've probably been revising all along, but at this point you can revise more thoroughly and deeply. You know your purpose, audience, and thesis—all of which will help you organize your paper more effectively.

8. **Proofread.** Look for surface errors and check spelling and punctuation. Run your text through the spelling checker, but question anything offered as a substitute—it may be the wrong word. As for punctuation, if you have a grammar checker on your computer, try it. It may be useful, but a handbook of grammar and usage will be much more helpful because the explanations are fuller with lots of examples. Just look up the key word in the handbook's index.

Describe and Narrate

The start of Lori Jakiela's "You'll Love the Way We Fly" puts the reader in her shoes and space:

1   I'm in the galley, making coffee. I try to look busy, not in the mood to talk or help. This is the fourth leg of a six-leg day, and already I'm tired. I immerse myself in counting and recounting stacks of styrofoam cups, tightening the handles on metal coffee pots, scrubbing the steel galley counter until I can see my face, distorted and greenish in the plane's fluorescent light, eyes flecked with dried mascara.

2   I hear him coming before I can see him: the rustle of his nylon bag, brushing against seat backs and the heads of other passengers. He is old, thin. He plops the bag on the floor of the emergency exit row, right across from where I'm standing. I'm engrossed now in stocking Cokes into the beverage cart. I watch him from behind the galley wall, a talent all flight attendants learn, covert ways to size people up.

Immediately you know Jakiela is a flight attendant and passengers are boarding the plane, but description gives that information life—the tasks she is carrying out, the way she looks, and the passenger's progress down the aisle. And with her last sentence, she sets the focus for the narrative to follow. The details add up to a passenger who will be trouble, sets up a conflict, and implys an eventual resolution—her "sizing up."

Essays use description to bring their subjects to life so that the reader can see and understand them, but for that description to have a point it often supports a **narrative,** a story. All the essays that follow use description and narration. All present conflicts, build to a point, and spring from personal experience—from the something that happened.

How can you shape description for different purposes and readers? If, like Jakiela, you want to convey the impact of a chance meeting, you would be writing **exposition**[1] and your purpose would

---

[1]Words printed in boldface are defined under "Useful Terms" at the end of each introductory section.

be expository. When you read the rest of Jakiela's essay, you'll see her focus is clearly on her subject: She is the narrator, telling you the story, analyzing it, and explaining it to you.

Jakiela writes for a broad audience, one directly or indirectly familiar with commercial flights. In general, you address the same sort of audience in your own writing. You have a good idea about what your readers do and do not know. Other essays in this chapter show ways to engage readers who are unfamiliar with a subject: Flavius Stan tells of a Christmas in Romania; Magdoline Asfahani writes about her heritage; Mary Roach shows us a "brain bank." All depend on description, details, and comparisons to explain the unfamiliar.

It also helps to know how your readers may feel about your subject and how you want them to feel. How you want them to feel is a matter of **tone,** your attitude toward the subject and the audience. Mary Roach's subject—that brain bank—would put off many a reader but she uses humor to connect with her audience.

How can you explore your subject?   *Who? What? Where? When? How? Why?*—all are standard questions used in journalism, and they can help you write narration. *What happened?* That's the essential question for narrative, and you'll probably find that the greater part of your essay supplies the answer. *How* and *why* will probably figure in as well, and *who* is obviously essential. But it's easy to neglect *where* and *when.*

If you think of both *where* and *when* as the **setting,** as ways to set the scene, you can remember them more easily and perhaps put them to good use. Jakiela's setting is the plane's interior that also contains the ill passenger. Flight attendant, passenger, and compartment supply a setting that builds the readers' interest in what will happen next.

How important are details?   Details drive description and narration. Note how many details are in the paragraphs by Jakiela, most of which are **concrete details:** *styrofoam* cups, *metal* coffee pots, *steel* counter. Nor is she satisfied with **abstract words.** She tells us her face is "distorted," an abstract word that has different meanings to different people, so she gives us a concrete sense of what the word means—"greenish in the plane's flourescent light, eyes flected with dried mascara."

How can you make details effective?   The words a writer chooses determine whether the description is more **objective** or **subjective,**

whether its tone is factual or impressionistic. Although total objectivity is impossible, description that leans toward the objective is called for when the writer wants to focus on the subject as opposed to emotional effect, on what something is rather than how it felt.

The second paragraph of Jakiela's essay presents an objective account of the passenger: "I hear him coming before I can see him: the rustle of his nylon bag, brushing against seat backs and the heads of other passengers. He is old, thin. He plops the bag on the floor of the emergency exit row, right across from where I'm standing." But then the next paragraph shifts:

> His hair is gray, and saliva has settled into the corners of his mouth. He holds a filthy handkerchief to his nose. He is coughing, a deep-lunged cough, the kind that fades into a feathery wheeze then begins again, a terrifying, endless loop. A pack of Marlboros is tucked into his left sock.

The more subjective description has an emotional effect.

What is the role of comparisons? Take any object and try to describe what it looks, feels, smells, sounds, and tastes like, and you'll quickly find yourself shifting over to comparisons. Comparisons enrich description in that they can:

- produce an arresting image
- explain the unfamiliar
- make a connection with the reader's own experience
- reinforce the major point in the essay

Comparing the unfamiliar to the familiar makes what is being described more real. The term *World Wide Web* evokes an electronic spider web that encompasses the globe. The image is a metaphor, and often comparisons take the form of **metaphor, simile,** or **allusion.**

Simile and *metaphor* both draw a comparison between dissimilar things; the terms differ in that a simile uses a comparative word such as *like* or *as*. Metaphor is often more arresting because it is a direct equation. If you were writing and got stuck—the classic writer's block—you might describe your state as "sinking in the quicksand of words."

Unfortunately, the first comparisons that often come to mind can be overworked ones known as **clichés:** *green as grass, hot as hell, mad* *as a hornet, red as a rose,* and the like. You can guard against them by being suspicious of any metaphor or simile that sounds familiar.

Analogy is another form of comparison. Think of it as a metaphor that is extended beyond a phrase into several sentences or a paragraph. You can understand how that can happen if you think of a metaphor for the way you write. Some may imagine a roller coaster; others might think of having to manage a busy switchboard; and for some it may be trying to build a house without having any blueprints or knowing what materials are needed. No matter which image, you can tell that it will take more than a sentence or two to develop the metaphor into an analogy.

What is the role of conflict?   Narratives are structured around a **conflict.** In its simplest form, conflict is x versus y, Superman versus the Penguin, the Roadrunner versus Wile E. Coyote. But rarely does conflict exist in such a clear-cut way. Put real people in place of any of those names, and you begin to understand that what seemed so simple is not; the defense versus the prosecution, a Republican candidate versus a Democrat—these conflicts are complex. The issues become even more complex when you substitute ideas, such as reality versus illusion, a distinction that even a postcard can blur (how many of us have been disappointed when a scene didn't live up to its photograph?). Even distinguishing good from evil isn't always clear, as the debates over capital punishment and abortion constantly remind us. When a writer explores the complexity involved in a conflict, the essay gains depth and substance, making the reader think. That exploration can be direct, such as naming the opposing forces, or indirect—implying them.

On the surface, Jakiela's conflict is *external*, flight attendant vs. passenger. But the conflict is *internal* as well: Jakiela feels repulsed yet sympathetic. When you read the entire essay, you'll discover other conflicts as well.

How do you choose a point of view?   A not-so-obvious question about any narrative is "Who tells it?" This question identifies the **point of view,** the perspective from which the narrative is related. Probably the first pronoun that comes to mind is *I*, first-person singular, and that's a good choice if you want your readers to identify with you and your angle on the narrative you're relating. When a reader sees first person, an automatic psychological identification takes place; you see Jakiela's passenger through her eyes. That sort of identification is strongest if you, like Jakiela, are part of the action. Obviously, there's a huge difference between "I was there" and "I heard about it."

But using first person can be a hazard, and that's why at some point in some classroom, you have probably been warned off using *I.* There are at least three reasons: it's easy to overuse the pronoun; it can modify your purpose in a way you hadn't intended; and it can lead to an overly informal tone. If you were to take a look at your first draft for an essay you wrote using *I,* odds are you used it too frequently. The result is apt to be short, choppy sentences that are similar in structure—subject (*I*) followed by a verb and its complement (the word or words that complete the sense of the verb). That's fine for a first draft, and you can revise your way out of the problem. You *need* to revise because too many *I*'s can shift the focus so that what becomes important is you, not your subject. Your tone may also change, becoming more informal than the assignment calls for, which is why you don't see many research papers that use first person.

Choosing to relate the narrative from the position of *he* or *she* (rarely *they*) puts more distance between the subject and the reader. Think of the difference between "I fell out of the window" and "He fell out of the window." The former enlists the reader's sympathy immediately, but the latter a bit less so. That's not the case with the second person, *you.* *You* is direct and that's what makes it a somewhat slippery choice. If you're going to use a second-person point of view, make sure the reader understands exactly who is meant by *you.* Many a teacher has been stopped short when reading an essay that has a sentence such as "When you graduate, you'll start looking for a job that can turn into a career." You can avoid that problem if you specify the audience in your paper. "All of us who are now in college worry about jobs" tells the reader just who the audience is, and the teacher then reads the essay from the perspective of a college student.

How can you organize your essay?   All the details and the narrative combine to create a **thesis.** Ask "What is the writer saying about the subject?" The answer, phrased as a complete sentence, is the thesis. If the thesis is explicit, it's apt to occur in the introduction; sometimes, however, the writer will reserve it for the conclusion. But if the organization isn't tight, the reader may wonder where the essay is going; with a delayed thesis, the reader needs to have the feeling that the essay is going somewhere, even though the final destination isn't apparent till the end.

Whether implicit or explicit, the *thesis* is what the writer builds the essay around. It's the main point. The writer must select the most important details, create sentences and paragraphs around them, and then sequence the paragraphs so that everything not only contributes to but also helps create the thesis.

The building block for the essay is the paragraph. And just as the essay has a controlling idea, an assertion that is its thesis, so, too, does the paragraph, usually in the form of a **topic sentence.** Like the thesis, the topic sentence can be explicit or implied, and it can be found in one sentence or deduced from the statements made in several. Because paragraphs frequently cluster around a central idea, particularly in a longer essay, one more than 600 words or so, a topic sentence often covers more than one paragraph.

There's no magic number for how many words make up a paragraph and no magic number for how many paragraphs make up an essay, but it is safe to say that all essays have a beginning, middle, and end. The same is true of a paragraph or group of paragraphs that function under one topic sentence. As you read, ask yourself why a given paragraph ends where it does and how it connects to the one that follows. You may discover that sometimes paragraph breaks are not set in cement and that they could occur in several different places and still be "right."

Useful Terms

Abstract words Words that are so general they mean different things to different people. A cereal box labeled "large" may be your idea of small.

Allusion An indirect reference to a real or fictitious person, place, or thing.

Analogy A point-by-point comparison to something seemingly unlike but more commonplace and less complex than the subject. An analogy is also an extended metaphor.

Cliché A comparison, direct or indirect, that has been used so often that it has become worn out, such as *cool as a cucumber* or *ice cold.*

Concrete details Words that stand for something that can be easily visualized and have fixed meaning. "Large" on the cereal box is abstract; "8 ounces" is concrete.

Conflict An element essential to narrative. Conflict involves pitting one force represented by a person, physical object, or abstract concept against another. It can be *internal*—"Should I or should I not?"—or *external*, as in St. George versus the Dragon.

Exposition Writing that explains; also called expository writing.

Metaphor An implied but direct comparison in which the primary term is made more vivid by associating it with a quite dissimilar term. "Life is a roller coaster" is a metaphor.

Narrative A narrative tells a story, emphasizing what happened.

Objective prose Writing that is impersonal.

Point of View The writer's use of personal pronouns that control the perspective from which the work is written. If the writer uses *I* or *we* (first-person pronouns), the essay will have a somewhat subjective tone because the reader will tend to identify with the writer. If the writer depends primarily on *he, she, it,* or *they* (third-person pronouns), the essay will have a somewhat objective tone because the reader will be distanced. Opting for *you* (second person) can be a bit tricky in that *you* can mean you the reader, quite particular, or you a member of a larger group, fairly general. In both cases, *you* brings the reader into the text.

Setting The *where* and *when* in the narrative, its physical context.

Simile A comparison that links the primary term to a dissimilar one with *like* or *as* to create a vivid image: "Life is like a roller coaster."

Subjective prose Writing that is personal.

Thesis A one-sentence statement or summary of the basic arguable point of the essay.

Tone A writer's attitude toward the subject and the audience.

Topic sentence A statement of the topic of a paragraph containing an arguable point that is supported by the rest of the paragraph.

POINTERS FOR USING DESCRIPTION AND NARRATION

Exploring the Topic

1. **What distinguishes your topic?** What characteristics, features, or actions stand out about your subject? Which are most important? Least important? What role does narrative play?

2. **What happened? Why and how?** What are the events involved in the essay? When does the action start? Stop? Which events are crucial? What caused them? How? What tense will be most effective in relating the narrative? What role does conflict play?

3. **Who or what was involved?** What does the reader need to know about the characters? What do the characters look like? Talk like?

(Continued)

POINTERS FOR USING DESCRIPTION AND NARRATION *(Continued)*

4. **What is the setting for your essay?** What does the reader need to know about the setting? What features are particularly noteworthy? How can they best be described?

5. **To what senses can you appeal?** What can you emphasize that would appeal to sight? Smell? Touch? Taste? Motion?

6. **What concrete details can you use?** What abstract words do you associate with each of the features or events you want to emphasize? How can you make those abstractions concrete?

7. **How can you vary your narrative?** Where might you use quotations? Where might you use dialogue?

8. **What can your audience identify with?** What comparisons can you use? What similes, metaphors, or allusions come to mind?

9. **What order should you use?** Is your description best sequenced by time? Place? Dramatic order? What happened when? Within that chronology, what is most important: time, place, or attitude?

10. **What is your tentative thesis?** What is the dominant impression you want to create? If your essay is primarily a narrative, what major assertion do you want to make? Do you want it to be implicit? Explicit?

11. **What is your relationship to your subject?** Given your tentative thesis, how objective or subjective should you be? Do you want to be part of the action or removed from it? What personal pronoun should you use?

Drafting the Paper

1. **Know your reader.** Try to second-guess your reader's initial attitude toward your essay so that if it is not what you want it to be, you can choose your details to elicit the desired reaction. A reader can be easily bored, so keep your details to the point and your action moving. Play on similar experiences your reader may have had or on information you can assume is widely known.

2. **Know your purpose.** If you are writing to inform, make sure you are presenting new information, offering enough detail to bring your subject to life. If you are writing to persuade, make

sure your details add up so that the reader is moved to adopt your conviction. Keep in mind that your reader may not share your opinions and indeed may even hold opposite ones.

3. **Establish the setting and time of the action.** Use descriptive details to make the setting vivid and concrete. Keep in mind the reaction you want to get from your reader, and choose your details accordingly. If, for instance, you are writing a narrative that depicts your first experience with fear, describe the setting in such a way that you prepare the reader for that emotion. If the time the event took place is important, bring it out early.

4. **Set out the characters.** When you introduce a character, immediately identify the person with a short phrase, such as "Anne, my sister." If a character doesn't enter your essay until midpoint or so, make sure the reader is prepared so that the person doesn't appear to be merely plopped in. If characterization is important, use a variety of techniques to portray the person, but make sure whatever you use is consistent with the impression you want to create. You can depict a person directly—through appearance, dialogue, and actions—as well as indirectly—through what others say and think and how they act toward the person. Keep in mind that the narrator, often the author, also conveys a sense of himself or herself.

5. **Clarify the action.** Make sure the time frame of your essay is clear. Within that time limit, much more action occurred than you will want to use. Pick only the high points to support your thesis and feel free to tinker, sacrificing a bit of reality to make your point. And if your essay deals with conflict, be sure it's clearly drawn.

6. **Choose an appropriate point of view.** Your choice of grammatical point of view depends on what attitude you wish to take toward your narrative and your audience. If you can make your point more effectively by distancing yourself from the action, you will want to use *he*, *she*, or *they*. But if you can make your point most effectively by being in the action, use first person and then decide whether you want to be *I* the narrator or *I* the narrator who is also directly involved.

7. **Vary sensory details.** Emphasize important details by appealing to more than just one sense.

(Continued)

POINTERS FOR USING DESCRIPTION AND NARRATION *(Continued)*

8. Show, don't tell. Avoid abstract terms such as *funny* or *beautiful*. Instead, use concrete details, quotations, and dialogue. Don't settle for vague adjectives such as *tall*; replace them with sharper details—*6 feet 7 inches*. Consider making description vivid with an occasional metaphor or simile. If you are writing about something quite unfamiliar, use literal comparison to clarify your description.

9. Arrange your details to create a single dominant impression or point. If your essay is primarily descriptive, check the order of your sentences to make sure they follow each other logically and support the impression you wish to create. If you are writing an essay that relies heavily on narrative, it should lead to a conclusion, an implicit or explicit point that serves as the thesis of the piece.

You'll Love the Way We Fly

Lori Jakiela

The title of Lori Jakiela's essay was for years the popular advertising slogan for Delta Airlines, a time when Jakiela worked for Delta as a flight attendant. She recounts some of her experiences in her memoir Miss New York Has Everything *(2006). One of those experiences forms the basis of the essay that follows. Jakiela now teaches in the writing program at the University of Pittsburgh at Greensburg and is an established writer whose work has been published in various newspapers—*The New York Times *and* The Chicago Tribune *among them—and in journals such as* Double Take, Creative Nonfiction, The Chicago Review, *and* Slipstream. *Winner of many awards for writing as well as one for her contributions to her university, Jakiela also writes a regular column called "Here and Now" for the Tribune Review Company. The following essay appeared in* Creative Nonfiction, *twenty-seventh issue, in 2005.*

What to Look For   As you read Jakiela's essay, you'll see how description and narration are interwoven. What happens in the essay supplies the narrative, but the descriptions bring it alive.

1   I'm in the galley, making coffee. I try to look busy, not in the mood to talk or help. This is the fourth leg of a six-leg day, and already I'm tired. I immerse myself in counting and recounting stacks of Styrofoam cups, tightening the handles on metal coffee pots, scrubbing the steel galley counter until I can see my face, distorted and greenish in the plane's fluorescent light, eyes flecked with dried mascara.

2   I hear him coming before I can see him: the rustle of his nylon bag, brushing against seat backs and the heads of other passengers. He is old, thin. He plops the bag on the floor of the emergency exit row, right across from where I'm standing. I'm engrossed now in stocking Cokes into the beverage cart. I watch him from behind the galley wall, a talent all flight attendants learn, covert ways to size people up.

3   His hair is gray, and saliva has settled into the corners of his mouth. He holds a filthy handkerchief to his nose. He is coughing, a deep-lunged cough, the kind that fades into a feathery wheeze then begins again, a terrifying, endless loop. A pack of Marlboros is tucked into his left sock.

23

4   I am afraid to go near him, afraid of what I might catch. When you make your living on an airplane, there are things you become afraid of, like germs and crashes and how cold the ocean is off LaGuardia in winter.

5   "They're not supposed to let them on like this," says my friend, who's working with me.

6   They're not supposed to let them on drunk, either, but this is how it is. That's what I think, but I don't say anything.

7   The man coughs, then follows with his wet-rattled breaths.

8   I think: This is serious, maybe not contagious, but serious. I call to him from the galley. "Sir, would you like water?"

9   He wheezes, coughs, shakes his head. I look at my friend, who's busy alphabetizing magazines and stacking pillows in the overhead bins.

10   "Excuse me, sir?" I say. "Can I get you something?

11   He coughs, points. Coffee.

12   "Cream and sugar?"

13   He nods, and so I bring him what he wants, along with some water.

14   "Thank you," he says and grabs hold of my hand. I feel myself pull back. His hand is damp and cold; the fingers are all bone. "Thank you, I—" he coughs again, and I don't get the rest, so I have to lean closer, "—really appreciate."

15   Later, he tries to give me a tip: two quarters wrapped in a wet dollar and held together with a rubber band. I say, "No, no," but he presses it into my palm, gasping, "You take it for taking care. I appreciate."

16   The effort of breathing has made him sound foreign. He's American, I'm sure, a New Yorker, though disease has taken the hardness out of his eyes. They are brown and damp, the whites yellowing like old paper. Still, he thinks small kindnesses are things you have to pay for.

17   I haven't really been kind. I've just done my job, against what I wanted, despite my own disgust. I am paid to smile, to talk to strangers about the latest issue of *People,* to bring coffee and water, to make people comfortable.

18   I take the money.

19   "What is it you say?" he's asking, but I don't understand. "What is it you say on TV?"

20   "You'll love the way we fly," my friend sing-songs from the galley.

21   The man nods gravely, repeats it.

22   I laugh now. I don't know what else to do. He's dying, I'm sure. Emphysema or lung cancer, probably, like my father.

23   The flight is only an hour, D.C. to New York. When the man gets up to leave, I keep my head down, eyes focused on my hand, checking off items on a list. What we need: tea bags, stir sticks, Band-Aids, first-aid cream, two bags of peanuts. I try not to think, but I can't help it.

24   Who will be there in the airport to meet him? What is his home like? Who brings him coffee the way he likes it? Who is not afraid to touch him?

ORGANIZATION AND IDEAS

1. In what ways does the essay relate to the slogan that provides the title?
2. Describe what the essay reveals about Jakiela. How would you characterize her?
3. In paragraph 2, Jakiela watches the passenger "from behind the galley wall, a talent all flight attendants learn, covert ways to size people up." How accurate is her initial impression?
4. The similar actions and details from paragraph 1 are repeated in paragraph 23. How effective is that framing device?
5. The essay is a good example of an implied thesis. Given what you now know about the situation, the passenger, and Jakiela, what thesis do you draw out?

TECHNIQUE AND STYLE

1. Reread the essay noting Jakiela's use of appeals to the senses. What do you find? Which ones stand out? What reasons can you find for that choice?
2. The essay incorporates a fair amount of dialogue. What does it add? How realistic do you find it?
3. What does the incident with the tip suggest? What does it add to the essay?
4. Given the essay as a whole, what do you learn about Jakiela? Do you find anything that is unnecessary, and if so, how so?
5. The essay ends with a string of questions. What answers, if any, are implied? How effective is the ending?

SUGGESTIONS FOR WRITING

Journal

1. Like Jakiela, you have probably had to do something you didn't want to do but felt obliged to do it. Select one example and describe it in your journal.
2. Reread the essay's last paragraph and supply your own answers, explaining them.

Essay

1. In a way, Jakiela's essay is about living up to what's expected of her as a flight attendant. That sort of pressure applies to many different situations. Consider your own experience from that perspective, one of having to meet expectations. Possible topics:
    as a parent, son, or daughter
    in a job
    as a student
    as an owner of an animal
    as a citizen

2. Doing one's job can be demanding. Think about the jobs you have had and their demands. What were they? What effect did they have? How did you respond to those demands? What did you learn or conclude from your experience? Choose one experience and describe it so that your reader understands your position and your conclusions.

Tommy

Kelly Ruth Winter

A recent graduate of the University of Iowa, where she majored in English as well as Journalism and Mass Communication, Kelly Ruth Winter is already on her way to a career in writing literary nonfiction. While at Iowa, her honors thesis earned her the university's Anderson Prize for Undergraduate Expository Writing. She has since gone on to graduate school at the university earning an MAT in English Education. At present, Winter is a high school English teacher in rural Iowa where she lives with her husband and their daughter. Her work has appeared in upstreet, *a literary anthology published annually, and in* Brevity, *a journal devoted to short essays by emerging and established writers. Winter's "Tommy" appeared in* Brevity's *twenty-fifth issue, published in the fall of 2007.*

What to Look For   When you read Winter's essay, note how she uses present tense and short paragraphs to recreate the different times within her narrative. Also, pause after each group of short paragraphs to think about how they function as a unit.

1   Tommy Schmidt does not drink milk. He is scrawny and freck-led and eight years old to my five. We are in love.

2   His mom pays my mom to watch him after school. I watch him from the kitchen as he sits Indian-style on the brown shag carpet in front of our T.V.

3   Later, in the entryway of our house, Tommy and I tap our feet on the linoleum, imitating the patterns of speech.

4   Tap, ta—p, tap, says the dirty sole of his white tennis shoe.

5   "I love you?" I guess.

6   He grins.

7   The next day, I draw a picture of us getting married, crisscross-ing the pencil over my face for the veil. I include a baby. My mom says I shouldn't have my baby at my wedding. Her eyebrows say I shouldn't marry Tommy.

8   A year later, I sit in the middle of the school bus while Tommy sits in back with the older kids. I lean into the aisle, pretend to look out the back window, but really look at him.

9   He's a bad boy now. I can tell from his ripped jeans and the number of times the bus driver makes him sit up front. His eyes meet mine, and he hands me a half-dollar-sized piece of leather covered in turquoise beads.

10   "Want it?" he asks.

11   "Sure. Thanks." I face the front and bite my smile. At home, I tuck the trinket in my pink plastic jewelry box, next to the beaded Indian figurine from my family's South Dakota vacation.

12   The summer after second grade, my family moves seven miles, from one tiny Iowa town to another, so I don't have to ride the bus anymore. My dad gives Tommy's dad our old record player—a big wooden box with a heavy hinged lid.

13   I miss listening to the Oakridge Boys and hopping until the re-cord skips and I am told to settle down.

14   My dad and Tommy's dad used to ride motorcycles out to Wyoming and Washington, sleeping in a tent along the way. I imagine our fathers each rolling a t-shirt to fit in the pouches on the backrests of their bikes.

15   If our fathers rolled their t-shirts, kept them in the leather pouches of motorcycles, if they listen to the same music on the very same record player, what made me good and Tommy bad?

16   When Tommy is in sixth grade and I am in third, he lights his house on fire and tries to kill himself with a pair of scissors.

17   During art class, I stare at a blue vein that snakes from my palm, then run the edge my scissors over it. A faint white line appears, then vanishes.

18   My mom says Tommy's in a mental institution.

19   Tommy's freckled mug smiles from his first-grade picture as my dad and I page through my photo book.

20   "You should probably rip that up and throw it away," he tells me. I am ten, struggling through multiplication tables, but taking straight A's in everything else. My dad wants me to stay away from the bad kids.

21   I tear up the picture, but feel guilty as I stare at the pieces of Tommy's face in my pink garbage can.

22   Later, I am relieved to find his second-grade picture farther back in the book.

23   When I'm in high school and Tommy has long since dropped out, he comes in the town hardware store where I work, dusting shelves and helping customers find pop rivets and three-eighths-sized bolts.

24   He's been in and out of boys' homes and jail, has long, frayed rust-colored hair, and is missing his front right tooth—but I still recognize him.

25   "Shotgun shells," he says, voice low.

26   I bite my lip and try not to look at him as I stride to the case. I want him to recognize me, to tell me that I grew up pretty. But he just follows me, stares at the floor.

27   Fumbling with the keys, I wonder if I should sell him shotgun shells at all—but there's no background check for ammunition. When I count back the change, my fingertips graze his palm. He just grabs his shells and saunters out the door.

28   After I graduate, I go to college with my scholarships and hand-me-down T.V.

29   Tommy dies alone at his parents' house in the country. Suicide, but I'll never know how. Sitting alone in my apartment, I find his obituary online, only five lines long.

ORGANIZATION AND IDEAS

1. The short paragraphs form seven distinct times in Winter's life. How old is Winter in each one?
2. In paragraph 17, what does the "white line" suggest about the relationship between Winter and Tommy?

3. The essay deals with scenes from different times of Winter's life, but those times also correspond to different stages of maturity. What are those stages?

4. What does Winter think about and feel toward Tommy? What can you infer that Tommy thinks and feels toward Winter?

5. Winter never states her thesis but instead describes Tommy and how she feels about him. What thesis can you deduce from what she says?

TECHNIQUE AND STYLE

1. In paragraph 9, Tommy gives Winter a "half-dollar-sized piece of leather covered in turquoise beads." What might it symbolize or represent? What is Winter's reaction?

2. Reread the essay looking for contrasts. What do you find and what meaning do they carry?

3. Winter poses a question in paragraph 15. What answers does the essay suggest?

4. Take a look at the last sentence in the essay. What impact does it have?

5. Throughout the essay, Winter manages to imply a great deal in only a few simple words as in her opening sentence: "Tommy Schmidt does not drink milk." Where else in the essay does she use this technique? How effective is it?

SUGGESTIONS FOR WRITING

Journal

1. What other titles can you think of for the essay? Which do you prefer and why?

2. Use your journal to describe your own encounter with a "bad boy" or "bad girl."

Essay

1. Winter describes various stages in her relationship with Tommy, starting with when she was five and ending with her going to college. Write your own essay in which you compare a "then" and a "now." If, like Winter, you want to spell out the stages in between, fine; but if you just want to focus on the contrast, that's fine, too. Possible topics:

friendship
political view
change of mind
taste in music
event

2. Readers may respond to Winter's essay in different ways, but most will agree it makes quite an impact. Reread the essay noting the various ways Winter creates that impact, and write an essay that analyzes her techniques. You will find that you need to quote from the essay, but remember that when you do you also need to comment on the quotation.

The Night of Oranges

Flavius Stan

Flavius Stan was 17 when this piece was published on Christmas Eve day, 1995, in The New York Times. *At the time, he was an exchange student at the Fieldston School in the Bronx, one of New York City's five boroughs. The time and place he writes about, however, is Christmas Eve in the city of Timisoara in the Romania of 1989, when the country was emerging from Communist rule. On December 16, government forces had opened fire on antigovernment demonstrators in Timisoara, killing hundreds. The president, Nicolae Ceausescu, immediately declared a state of emergency, but that did not stop antigovernment protests in other cities. Finally, on December 22, army units also rebelled, the president was overthrown, and civil war raged. The new government quickly won out, and Ceausescu was tried, found guilty of genocide, and executed on December 25.*

Since that time, Stan has earned degrees in political science (Columbia University), European Politics and Policy (New York University), and public management (SDA Bocconi School of Management, Milan). When Stan was at Columbia, he set up a nongovernmental agency "to address issues of children in orphanages in Romania...[that was] a big success." He adds: "throughout the years I [have] been involved in humanitarian and reform initiatives in Romania and elsewhere, focused on children and their environments."

What to Look For   Few of us reading this essay have had firsthand experience of a revolution, nor have many of us lived under Communism or a dictatorship, much less a government whose leader was not only overthrown but also executed. But all of us know oranges. What is familiar to us was strange to Stan, and what is strange to us was his everyday world. The resulting gap between Stan's society and ours is huge, yet in this essay he is able to bring his readers into the cold, postrevolution world of a city in Romania and make us see our familiar orange in a new way. Read the essay once for pleasure and then read it again, looking for the ways in which he makes the unfamiliar familiar and vice versa.

1   It is Christmas Eve in 1989 in Timisoara and the ice is still dirty from the boots of the Romanian revolution. The dictator Nicolae Ceausescu had been deposed a few days before, and on Christmas

Day he would be executed by firing squad. I am in the center of the city with my friends, empty now of the crowds that prayed outside the cathedral during the worst of the fighting. My friends and I still hear shots here and there. Our cold hands are gray like the sky above us, and we want to see a movie.

2 There is a rumor that there will be oranges for sale tonight. Hundreds of people are already waiting in line. We were used to such lines under the former Communist Government—lines for bread, lines for meat, lines for everything. Families would wait much of the day for rationed items. As children, we would take turns for an hour or more, holding our family's place in line.

3 But this line is different. There are children in Romania who don't know what an orange looks like. It is a special treat. Having the chance to eat a single orange will keep a child happy for a week. It will also make him a hero in the eyes of his friends. For the first time, someone is selling oranges by the kilo.

4 Suddenly I want to do something important: I want to give my brother a big surprise. He is only 8 years old, and I want him to celebrate Christmas with lots of oranges at the table. I also want my parents to be proud of me.

5 So I call home and tell my parents that I'm going to be late. I forget about going to the movie, leave my friends and join the line.

6 People aren't silent, upset, frustrated, as they were before the revolution; they are talking to one another about life, politics and the new situation in the country.

7 The oranges are sold out of the back doorway of a food shop. The clerk has gone from anonymity to unexpected importance. As he handles the oranges, he acts like a movie star in front of his fans.

8 He moves his arms in an exaggerated manner as he tells the other workers where to go and what to do. All I can do is stare at the stack of cardboard boxes, piled higher than me. I have never seen so many oranges in my life.

9 Finally, it is my turn. It is 8 o'clock, and I have been waiting for six hours. It doesn't seem like a long time because my mind has been flying from the oranges in front of me to my brother and then back to the oranges. I hand over the money I was going to spend on the movie and watch each orange being thrown into my bag. I try to count them, but I lose their number.

10 I am drunk with the idea of oranges. I put the bag inside my coat as if I want to absorb their warmth. They aren't heavy at all, and I feel that it is going to be the best Christmas of my life. I begin thinking of how I am going to present my gift.

11   I get home and my father opens the door. He is amazed when he sees the oranges, and we decide to hide them until dinner. At dessert that night, I give my brother the present. Everyone is silent. They can't believe it.

12   My brother doesn't touch them. He is afraid even to look at them. Maybe they aren't real. Maybe they are an illusion, like everything else these days. We have to tell him he can eat them before he has the courage to touch one of the oranges.

13   I stare at my brother eating the oranges. They are my oranges. My parents are proud of me.

ORGANIZATION AND IDEAS

1. Paragraphs 1–3 introduce the essay. Explain how they do or do not fit the journalistic questions establishing *who, what, where, why, when, how.*

2. The central part of the essay takes the reader from the time Stan decides to buy the oranges to his presenting them to his brother. What is the effect of presenting the narrative chronologically?

3. The last paragraph functions as the essay's one-paragraph conclusion, a conclusion presented in three short sentences. Explain whether you find the ending effective.

4. On the surface, Stan's essay has a simple thesis—that finding the rare and perfect gift for his brother fills him with pride, pride also reflected by his family. If you dig a bit, however, you may also discover other less obvious theses. What, for instance, might Stan be implying about Christmas? About Romania's future?

5. How would you characterize the conflict or conflicts in this essay?

TECHNIQUE AND STYLE

1. Although the essay was written in 1995, it is set at a previous time, 1989. Many writers would, therefore, opt for the past tense, but Stan relates his narrative in the present. What does he gain by this choice?

2. Trace the number of contrasts Stan has in his essay. What do you discover? How do they relate to the thesis?

3. Paragraphs 7 and 8 describe the clerk in charge of selling the oranges in some detail. What does this description add to the essay?

4. Why is it important that the money Stan spends on the oranges is the money he was going to spend on the movies?

5. Reread the first paragraph, one that sets not only the scene but also the atmosphere, the emotional impression arising from the scene. In your own words, describe that atmosphere.

SUGGESTIONS FOR WRITING

Journal

1. Choose a common object and describe it as though you were seeing it for the first time.

2. In a sense, Stan's essay is written from the perspective of an 11-year-old, the age he was at the time of the narrative. Leaf through your journal to find a short narrative and then try rewriting it from the perspective of a much younger person.

Essay

1. Sift through your memory to find several times when you felt proud. Choose one to turn into a narrative essay. Perhaps, like Stan, you may want to retell the event in the present tense, placing yourself in the position of reliving it. If you do, check your draft to see if you have an implied thesis that is larger than the apparent one, because you want your essay to have some depth to it. For ideas of what might have made you feel proud, consider something you

    did

    didn't do

    saw

    owned

    said

2. For a more generalized essay, consider the times you felt pride and list them. What were the occasions? What do they have in common? In what ways are those examples similar? Different? Write an essay in which you define *pride*, using your experiences as examples and keeping first person to a minimum so that you emphasize the subject, not yourself.

A Terrible Thing to Waste

Mary Roach

If you'd like to be entertained by and also informed about Mary Roach, visit her web page maryroach.net *where a giant roach will greet you. You'll also discover that she has a long list of curious interests, many of which she has written about: earthquake-proof bamboo houses, amputee bowling leagues, and bursting human stomachs. Her articles have appeared in varied magazines such as* Wired, National Geographic, *and* New Scientist, *and her books contain even more interesting information*: The Curious Lives of Human Cadavers (2003); Spook: Science Tackles the Afterlife (2005); Bonk: The Curious Coupling of Science and Sex (2008); and Packing for Mars: The Curious Science of Life in the Void (2010), *the latter a look at space travel and answers to all the questions you never got to ask. The essay printed here first appeared in* Salon *in 1999 where it was subtitled* "You do not need brains to go to the Harvard Brain Bank, only a brain."

What to Look For One way to get a reader interested in an unpleasant subject is to use a humorous tone. As you read Roach's essay, try to pin down the kind of humor she adopts.

1   There are many good reasons to become a brain donor. One of the best is to advance the study of mental dysfunction.

2   You see, researchers cannot study animal brains to learn about mental illness, because animals don't get mentally ill. While some animals—cats, for example, and dogs small enough to fit into bicycle baskets—seem to incorporate mental illness as a natural personality feature, animals are not known to have diagnosable brain disorders like Alzheimer's and schizophrenia. So researchers need to study brains of mentally ill humans and, as controls, brains of normal humans like you and me (OK, you).

3   My reasons for becoming a brain donor aren't very good at all. My reasons boil down to a Harvard Brain Bank donor wallet card, which enables me to say "I'm going to Harvard" and not be lying. You do not need brains to go to the Harvard Brain Bank—only *a* brain.

4   One fine fall day, I decided to visit my final resting place. The Brain Bank is part of Harvard's McLean Hospital, which sits on a rolling estate of handsome brick buildings just outside Boston. I was directed to the third floor of the Mailman Research Building. The woman pronounced it "Melmon," so as to avoid having to answer stupid questions about what kind of research is being done on mailmen.

5   If you are considering becoming a brain donor, the best thing for you to do is stay away from the Brain Bank. Within 10 minutes of arriving, I was watching a 24-year-old technician named Al slice up a piece of a 67-year-old named Fran. Fran's brain had been flash-frozen and did not slice cleanly. It sliced as does a Butterfinger, with little shards crumbling off. The shards quickly thawed and looked less Butterfinger-like. Al wiped them up with a paper towel: "There goes third grade."

6   Al has gotten into trouble for saying things like this. I read a newspaper story in which the reporter asked Al if he planned to donate his brain and he replied, "No way! I'm going out with whatever I came in with!" Now when you ask him, he says quietly, "I'm only 24. I really don't know."

7   The Brain Bank's associate director, Steven Vincent, was showing me around. Down the hall from the dissection room was the computer room. Vincent referred to it as "the brains of the operation," which in any other operation would have been fine, but in this case was a tad confusing. At the end of the hall were the real brains. It wasn't quite what I had imagined. I had pictured whole, intact brains floating in glass jars. But the brains are cut in half, one side being sliced and frozen, the other side sliced and stored in formaldehyde inside Rubbermaid and Frezette food savers. Somehow, I'd expected more of Harvard. If not glass, at least Tupperware. I wondered what the dorms look like these days.

8   Vincent told me there are currently 4,600 specimens in the formaldehyde room. I wrote the number down and then, seconds later, I said, "How many half-brains are in here altogether?" Vincent politely repeated 4,600, though you could tell that what he wanted to say was, "4,601." Earlier I'd asked Fran's age after I'd just been told it. I began to worry that perhaps there wouldn't be a place for my brain at Harvard. "Of course there is," deadpanned Vincent. "See those tiny little freezers down there?"

9   The more I learned, the more I wasn't so sure about this. I made the mistake of reading the Nurses Procedure Sheet, which includes the line "If mortuary refrigeration is not immediately available, pack the decedent's head in wet ice...." It was not clear from the wording whether the head was to be left attached to the remainder of the decedent, and I could imagine many a harried nurse reaching for the bone saw. On the other hand, brain donation does present the novel experience of getting to travel by Fed Ex. Plus, I was told, brains are spared the rigors of the cargo hold and often get to sit up in the cockpit with the pilot. It doesn't make up for an eternity spent in Rubbermaid, but still.

10   My problem now was that I was picturing myself brainless in a coffin, seeping spinal fluid onto my satin casket pillow. Vincent assured me that no one would even be able to tell that my brain was missing. He assured me in a way that assured me and at the same time didn't bring me any closer to being a committed brain donor. "First," he began, "they cut the skin like this." On his head he traced a line from one ear back around to the other.

"Then they pull the skin up over the face." Here he made a motion as though taking off a (particularly effective) Halloween mask. "They use a saw to cut the top of the skull off, the brain is removed and the skull is put back and screwed in place. Put the skin flap back, and comb the hair back over." Vincent used the peppy how-to language of an infomercial host, making brain harvesting sound like something that takes just minutes and wipes clean with a damp cloth.

11   Vincent sensed I was slipping from his grasp. He went earnest on me, talking of how the bank got only 40 "normals" a year, and how less than 15 percent of the people he sends brochures to wind up being donors. "A lot of people think they're signed up but they're not," he said. "They ask for information but they never send the form back. They have the papers, so they think they're signed up." Clearly, I wouldn't want for company in the little-tiny-brain freezer.

12   Vincent inquired as to whether I was still game. I considered. "Can I have one of those Brain Bank refrigerator magnets on your file cabinet?" He handed me a stack. On his monitor sat a gray squishy Brain Bank miniature brain, one of those palm-size squeeze toys. Vincent followed my gaze. "Oh no," he said. "We have a very limited promotional budget, and those are being used to motivate the mental illness community."

13   "Which would of course include journalists."

14   Vincent tossed me a squeeze brain. I promised to keep the donor card in my wallet.

15   Before I left, Vincent advised me to talk to my husband, for next-of-kin have final say about brain donations. When you die, your body becomes the property of your spouse. Legally, spouses can do whatever they please with their dead mate's body.

16   So I talked to Ed. He had some lively and novel ideas, but brain removal wasn't on the list. Ed is a squeamish guy: "Ixnay on the ainbankbray." Unless, he added, there was a chance they could one day revive my brain and put it on someone else's body. "Provided I get to choose the body."

ORGANIZATION AND IDEAS

1. How would you describe the tone of paragraph 1? Of paragraph 2? What reasons can you think of for the change?
2. Reread paragraphs 4–15 and you'll see the essay is structured by chronology and place, a choice that can be boring. How does Roach try to keep your interest?

3. Aside from Roach, the essay includes three others: Al, Steven Vincent, and Ed. What do they contribute to the essay? Why might Roach have decided to omit last names for Al and Ed?

4. The idea that a dead body is treated by law as property may never have occurred to you, but legally you have no say over what happens to your body. What reasons can you think of for law overruling personal choice?

5. Paragraphs 5, 6, and 10 are filled with details may readers would find quite unpleasant. What effect do they achieve? How could they be toned down? What would be gained? Lost?

TECHNIQUE AND STYLE

1. How would you describe the Mary Roach who is the narrator of the essay? To what extent does she seem the kind of person you would like to know?

2. Although there's no mistaking the humorous tone of the essay, does Roach have a serious point? What? How effectively does she make it?

3. A "Brain Bank" is hardly a familiar place. What details does Roach include that relate to common experience? To what extent do they achieve their purpose?

4. Paragraphs 12 and 14 describe the Brain Bank's version of refrigerator magnets and squeeze toys. What does including them imply about Roach? Vincent? The Brain Bank?

5. If someone says *Harvard* to you, what do you associate with the word? Why might Roach have chosen this particular brain bank?

SUGGESTIONS FOR WRITING

Journal

1. If you had to edit the essay, what would you add? Omit? Change? Explain your decisions.

2. Explain in some detail why you would or would not become a brain or organ donor.

Essay

1. Roach's subject presents a number of challenges. If, like Roach, you choose a subject that can both intrigue and repell the reader, tone and details are crucial. For such a subject, think, for instance, about a
   car crash
   operation
   hospital visit
   bizarre situation
   friend you both love and hate

2. Scientific research sometimes involves what most people would find distasteful, immoral, or illegal. The Nazi concetrations camps of World War II carried out experiments on prisoners, and in the United States the Public Health Service conducted a forty-year clinical study on syphillis using African Americans without their consent or knowledge. Using the Internet or college library, examine the misuse of human subjects for scientific study, selecting one example to explore in detail.

What Is So Close, Yet So Far, Alex?

Mark Abadi, The Daily Tar Heel

If you've ever watched "Jeopardy" (who hasn't?), you're used to the show's fast pace and the excitement it generates among its contestants, audience, and television viewers. That's the emotion Mark Abadi recreates in his essay. The essay was published in The Daily Tar Heel, *the student newspaper of the University of North Carolina, where Abadi is now a senior majoring in Linguistics. For Abadi, "Language is a fascinating thing. As newborns, we don't know the slightest thing about it, yet by adulthood, we're fluent speakers who can tell jokes, make rhymes, judge whether something is grammatically correct and determine where someone is from by listening to their accent. I view language as the essence of the human experience, and that's why I study linguistics." The essay was published on October 23, 2011, in Opinion.*

What to Look For   When you are working on an essay, it's helpful to imagine a specific audience, often your peers. That's who Abadi is writing for, so some of the techniques he uses can carry over to your own writing. As you read Abadi's essay, note the diction level he chooses, his references, and his word choice—all are aimed at a particular group of readers.

1   I entered the cozy, well-lit conference room in a Los Angeles hotel and surveyed my competition.

2   There were 14 students seated inside. Each shared a common goal: becoming a contestant on the Jeopardy College Championship.

3   You know, the game where students answer in the form of a question while donning their nicest college crew-neck sweatshirts.

Qualifying for the show has been a goal of mine since my freshman year. I even had a dream one night in which I couldn't decide between a navy or Carolina blue sweatshirt—five minutes before showtime.

4   Each student in the room had passed an online test in March to earn the callback invitation. For months, the Jeopardy crew had been traveling across the country to rooms like this one to whittle 200 or so hopefuls down to 15. The ultimate prize: $100,000.

5   In other words, I didn't take the audition lightly. I had spent countless hours this summer holed up in my local library, poring over *The World Almanac*, studying European monarchs, state nick-names, birthstones, thermodynamics, Greek gods and anything else that qualifies as "general knowledge."

6   In the hotel conference room, there was a student with a Brown University crew-neck and two Stanford students in Cardinal red. I had no school spirit, just a killer's mentality. The kid from Duke seemed nice enough, but he nevertheless became my arch nemesis for those two hours.

7   After a few introductions, our hostess kicked off the competition with some practice questions to familiarize us with Jeopardy's famous wordplay categories. For "Rhyme Time," the clue was "Chewbacca's dessert treat."

8   Brown crew-neck slammed his hand on the table. This dude was eager. "What is a Wookiee cookie?"

9   I soon got my chance. Before and After: "This early Supreme Court justice raps under the name Eminem." Who is John Marshall Mathers? Yes sir.

10   But enough of the warm-ups. The reason we were here was to take a 50-question test, with eight seconds for each answer.

11   The first question was a blur. So were the next 49. All I remember was hearing the questions and either immediately knowing the answers or staring down as others scribbled furiously beside me.

12   My ideal scenario, in which every piece of trivia somehow related to my life story with Slumdog Millionaire-like convenience, never came to fruition.

13   I came up with nothing for questions on Depression-era theater and obscure British authors. I bungled an astronomy question and confused my Shakespeare plots. In a cruel twist, precisely none of my study material proved relevant to the 50 questions.

14   Still, I managed to salvage my audition during the mock game—in which I out-buzzed the Duke kid—and during the personality interview, in which I refrained from meowing (unlike Brown crew-neck, who was demonstrating one of his "talents").

15   And just like that, it was over. I picked my heart up off the ground, took my souvenir Jeopardy pen and left the room.

16   I'm not counting on getting the call this winter. But when the episodes air, I'll at least be playing at home, clicking my pen like a buzzer and answering in the form of a question—crew-neck optional.

ORGANIZATION AND IDEAS

1. Assume you know little or nothing about "Jeopardy." What information does Abadi provide and how adequate is it?
2. Abadi deals with two different time frames—before and after the show and the show itself. Where and how does he shift between them?
3. The word *competition* occurs in paragraphs 1 and 7. Where else in the essay does the idea crop up? To what extent is it important?
4. Consider the essay as a whole. What is its main subject and what statement is Abadi saying about it? How might that statement relate to a college audience? To the general reader?
5. Take another look at the title. How effective is it? What other titles might work as well or better?

TECHNIQUE AND STYLE

1. Reread paragraph 3 and compare the style and tone to that in paragraphs 15 and 16. What do you notice and what does that contribute to the essay as a whole?
2. You will have noticed that Abadi uses short paragraphs, some times only a sentence long. What is the effect on the reader?
3. Abadi combines description and narration in his essay. Which do you find predominates and why?
4. How would you describe the level of diction in the essay? On a scale ranging from 1 (slang) to 10 (academic), where would you put it and why?
5. Not that many college students get to compete on game shows. How effective is Abadi's account of his experience? What particular examples can you find to support your opinion?

SUGGESTIONS FOR WRITING

Journal

1. Use your journal to explain why you would or would not like to compete on "Jeopardy."
2. If you were going to be on a game or reality show of your choice, which would it be and why?

Essay

1. You could read Abadi's essay as an example of how to deal with disappointment, what was expected versus what happened. Think about your own experiences from that perspective. Narrow down your choice to one example and write an essay in which you explore what you learned, where, and why. Suggestions:

   working part-time
   signing up for a course
   participating in a sport
   participating in an extracurricular activity
   being responsible for someone

2. Think about the degree to which competition is a part of college life. Where do you find it? How does it affect you? What is its negative impact? What positive effects might it have? How does it differ from competition in high school? The work place? Life in general? Given your experiences, select one that involves competition and then use description and narration to explore the topic in an essay.

Internet Plagiarism: We All Pay the Price

Ellen Laird

Ellen Laird is a Professor of English at Hudson Valley Community College, where she has been teaching since 1987 and teaching very well indeed. In 2001, she was honored with the College's President's Award for Excellence in Teaching, and in 2009 she received the SUNY Chancellor's Award for Excellence in Teaching. The news story announcing the 2001 award stated that she "is known as an innovative classroom teacher who melds the use of technology with a rigorous and caring teaching style." You can judge for yourself in the essay that follows. It was published in the "The Chronicle Review," the "Opinion and Ideas" section of The Chronicle of Higher Education, *July 13, 2001.*

What to Look For As you read Laird's essay, keep in mind how and where she shifts from the particular—Chip's essay—to the general. As a result, the essay, although based on personal experiences, makes a larger point.

1   When I first read Chip's essay last year, I was ecstatic. Chip (an alias) had clearly absorbed class lessons on specificity, readership, and organization in writing. In fact, he had gone further. He had shown that he could write a clever thesis and select examples perfectly suited to the topic. My enthusiasm darkened to suspicion upon a second reading, however. Chip was an A student in the course, but his essay seemed a bit too mature in content and focus, compared with his previous work. His rhetorical voice was deeper than what I had come to expect of his prose.

2   A 60-second AltaVista search brought me to the full essay. A Dave Barry-like piece available at BigNerds.com, the text was filtered through life experience that Chip, at 18, would be lacking. I was crushed.

3   Like so many problems—cheating spouses, I.R.S. audits, sun-induced cancers—this was supposed to happen only to others.

4   Except for a small number of individuals over the years, my students don't intentionally plagiarize. After all, in both our actual and virtual English-composition class meetings, I am a witness to their writing process, not just a reader of their written products. I keep their rhetorical fingerprints—their in-class writing samples—in the front of my file cabinet. And I teach them what it means to be honest in college.

5   In an effort to be especially thorough last year, I reinforced my instruction with a repertoire of stories—about dethroned and dishonored college presidents and six- and seven-figure damage awards—to demonstrate the price paid, even by the high and mighty, for the theft of words and ideas. And after sculpting a lesson on academic honesty, based on an article by an English professor, Richard Fulkerson, in the journal *The Writing Instructor*, I pointed out my bold-faced statement of attribution on the handout. I explained to students, "Even in the relaxed setting of this class, I must tell you whose idea this lesson was originally. Fulkerson owns it; I borrowed it."

6   Yet, the day after the Fulkerson-based lesson, Chip submitted as his own an essay he had downloaded from the Internet. Not for a researched essay or an important course grade, but for a portfolio piece he could have chosen to leave ungraded.

7   Chip committed his academic felony in April 2000, but he and his essay remain for me in the present tense, still an interrogative sentence. Surely, with all my harping and haranguing, he knew better. His act had none of the fuzziness of what might be called

unintentional plagiarism—unattributed text too close to the spirit and structure of the original. His was a clear-cut point, click, and save theft.

8   I am struggling to understand what happened. Which of the usual explanations for academic dishonesty apply in this instance? Pressure to succeed? Not Chip, and not this assignment. Lack of clarity about plagiarism in our learning environment? Not in the English department at Hudson Valley Community College. Lack of a clear position on the instructor's part? Not with this fanatic teaching the course. An assumption that I lacked Web savvy? Not with a Web site, linked syllabus, online discussion of readings, and interactive lessons for the course. Lack of personal connection in a large institution? Chip and I had just seen each other at a local event over the weekend, and he had introduced his mother to me.

9   To save face with myself, I must assume that Chip understood that downloading an essay and submitting it as his own was an egregious act. Why, then, did he do it?

10   Chip explained that he had been "mentally perturbed" the weekend before the paper was due, and that the essay he had written failed to meet his high standards. But I sensed that Chip felt that he had made a choice akin to having a pizza delivered. He had procrastinated on an assignment due the next day, had no time left in which to prepare his work from scratch, and had to get on to those pressing matters that shape the world of an 18-year-old. He dialed his Internet service provider, ordered takeout, and had it delivered.

11   Twenty-some years of teaching in two-year colleges have taught me that cheating on research papers is fairly straightforward. Most of my plagiarists (a tiny pool to begin with), despite lessons like that mentioned above, borrow words and ideas too often, with too little attribution, from sources included in their lists of "Works Cited." The result is criminal; the intent clearly is not. A few omit citations or fail to indicate that quoted material is, in fact, quoted. The final 1 percent—class felons all—submit papers written by friends or professionals on unapproved topics switched 10 minutes before the deadline. Such theft most often is an act of desperation: "I won't be able to play football if I fail your course."

12   Chip's cheating feels different. The assignment, specific to the class and based on an essay in our reading materials, did not require the rigor of a typical freshman research paper. Students should have been able to complete it comfortably within a relatively short time, with careful thought but without research or

Con Viment

hand-wringing. Like delivered pizza, Chip's download, I truly think, was an act of <u>expediency</u>, not desperation. And here, of course, the metaphor fails. Ordering takeout prose is not an acceptable alternative to composing, but I wonder if Chip even flinched.

13   My sense is that Internet plagiarism is becoming more dangerous than we realize. In the comfort of a student's home or dorm room, questions of ethics may be coming to seem academic only. From his own bedroom, Chip has access to an unprecedented wealth of resources. He is not sitting in a library, which might, like a church, prompt behavior worthy of the setting.

14   Might Chip's download be related to a certain slipperiness, only partly Internet fueled, that characterizes our culture? I think of runners, myself included, arriving mid-pack at the finish line of a recent 5K Race for a Cause. A table is laden with water, juice, fruit, and all the energy bars a person could want. Race etiquette, if not regulation, instructs us to take only what we will consume on the spot. But most of us squirrel away rations for family on the sidelines, next week's school lunches, or next month's ski trip. Such bounty, free for the taking, seduces us to step over the line of self-regulation.

15   Students have now reached the food table. They are taking what is there, without regard for whether they can handle it, whether they need it, whether they even know what it is. They are copying, pasting, wallpapering, and MP3-ing their academic existences. Such activity used to seem wrong, but now I wonder whether we all have become inured to the concept of ownership, as we enhance our PowerPoint notes or Web sites.

16   The allure of and easy access to abundance, and the absence of the cues that physical settings provide, work in concert with another factor. In most cases, Internet cheating, while surprisingly easy to trace, is dishearteningly tricky to spot. The majority of papers plagiarized from the Internet are devoid of the professional gloss—an instant tip-off—characteristic of the products of research-paper mills. Writing of all kinds is taken from student and class Web sites, where text has been shared and "published" for laudable purposes. In other words, text that students download from the Web is written by students just like them, so it appears student written—exactly what we instructors want it to be.

17   In addition, the limits of a library's physical collection no longer signal possible problems. Seemingly limitless sources for the researched writing published online are collected in electronic databases available to most students who have a college I.D. card. Thus, the appearance of those sources on a Works Cited page

raises no red flags, making the plagiarism even more convincing. And the sheer volume of online material and the sophistication of search tools mean that the casual plagiarist can finish his or her "work" in a matter of seconds.

18   A chance meeting with my friend Jane, a high-school English teacher, in Aisle 4 of the local supermarket confirmed my sense that teaching and learning are being profoundly altered, and that Internet plagiarism may be gathering sufficient force to become an academic hurricane.

19   Jane's frown lines matched her sharp tone as she explained that she now has to conduct an Internet search before she selects required reading of any sort. She then ticked off a list of works she will no longer assign to her Advanced Placement English class, because of the ease with which students can—and do—download chat content, journal entries, chapter notes, and essays. Sylvia Plath's "Mirror" and David Guterson's *Snow Falling on Cedars* were the latest cross-outs on her list. Students must complete assignments on classic texts for the course, like *The Great Gatsby* and *The Grapes of Wrath*, in front of Jane, in class, in longhand.

20   Like Jane, I found myself hesitating over an essay or two on my reading list while preparing my last batch of syllabuses. I fear that academic takeout will soon begin to drive course content. I worry that these new student practices will shape our reading lists right down to the individual poems we select. In years past, plagiarists suffered loss in learning, if not in grades. After entering his guilty plea, Chip received an F where his A might have been and forfeited his stature in the class. To his credit, he tried to mend our academic friendship. But the consequences of cheating like Chip's ripple far beyond a transcript or a conscience. This new taking, which costs student-thieves neither time nor money, will cost us all.

ORGANIZATION AND IDEAS

1. What paragraph or paragraphs introduce the essay? Why do you make that choice?
2. Paragraphs 8–14 explore possible reasons for Chip's actions. Why might Laird have provided so many possibilities? Which seems most accurate and why?
3. In paragraph 14, Laird analyses Chip's action as part of our society's "slipperiness." What other examples of slipperiness can you think of?
4. What does Laird's encounter with her friend Jane contribute to the essay?
5. Given the topic of plagiarism in the classroom, what is Laird's thesis?

TECHNIQUE AND STYLE

1. How would you describe the Ellen Laird who is the main character in the essay? What evidence supports your ideas?
2. How would you characterize Chip? How fair or unfair is Laird's description of him? His motives?
3. Laird uses pizza as a metaphor for Chip's actions. To what extent is it effective?
4. Paragraphs 3 and 9 are short. What is their function? What is their effect?
5. Laird's essay originally appeared in "The Chronicle Review," the "Opinion and Ideas" section of *The Chronicle of Higher Education*, a journal, according to its Website, that delivers "news, information, and jobs for college and university faculty members and administrators." What evidence can you find to show she is writing for that audience?

SUGGESTIONS FOR WRITING

Journal

1. Use your journal to explore whether Laird's actions were justified.
2. Chip's plagiarism took place in 2000, and Laird's essay was published in 2001. What does your own experience in school and college suggest about the extent of plagiarism?

Essay

1. In paragraph 15, Laird muses over "whether we all have become in-ured to the concept of ownership, as we enhance our PowerPoint notes or Web sites." Consider the idea of "ownership" in general. To what extent, if any, has it eroded when applied to a subject of your own choosing or to
   borrowing or using without asking
   giving out recipes
   telling jokes or stories
   inflating resumés
   changing facts
2. In paragraph 20, Laird states, "the consequences of cheating like Chip's ripple far beyond a transcript or a conscience. This new taking, which costs student-thieves neither time nor money, will cost us all." She also points out how Chip's plagiarism "may be related to as a certain slipperiness, only partly Internet fueled, that characterizes our culture" and that plagiarism also affects what both students and teachers do in the classroom. Think of times when you noticed what Laird calls "slipperyness," and choose one example to analyze in an essay that uses description and narration.

Coming to America

Matthew Gooi

Every fall, the University of Iowa's Office of International Students and Scholars invites the university's international students to submit essays about "their experiences of coming to the U.S.—the high points, low points, pleasant and not-so pleasant surprises, disappointments, unexpected successes, frustrating and positive encounters." The results are published in Coming to America *so "By reading these essays, we can gain a better knowledge of what it is like to suddenly be a foreigner in a Midwestern university town." Matthew Gooi's piece was one of the essays in the collection and it will tell you much about him. What it doesn't say, however, is that he studied Biomedical Engineering, survived life in Iowa, and returned to Indonesia where he presently lives in Penang and works for Motorola Solutions.*

What to Look For   Although narrative and descriptive essays lend themselves to first person, shortening the distance between reader and writer, Gooi shortens it even more. As you read his narrative, look for how he addresses the reader directly.

1   Corn. That's all I was told to expect if I came to Iowa. Well, that and the longer-than-necessary-and-don't-bet-on-them-being-mild winters—in fact, the Consular Officer in the American Embassy back home even went as far as to bid me welcome to "the frozen wastelands of Iowa." Boy was that reassuring. Add to that the news of the tornado that had hit Iowa City and you had one slightly worried me.

2   Speaking of which, I haven't introduced myself yet. You can call me Matt; long story short, I'm a Chinese-Polish Malaysian. Before January this year, I had never set foot in America, hadn't a clue about the Midwest, and was therefore quite susceptible to believing almost anything I heard about Iowa. Fortunately, my love for traveling kept me excited about coming here regardless of my newfound feelings of foreboding. It was ironic then, I suppose, that the act of traveling here itself proved to be my worst experience to date.

3   Let me start off by saying that the entire journey from my home in Malaysia to Iowa City took more than 38 hours. Of those 38 hours, only around 7 were spent on sleep. Needless to say, when I arrived at the Cedar Rapids airport, I was asleep on my feet, had a steadily dripping nose (courtesy of a contagious passenger on the plane from Japan), and was weary from lugging my luggage around. You can only imagine how relieved I was to see the driver of the shuttle I had booked.

4   After helping him load my luggage in the trunk, I stood expectantly by the door, dying to be let in. After a minute of silence, in which the door remained locked, I chanced a puzzled look at the driver. He was giving me a strange look as well. We both stared at each other for a while, until he finally said with a nervous laugh, "I'm not allowed to let *you* drive." I looked down at the car, still confused, and then, when realization finally hit me, muttered a sheepish apology and switched sides with him—oh you Americans and your driving on the other side of the road.

5   As the car left the airport, I realized with a jolt of excitement that I was about to see Iowa for the first time (I had been in a semi-comatose sleep during the flight from Chicago to Cedar Rapids). I won't lie to you; it was quite anti-climactic to see nothing—At all. No buildings, no billboards, no signs of human habitation anywhere on either side of the freeway—just darkness. At that point I was even slightly disappointed that I couldn't see any corn.

6   Eventually, however, we neared Iowa City, and I was mollified by the lights of the mall, and my sudden fear that the Consular Officer hadn't been joking, vanished. I honestly can't quite remember the details of the remainder of that night, as it passed in a happily fuzzy blur of anticipation for a warm bed (though at that point, the cold ground was looking pretty anticipatory), but it consisted mainly of arriving at Mayflower Hall, being let in from the cold by a saint of a receptionist, checking into my new room, and collapsing onto the aforementioned bed.

7   With that adventure thankfully behind me, I spent the weekend before orientation exploring however much of Iowa City my legs could take me, and even though it was early winter, and all the trees were bare, I really liked (and still do) what I saw—probably more so than most people, just because it was all so different from what I was used to. I mean, I even got a kick out of every chance sighting of a squirrel or rabbit, and literally came to a standstill whenever I saw a bird that was any color other than black or

brown (the city wildlife back home is usually more limited to stray dogs and cats that evoke more pity than awe).

8   I suppose my transition here was a lot easier than it is on many other internationals, if only because English is my first language (so no amusing stories there I'm afraid). But one thing that took ages to adjust to was the reversal of almost everything that I had learnt to do as second nature—from small things like flipping light switches and turning keys and doorknobs, to the more life-threatening crossing of roads and driving. It was enough to convince me that either Britain or America had deliberately tried to make things harder for each other some time in the past. You might not think that having to turn things the other way round is much of an issue, but try fumbling with it 20 times a day; it also took me about 2 weeks to stop standing on the wrong side of the road when I was waiting for the bus.

9   Aside from my complaining, however, Iowa really has been great. At the risk of sounding corny, I'd have to say that one of the best things I've experienced here is meeting so many amazing people (Iowans and otherwise) who've made time fly by at an unbelievable speed and ensured that I haven't yet become homesick (though the lack of an urge to return home might be due, in part, to the memory of what that journey would be like; which is still fresh in my mind).

10   Some other highlights? Coming from a country with an almost never-varying climate of Hot and Humid (the capital H's don't do the words justice), I'd have to say that the weather variations are—for now at least—a breath of fresh air. There's nothing like the uncertainty of tomorrow's weather and the ever-looming threat of a tornado to add a little spice to your weekdays, I say. Plus, each season so far has been a new experience for me: I saw and fell in love with snow for the first time last winter, thoroughly enjoyed the new life of spring (before the bugs descended in clouds upon me that is), was reminded of home during summer and am right now experiencing the beauty of autumn, my favorite season thus far.

11   I guess in the end, it all comes down to a little give and take— crossing roads may take me a little more thinking and hesitation than it would have back home, but on the other hand, I don't have to run for dear life whenever I *do* cross one, because while over here, pedestrians seem to have the upper-hand, back home, drivers realized long ago that cars are much bigger, faster and scarier than pedestrians. And though I miss the sea (you tend to take it for granted

when you come from an island), the food and the familiarity with all aspects of my country's customs and cultures, I get to experience things here that would never happen back home, like the ice storm last winter that coated everything with a crystalline layer (which in my opinion had to be seen to be believed) and Halloween, which I never had the chance to celebrate as a child (so I'll just have to relive those non-existent memories as a young adult).

12   So all in all, I'd have to say that I'm pretty much in love with Iowa and all it has to offer, that I'm proud to be a Hawkeye, and that in 50 years or more, I'm positive that I'll look back on these times with great fondness.

ORGANIZATION AND IDEAS

1. Gooi uses chronology to organize his essay but does so somewhat subtly. Trace what happens when. What is the general time span and how does Gooi indicate the passage of time?
2. Reread the essay looking for Gooi's different moods. What progression do you find?
3. What sort of person does Gooi appear to be? How "foreign" or "International" is he?
4. Paragraphs 1–6 take Gooi from Indonesia to the University of Iowa's Mayflower Hall in Iowa City, fully half of the essay. Why might he have devoted that much space to that part of his narrative?
5. Given the essay as a whole, use your own words to state what you find to be the thesis. Is there anything more you would like to know about Gooi's experiences at the University of Iowa? If so, what?

TECHNIQUE AND STYLE

1. What unusual sentences do you find in the essay? Choose three or four and explain what's different about them and the effect they have on the reader.
2. Given that prose styles fit somewhere along a line stretching from informal to formal, where would you place Gooi's style and why? What examples do you find to support your opinion?
3. Gooi uses a greater variety of punctuation than you might expect. Note his use of dashes, hyphens, and parentheses. What do these choices add or detract from the essay? What effects do they achieve?
4. Where in the essay do you find comparisons? Which are surprising and how so?
5. Gooi's comparisons lend coherence to the essay, but he also uses other ways to link ideas. What links can you spot? Explain how they are or are not effective.

SUGGESTIONS FOR WRITING
Journal
1. Explain how Gooi's impressions of Iowa make you want to visit or avoid it. In what ways do they differ from where you live?
2. Reread the essay paying particular attention to the last paragraph. Using what you know about Gooi and his experiences, write a new concluding paragraph.

Essay
1. In many ways, Gooi's narrative is the classic "new experience" essay, and though you may not have had as extreme an adventure, you probably have several of your own, one of which can serve as the subject for your narrative. Consider what you expected and what you found out. Suggestions:
   class or job
   sport
   something you feared
   something you thought you liked
   friendship
2. Imagine that you are offered a full scholarship as an international student in the place and university of your choice. Use the Web to research your selection and write an essay that explains your choice, documenting your reasons.

Time to Look and Listen
Magdoline Asfahani

Magdoline Asfahani's essay originally appeared in the weekly news magazine Newsweek. *Although the magazine has now merged with* The Daily Beast, *it still runs a regular column called "My Turn," one that you can check out by going to* http://www.thedailybeast.com/search.html?q=My+Turn. *You'll see that more than six thousand stories are archived there, among which is "Time to Look and Listen." Asfahani was a student at the University of Texas at El Paso when the essay was published on December 2, 1996. Then, she was trying to balance her identity in ways that honored her parents' Syrian and Lebanese cultures while embracing her American-born values. It wasn't easy. Reflecting on what she wrote, Asfahani now finds "the piece is probably more meaningful now than it was when I wrote it." See if you agree.*

What to Look For If you have ever written about a painful experience, you know that it's hard to keep your emotions under control. Anger, resentment, and pain can break through and overwhelm what you are trying to portray in a cool, rational manner. As you read Asfahani's essay, look for the ways she keeps her emotions from engulfing her ideas.

1 I love my country as many who have been here for generations cannot. Perhaps that's because I'm the child of immigrants, raised with a conscious respect for America that many people take for granted. My parents chose this country because it offered them a new life, freedom and possibilities. But I learned at a young age that the country we loved so much did not feel the same way about us.

2 Discrimination is not unique to America. It occurs in any country that allows immigration. Anyone who is unlike the majority is looked at a little suspiciously, dealt with a little differently. I knew that I was an Arab and a Muslim. This meant nothing to me. At school I stood up to say the Pledge of Allegiance every day. These things did not seem incompatible at all. Then everything changed for me, suddenly and permanently, in 1985. I was only in seventh grade, but that was the beginning of my political education.

3 That year a TWA plane originating in Athens was diverted to Beirut. Two years earlier the U.S. Marine barracks in Beirut had been bombed. That seemed to start a chain of events that would forever link Arabs with terrorism. After the hijacking, I faced classmates who taunted me with cruel names, attacking my heritage and my religion. I became an outcast and had to apologize for myself constantly.

4 After a while, I tried to forget my heritage. No matter what race, religion or ethnicity, a child who is attacked often retreats. I was the only Arab I knew of in my class, so I had no one in my peer group as an ally. No matter what my parents tried to tell me about my proud cultural history, I would ignore it. My classmates told me I came from an uncivilized, brutal place, that Arabs were by nature anti-American, and I believed them. They did not know the hours my parents spent studying, working, trying to preserve part of their old lives while embracing, willingly, the new.

5 I tried to forget the Arabic I knew, because if I didn't I'd be forever linked to murderers. I stopped inviting friends over for dinner, because I thought the food we ate was "weird." I lied about where my parents had come from. Their accents (although they spoke

English perfectly) humiliated me. Though Islam is a major mono-
theistic religion with many similarities to Judaism and Christianity,
there were no holidays near Chanukah or Christmas, nothing to tie
me to the "Judeo-Christian" tradition. I felt more excluded. I slowly
began to turn into someone without a past.

6   Civil war was raging in Lebanon, and all that Americans saw
of that country was destruction and violence. Every other movie
seemed to feature Arab terrorists. The most common questions
I was asked were if I had ever ridden a camel or if my family
lived in tents. I felt burdened with responsibility. Why should an
adolescent be asked questions like "Is it true you hate Jews and
you want Israel destroyed?" I didn't hate anybody. My parents
had never said anything even alluding to such sentiments. I was
confused and hurt.

7   As I grew older and began to form my own opinions, my embarrassment lessened and my anger grew. The turning point came
in high school. My grandmother had become very ill, and it was
necessary for me to leave school a few days before Christmas
vacation. My chemistry teacher was very sympathetic until I said
I was going to the Middle East. "Don't come back in a body bag,"
he said cheerfully. The class laughed. Suddenly, those years of
watching movies that mocked me and listening to others who
knew nothing about Arabs and Muslims except what they saw
on television seemed like a bad dream. I knew then that I would
never be silent again.

8   I've tried to reclaim those lost years. I realize now that I come
from a culture that has a rich history. The Arab world is a med-
ley of people of different religions; not every Arab is a Muslim,
and vice versa. The Arabs brought tremendous advances in the
sciences and mathematics, as well as creating a literary tradition
that has never been surpassed. The language itself is flexible and
beautiful, with nuances and shades of meaning unparalleled in
any language. Though many find it hard to believe, Islam has
made progress in women's rights. There is a specific provision
in the Koran that permits women to own property and ensures
that their inheritance is protected—although recent events have
shown that interpretation of these laws can vary.

9   My youngest brother, who is 12, is now at the crossroads
I faced. When initial reports of the Oklahoma City bombing pointed
to "Arab-looking individuals" as the culprits, he came home from
school crying. "Mom, why do Muslims kill people? Why are the
Arabs so bad?" She was angry and brokenhearted, but tried to

handle the situation in the best way possible through education. She went to his class, armed with Arabic music, pictures, traditional dress and cookies. She brought a chapter of the social-studies book to life and the children asked intelligent, thoughtful questions, even after the class was over. Some even asked if she was coming back. When my brother came home, he was excited and proud instead of ashamed.

10   I only recently told my mother about my past experience. Maybe if I had told her then, I would have been better equipped to deal with the thoughtless teasing. But, fortunately, the world is changing. Although discrimination and stereotyping still exist, many people are trying to lessen and end it. Teachers, schools and the media are showing greater sensitivity to cultural issues. However, there is still much that needs to be done, not for the sake of any particular ethnic or cultural groups but for the sake of our country.

11   The America that I love is one that values freedom and the differences of its people. Education is the key to understanding. As Americans we need to take a little time to look and listen carefully to what is around us and not rush to judgment without knowing the facts. And we must never be ashamed of our pasts. It is our collective differences that unite and make us unique as a nation. It's what determines our present and our future.

ORGANIZATION AND IDEAS

1. In paragraphs 3–6, Asfahani recreates her experiences as a seventh-grader. How well does she do it?
2. It's possible to find a number of subjects in Asfahani's essay: discrimination, education, U.S. values, and stereotyping. Which is the most important? What evidence can you find to support your opinion?
3. What statement is Asfahani making about that subject?
4. How would you characterize the essay's aim: Is Asfahani trying to persuade the reader? Explain her position? Let off steam? If some combination, which dominates?
5. The essay was published in 1996 just after Thanksgiving. To what extent, if any, is it dated?

TECHNIQUE AND STYLE

1. Asfahani describes her "political education" (paragraphs 2–9). Which example is the most telling and why?
2. In paragraph 8, Asfahani asserts that she comes "from a culture that has a rich history." How well does she back up that claim?

3. Asfahani never told her parents what she was going through when she was in the seventh grade, keeping it to herself. How realistic is that reaction?
4. According to Asfahani, "Education is the key to understanding" (paragraph 11). What evidence does she present to back up that idea?
5. What examples can you find of Asfahani appealing to the reader's emotions? To reason? Which predominates?

SUGGESTIONS FOR WRITING

Journal

1. Use your journal to record the time you first recognized or experienced discrimination.
2. Think of how culture is expressed through language, food, celebrations, dress, gestures, relationships, and the like. Write a brief entry in which you tell of a time when you first experienced a culture different from your own.

Essay

1. "Know thyself" was a basic belief of the ancient Greeks, and it is as difficult to do today as it was then. You can define yourself, for example, in any number of ways by associating yourself with a group or belief or heritage, to name just a few. Think about the various ways in which you define yourself and write an essay in which you explain who you are. To generate some ideas, try thinking about who you are in relation to

   family
   ethnic heritage
   friends
   religion
   political beliefs

   Choose one of these ideas, or any other, and consider the conflicts you encountered in becoming who you are. The danger here is taking on too much so that you have the first chapter of your autobiography instead of an essay, so be sure you narrow down your topic.
2. Asfahani says that in high school, she reached a "turning point" and "would never be silent again" (paragraph 7). Think of such turning points in your own life and select one to explore in an essay. Like Asfahani, you should try to distance yourself from the time so that you can balance the emotional and the rational.

The Flag

Ann Telnaes

A syndicated editorial cartoonist, Ann Telnaes is unusual for a number of reasons. Born in Sweden, educated at the California Institute of the Arts, winner of a Pulitzer Prize for Editorial Cartooning (2001) as well as numerous other awards, she is one of few women who has pursued a career as an editorial cartoonist. You can see her work in newspapers such as The New York Times, Chicago Tribune, Washington Post, *and* USA Today. *A collection of her work was exhibited at the Library of Congress and then published as* Humor's Edge *(2004). The following cartoon was published Feburary 7, 2004. Telnaes now lives in Washington, D.C., a good place for anyone in her line of work.*

FOR DISCUSSION

1. Telnaes depicts the U.S. flag atop a flagpole that has four cameras attached to it. What is her point?
2. Why might Telnaes have chosen not to include any people?
3. Telnaes tries to draw attention to the flag by indicating it is waving while everything else is still. What does she imply by that choice?
4. What connections do you find between the essays by Stan and Gooi and Telnaes's cartoon?
5. What connections do you find between Asfahani's essay and Telnaes's cartoon?

SUGGESTIONS FOR WRITING

Journal

Take another look at Telnaes's cartoon and think about what it is saying. What possible subjects might she be addressing? Which one do you think is the most important and why?

Essay

Cameras are now fairly commonplace in stores, and some cities have installed them to catch speeders and people who run traffic lights. Cities such as London use them in areas where crowds congregate as a measure to thwart terrorists. Are such uses legitimate? Necessary? An infringement on personal freedom? What? Pick one of these questions or one of your own choosing and then use the Web to research it. Write an essay that either reports on the topic or takes a stand.

Give Examples 2

1 I heard that Reba McEntire's new album, "Read My Mind," shot to No. 5 on the Billboard chart the first weekend of its release.

2 Well, she got my $11.95.

3 I'm a 40-something black woman who spent her youth in Washington, lip-syncing to the Supremes and slow dancing to the Temptations. Now I often come home to my Manhattan apartment and put on Vince Gill, Randy Travis or Reba. Consider me a fan of country music. So there. Deal with it.

Lena Williams titles her essay "A Black Fan of Country Music Finally Tells All," suggesting a confessional and humorous tone. The three paragraphs that follow give the reader a lot of information but also work more subtly to hint at her thesis and set up the essay's structure. From that point on, you expect lots of **examples** and a sharp look at tastes in music.

Examples also

- develop
- illustrate
- clarify
- support and
- emphasize

a main point. A basic building block, examples pin down generalizations with specifics.

What types of examples are there? Examples generally fall into two categories: extended and multiple. An essay that rests its assertion on only one example is rare, but you will run across one now and then. When you do, the example often takes the form of a narrative in support of the author's thesis. To show that a minimum-wage job can be a fulfilling one, you might support your thesis by telling about a typical day on the job. Although you are relying on only one example, you will have developed it in depth and probably included a sentence or two to indicate that other experiences may contradict yours. That way your readers will accept your extended example as valid. Far more frequent are multiple examples—the kind you see in Williams' first paragraphs. They add clarity, support, and emphasis. Sometimes the examples will be drawn from your own experience and the experiences of others, but often you will find you want more generalized sources, so you consult books, magazines, the Internet, interviews, reports, and so on. Examples drawn from outside sources give your essay a more objective, reasoned *tone*. If you think of that term as similar to tone of voice, you will realize that it means the writer's attitude toward the subject and audience. Examples drawn from outside sources often provide a cooler, more formal tone; those drawn from personal experience are apt to create an informal, conversational one. No matter where you find your examples, however, present them with some variety, summarizing some, and at times quoting others.

How do you find examples?   Start with your own experience, but don't stop there. You need to connect with readers who may have little in common with you. The Internet is an obvious source. Perhaps you're a NASCAR fan and want to find out more about its appeal. Try searching "NASCAR fan" and you'll find millions of hits. You'll also discover photographs and videos that may help with your topic by providing visual information: what the fans look like, the size of the crowds, and the excitement a race can generate. After you've looked at a few sites, you can form a working thesis to refine and illustrate through examples based on your own experience and that of others.

How do you structure your essay?   In your first draft, you may want to state your thesis in one sentence and in an obvious spot: the end of your introduction. When you revise, however, you may want to delay the thesis until the conclusion. If that's where you want it, check to make sure that everything preceding the conclusion leads up to it and that along the way the reader has a clear focus on your subject.

Delaying your thesis or weaving it into your introduction is a subtle way of treating your major assertion, but if you are worried these techniques are too subtle, consider getting some mileage out of a title. An imaginative title can arouse the reader's curiosity, set the tone, highlight the subject, reveal the essay's organization, and pave the way for the thesis. That's what Lena Williams does with "A Black Fan of Country Music Finally Tells All."

Examples not only illustrate generalizations; they also expand and develop them. After you have written a draft of an essay, you may find it useful to double-check each of your examples: How does the example support the generalization? Is the source of the example clear? How does it connect to the readers' experiences? If the example is an extended one, is it sufficiently developed so that it can support the thesis by itself? Then you might think about the examples as a whole: Do they draw on a variety of sources? Do they incorporate both summary and quotation?

When examples structure an essay, they are usually in chronological or dramatic order, moving from what came first and ending with what came last, or beginning with the least dramatic and finishing with the most. To decide which example is the most dramatic, ask some obvious questions: Which is the most important? Which is most likely to affect the reader? Which carries the most impact? You'll probably come up with the same answer for each question and that's the example you should use to cap your essay.

How do you link your examples? After you have found good examples and sequenced them logically, you should check your **transitions** to avoid overusing terms such as *for example.* Think of what transitions do:

- add: *and, also, again, besides, moreover, next, or finally*
- shift or concede: *but, yet, however, instead, in contrast, of course, certainly,* or *granted*
- emphasize a result or summarize: *therefore, thus, as a result, so, finally, in conclusion, hence,* or *in brief*

Less obvious and apt to be more effective are transitions that don't call attention to themselves, such as repeating a key word from the previous sentence or using a personal or demonstrative pronoun. If you use pronouns, however, make sure what they refer to is clear. The demonstrative pronoun *this,* for instance, should usually be followed by a noun, as in *this sentence* or *this idea.* A *this* standing by itself may force your reader to stop and reread to understand the reference.

Although all the essays in this chapter have a thesis developed by examples, the examples themselves often cross over into other categories. You will discover that is also the case with your own writing. You may well find yourself using an example that is also description, or, to put it more precisely, a description that functions as an example. A description of a crowd watching the Daytona 500 can serve as an example of car racing's popularity. Other patterns of organization, such as narrative, causal relationships, comparison, definition, or analysis of a process, can also serve as examples. The function—to support and develop an assertion—is more important than the label.

Useful Terms

Example An illustration that supports a generalization, usually an assertion, by providing evidence that develops or clarifies it.

Transition A word, phrase, sentence, or paragraph that carries the reader smoothly from point A to point B. Some transitions (*first, next,* and the like) are obvious; others are more subtle, such as a repeated word or phrase or a synonym for a key term. See also list on page 60.

POINTERS FOR USING EXAMPLE

Exploring the Topic

1. **What examples can you think of to illustrate your topic?** Are all from your own experience? What can you use from other sources?
2. **Are your examples pertinent and representative?** Do they fit? Do they illustrate? Are they of equal weight? Which are relatively unimportant?
3. **How familiar is your audience with each of your examples?**
4. **Which examples best lend themselves to your topic?** In what order would they best be presented?
5. **What point do you want to make?** Do your examples all support that point? Do they lead the reader to your major assertion?
6. **What is your purpose behind your point?** Is your primary aim to inform, persuade, or entertain?

Drafting the Paper

1. **Know your reader.** It may be that your audience knows little about your subject or that the reader simply hasn't thought

(Continued)

POINTERS FOR USING EXAMPLE *(Continued)*

much about it; on the other hand, maybe the reader knows a great deal and holds a definite opinion. Once you have made an informed guess about your readers' attitudes toward your topic and thesis, reexamine your examples in light of that information. Some may have to be explained in greater detail than others, and the more familiar ones need to be presented in a new or different light. Use the techniques you learned from writing descriptive papers.

2. **Know your purpose.** Personal experience papers are often difficult to write because you are so tied to your own experience. If you are writing with this aim in mind, try making yourself conscious of the personality you project as a writer. Jot down the characteristics you wish to convey about yourself and refer to this list as you revise. Although this is a highly self-conscious trick, when done well, the result appears natural. Also double-check your examples, making sure that you present them in sufficient detail to communicate fully to your audience. That warning serves as well for informative and persuasive papers. Again, use description to make your examples effective: Use sensory detail, compare the unfamiliar to the familiar, and be concrete. If you are writing a persuasive paper, use these techniques to appeal to emotions.

3. **Consider multiple examples.** Most essays rely on multiple examples to support their points; nevertheless, some examples will be more developed than others. Figure out which ones are particularly striking and develop them, reserving the others for mere mention. To lend breadth and credibility to your point, consider citing statistics, quotations, authorities, and the experience of others. Comment on what you take from sources to make it more your own.

4. **Consider extended example.** If an essay rests on one example, choose and develop that illustration carefully. Make sure it is representative and that you provide all relevant information. Make as many connections as you can between your example and the category it represents. During revision, you may eliminate some of these references, but at first it's best to have too many.

5. **Arrange your examples effectively.** Most essays move from the less dramatic, less important to the most, but examples can also be arranged chronologically or in terms of frequency (from least to most frequent). Like the essay itself, each paragraph should be developed around a central assertion, either stated or implied. In longer papers, groups of paragraphs will support a unifying statement.

6. **Check your transitions.** Take a hard look at what links one example and paragraph to another. The transitions should perform the appropriate function, so check them against the list on page 60.

7. **Make a point.** Examples so obviously need to lead up to something that it's not hard to make a point. But your point may not be an assertion. Test your thesis by asking whether your point carries any information. If it does, it's an assertion. Say you come up with, "We live in a world of time-saving technology." You can think of lots of examples and even narrow down the "we" to "anyone who cooks today." The setting is obviously the kitchen, but is the revised thesis an assertion? Given the information test, it fails. Your audience knows what you are supposedly informing them about. But if you revise and come up with "Electronic gizmos have turned the kitchen into a laboratory," you've given the topic a fresher look, one that does contain information.

A Black Fan of Country Music Finally Tells All

Lena Williams

While a student at Howard University, Lena Williams started her career in journalism as a reporter for a radio station. After earning her BA, she entered the Columbia University Graduate School of Journalism, from which she received an MSc. She worked as a reporter while interning at the Washington Post, *then as an associate editor at* Black Sports Magazine. *In 1974, she joined the staff of* The New York Times, *first as a clerk, then trainee, and finally senior writer, retiring in 2005. She has written on civil rights, lifestyles, metropolitan news, and sports, winning various publishing awards along the way. An article she originally wrote for the* Times *in 1997 she then developed as a book,* It's the Little Things: The Everyday Interactions That Get under the Skin of Blacks and Whites *(2000). The essay that follows appeared on June 19, 1994, in the* Times's *"Arts and Leisure" section's coverage of "Pop Music." The column was titled "Pop View."*

What to Look For   At times, you may find yourself writing an essay on a subject that you're somewhat embarrassed about, which is the position Lena Williams found herself in when she wrote the essay that follows. In that case, you'll need to make a decision about your tone, the attitude you take toward your subject and your audience. Williams, as you will see, takes an unapologetic stance, almost daring her readers to challenge her. Yet the overall tone of the essay is not antagonistic because she takes the edge off of her "challenge" with humor and personal narrative, techniques that you can incorporate into your own writing.

1   I heard that Reba McEntire's new album, "Read My Mind," shot to No. 5 on the Billboard chart the first weekend of its release.

2   Well, she got my $11.95.

3   I'm a 40-something black woman who spent her youth in Washington, lip-syncing to the Supremes and slow dancing to the Temptations. Now I often come home to my Manhattan apartment and put on Vince Gill, Randy Travis or Reba. Consider me a fan of country music. So there. Deal with it.

4   For most of my adult life, I was a closet country music fan. I'd hide my Waylon Jennings and Willie Nelson albums between the dusty, psychedelic rock. I'd listen to Dolly Parton on my earphones, singing along softly, afraid my neighbors might mistake my imitation twang for a cry for help. I'd enter a music store, looking over my shoulder in search of familiar faces and flip through the rhythm-and-blues section for about five minutes before sneaking off to the country aisle where I'd surreptitiously grab a Travis Tritt tape off the rack and make a beeline for the shortest cashier's line.

5   Just when I'd reached for my American Express card, I'd spot a tall, dark, handsome type in an Armani suit standing behind me with a puzzled look. What's he going to think? "The sister seems down, but what's she doing with that Dwight Yoakum CD?"

6   So now I'm publicly coming out of the closet and proclaiming my affection for country perennials like Ms. McEntire.

7   When I told a friend I was preparing this confessional, he offered a word of caution: "No self-respecting black person would ever admit to that in public."

8   I thought about his comment. As a child growing up in the 1950s, in a predominantly black community, I wasn't allowed to play country-and-western music in my house. Blacks weren't supposed to like country—or classical for that matter—but that's another story. Blacks' contribution to American music was in jazz, blues and funk. Country music was dismissed as poor white folks' blues and associated with regions of the nation that symbolized prejudice and racial bigotry. Even mainstream white America viewed country as lower class and less desirable, often poking fun at its twangy chords and bellyaching sentiments.

9   But I was always a cowgirl at heart. I liked country's wild side; its down-home, aw-shucks musicians with the yodel in their voices and the angst in their lyrics. I saw an honesty in country and its universal tales of love lost and found. Besides, the South didn't have a monopoly on racial hatred, and country artists, like everybody else, were stealing black music, so why should I hold it against country?

10   And while snickering at country, white America also demonstrated a similar cultural backwardness toward black music, be it gospel, ragtime or the blues. So I allowed country to enter my heart and my mind, in spite of its faults. Indeed, when prodded, some blacks who rejected country conceded that there was a spirituality that resounded in the music and that in its heartfelt sentiment, country

was a lot like blues. Yet they could never bring themselves to spend hard-earned dollars on Hank Williams Jr.

11   The 1980s saw country (western was dropped, much to my chagrin) become mainstream. Suddenly there was country at the Copa and at Town Hall. WYNY-FM radio in New York now claims the largest audience of any country station, with more than one million listeners. Dolly Parton and Kenny Rogers became movie stars. Garth Brooks became an American phenomenon.

12   Wall Street investment bankers bought cowboy boots and hats and learned to do the two-step. And black and white artists like Patti LaBelle and Lyle Lovett and Natalie Cole and Ms. McEntire now sing duets and clearly admire one another's music.

13   Perhaps the nation's acceptance of country has something to do with an evolutionary change in the music. Country has got edge. It has acquired an attitude. Womens' voices have been given strength. Oh, the hardship and misery is still there. But the stuff about "standing by your man" has changed to a more assertive posture.

14   In "I Won't Stand in Line," a song on Ms. McEntire's new album, she makes it clear to a skirt-chasing lover that "I'd do almost anything just to make you mine, but I won't stand in line." That line alone makes me think of Aretha Franklin's "Respect."

15   One other thing: I don't like sad songs. I've cried enough for a lifetime. Country makes me laugh, always has. Maybe because it never took itself so seriously. Think about it. "Drop-Kick Me, Jesus, Through the Goal Posts of Life." "A Boy Named Sue."

16   Ms. McEntire serves up a humorous touch in "Why Haven't I Heard From You." "That thing they call the telephone/Now there's one on every corner, in the back of every bar/You can get one in your briefcase, on a plane or in your car/So tell me why haven't I heard from you, darlin', honey, what is your excuse?" Call it Everywoman's lament.

17   Well it's off my chest; and it feels good.

18   I will no longer make excuses for my musical tastes. Not when millions are being made by performers exhorting listeners to "put your hands in the air and wave 'em like you just don't care."

19   Compare that with the haunting refrain of Ms. McEntire's "I Think His Name Was John," a song about a woman, a one-night stand and AIDS: "She lays all alone and cries herself to sleep/'Cause she let a stranger kill her hopes and her dreams/And in the end when she was barely hanging on/ All she could say is she thinks his name was John."

ORGANIZATION AND IDEAS

1. What paragraph or paragraphs introduce the essay?
2. Paragraphs 4 and 5 detail a short narrative. What is Williams' point?
3. Paragraphs 8–12 sketch the evolution of country-and-western music. Trace the chronology and the changes in attitude toward the genre.
4. The essay ends with a comparison in paragraphs 18 and 19, one that Williams doesn't spell out. What is it? How does it relate to her thesis?
5. Williams maintains that since the 1980s, country music has "become mainstream" (paragraph 11). How accurate is that assertion?

TECHNIQUE AND STYLE

1. Paragraphs 2 and 17 consist of one sentence each. What effect does Williams achieve with a one-sentence paragraph?
2. Is the essay addressed primarily to a black or white audience or both? What evidence can you find to support your view?
3. Although the essay expresses Williams' personal opinion and is subjective, she achieves a balance between the personal and the general. How does she do that?
4. Williams supports her thesis with examples from popular music, both country-western and black. Explain whether you find her examples sufficient evidence for her thesis.
5. Analyze the effectiveness of the essay's title. What other titles can you think of? Which is the more effective and why?

SUGGESTIONS FOR WRITING

Journal

1. Taste in music, as in most everything else, is apt to be idiosyncratic. Think of a band or song or type of music that represents your particular taste and explain why you like it, using examples to support your ideas.
2. Make a list of the names and titles Williams uses as examples. What examples can you provide to update that list?

Essay

1. If you look back on your tastes, you will probably find that they change over time. Perhaps a type of music that you liked some years ago you would now have a hard time listening to. Or perhaps you were disappointed in a film you recently saw again or a book that you reread, one that had impressed you in the past and belonged to a particular genre such as horror films or adventure stories. You might start by drawing up two columns—*Then* and *Now*—and jotting

down examples representing your previous tastes and your present ones. Like Williams, you may want to write about how your taste has evolved or explain why you like what you like. For a general category, you might think about

music
food
films
books
heroes
sports

2. Williams's essay is an assertive defense of her taste in music. Write an essay in which you evaluate the essay's effectiveness. You might start by asking yourself questions such as, "Does she present enough evidence?" "Are her examples apt?" "Does she provide enough background for her explanations?"

Why English Professors Love Country Music

Gina Barreca

Feminist, humorist, scholar, editor, and author, Gina Barreca is also a Professor of English at the University of Connecticut. Starting with the scholarly They Used to Call Me Snow White...But I Drifted: Women's Strategic Use of Humor *(1991), Barreca has edited sixteen books and written eight, the latest of which is a collection of short essays:* It's Not That I'm Bitter, or How I Learned to Stop Worrying About Visible Panty Lines and Conquered the World *(2009).* Babes in Boyland: A Personal Hisory of Co-education in the Ivy League *(2005) is her memoir whose title says it all. Her articles have appeared in numerous newspapers and magazines, and she also writes for the "Brainstorm" section of* The Chronicle of Higher Education *where the following essay appeared on May 30, 2011.*

What to Look For   One of the hazards of an essay that's built on example is ending up with a list, not an essay. As you read Barreca's piece, note how she avoids that trap.

1   Maybe not every English professor loves country music, but I do—and I know I'm not the only one.

2   Country starts where pop stops. It's grown-up music insofar as it begins when innocence is lost, or, to be more precise, when innocence throws its polka-dot panties out of the Chevy's back window.

3   It hates phrases like "insofar."

4   It's about life as it's actually lived: days filled by work ("9–5"; "Take This Job and Shove It"; "Down at the Factory") and evenings spent with family ("That Silver-Haired Daddy Of Mine"; "Cleaning This Gun—Come On In, Boy": "My Woman, My Woman, My Wife") or perhaps with the dissolving of families ("She's Actin' Single (I'm Drinkin' Doubles)"; "Sleeping Single in a Double Bed"; "If You've Got The Money, I've Got The Time").

5   It's about the fact that when one's poet days are over and one goes back to being one's self (country music hates this sentence), one learns that the only important things in life are "Faster horses, younger women, older whiskey, and more money."

6   Country music teaches us all about the triangularization of desire, a la Rene Girard: "You're on the phone with your girlfriend, she's upset/ she's going off about something that you said/ 'Cause she doesn't get your humor like I do" sings Taylor Swift (who was lovely and gracious when I asked to have a picture taken with her in Nashville); "Your beauty is beyond compare/ With flaming locks of auburn hair/ With ivory skin and eyes of emerald green/ Your smile is like a breath of spring/ Your voice is soft like summer rain/ And I cannot compete with you, Jolene" sings Dolly Parton, in a song that sounds like a sonnet.

7   Country songs are familiar, yet defiant. The first line of any respectable country song starts up after the traditional romance plot ends (*"She got the goldmine, I got the shaft"*) or after the singer realizes the complexity of the worker's situation within capitalism's oppressive system, etc. (*"You load sixteen tons, and what do you get?/ Another day older and deeper in debt"*).

8   It threatens or promises—depending on your perspective—that "Heaven's Just A Sin Away" and it warns you about what might happen if you lay off the bottle: "I sobered up, and I got to thinkin'/ You ain't much fun since I quit drinkin.'"

9   There are innumerable songs about fiercely independent women—including "Independence Day" ("he was a dangerous man/ But mama was proud and she stood her ground/ she knew she was on the losin' end/...Well, she lit up the sky that Fourth of July/ by the

time the firemen come they/ Just put out the flames and took down some names/ and send me to the county home/ Now I ain't sayin' it's right or it's wrong but maybe it's the only way/ Talk About your revolution/ It's Independence Day").

10   There's Miranda Lambert's "Gunpowder and Lead" where we learn that the guy who slapped her face and "shook (her) like a rag doll" is going to learn what "little girls (are) made of/ Gunpowder and lead" because, after all, "His fist is big but my gun's bigger/ He'll find out when I pull the trigger."

11   The classic Dixie Chicks fun-homicide song "Good-Bye, Earl" concerns another abusive guy ("he walked right through that restraining order and put her in intensive care") who, once poisoned by the black-eyed peas (the food, not the band), turns out to be "a missing person who nobody missed at all."

12   Country music talks about loss, jail, longing, grief, childhood, autonomy, adultery, trains, ambition, fighting, camaraderie, death, and all forms of vehicular transportation.

13   And, finally, country music talks about reading about a boy "in a Faulkner novel" and "meeting him once in a Williams play" while expecting—or at least hoping—its listeners will understand.

ORGANIZATION AND IDEAS

1. Paragraph 1 announces the subject and Barreca's attitude toward it, but as a thesis it seems incomplete in that it does not state the reasons. In your own words, what are they?
2. Look at the opening sentences of paragraphs 2–11. Why might Barreca have presented them in the order she does?
3. Although it's obvious that Barreca "loves country music," the essay also contains wording that shows she is an academic. What examples can you find? What do they add?
4. To what extent does Barreca's title invite your to read what follows? What other titles can you think of? Which do you prefer and why?
5. In paragraph 2 Barreca states: "Country starts where pop stops." Does the rest of the essay support that claim? Why or why not? Given your own experience, is the claim valid?

TECHNIQUE AND STYLE

1. Paragraphs 4–9 have the same structure—topic sentence followed by examples. How effective is the repetition? Why?
2. In what ways does paragraph 12 summarize what has gone before? Is anything added? How successful is the paragraph?

3. What is Barreca's point in paragraph 13? Why might she have saved it for last?
4. Barreca uses parentheses extensively. Choose a paragraph and rewrite it in your own words without parentheses. What did you have to add? What is gained? Lost?
5. How would you describe the diction level in the essay? Explain what it adds to or detracts from the essay.

SUGGESTIONS FOR WRITING

Journal

1. Barreca's essay first appeared in her blog for *The Chronicle of Higher Education*. Explain why you do or do not read blogs.
2. What is your favorite kind of music and why? Jot down the reasons in your journal. If you want to turn your notes into an essay, add some examples and you have a working draft.

Essay

1. Country music falls into the category of popular culture, but that's a grab bag of a category in which almost anything fits: music, film, video games, YouTube, fashion, and fads—you name it. Think about something you "love" that's part of popular culture and analyze the reasons behind your choice, supporting your ideas with examples.
2. Aside from country music, the essays by Gina Barreca and Lena Williams have a lot in common. Reread both, paying particular attention to tone, structure, thesis, claims, examples, and effect. Choose the essay you find the more effective and defend your thesis by drawing on examples from both essays. Make sure you comment on and analyze anything you quote.

A Bleak Future

Samantha Magaña

Shasta College, part of the California Community College system, is in Redding, California, but reaches out to students in an area larger than Massachusetts. Samantha Magaña is one of those students. Originally from Fairfield, California, she moved to Redding where she is now a freshman at Shasta. On graduation, she hopes to continue at the University of California, Davis to continue working toward her major in medical sciences, and in the meantime, she enjoys cross-country and track.

"A Bleak Future" was written for extra credit in a writing class taught by Dionne Soares Palmer who designed the assignment as a letter to the editor, with the students choosing their own topics to support their opinions. Palmer wanted the students "to experience the process of preparing a piece of writing for publication, write for a real general audience (rather than just an instructor), and possibly have an impact on their community by persuading Redding residents to accept their points of view." Magaña's essay, along with those by several other students, was published on December 5, 2012, by aNewsCafe.com.

What to Look For   As you read Magaña's essay, note how she uses both personal experience and outside sources, a combination that strengthens her argument.

1   As we all know, California is currently in the midst of a recession. This recession has forced funding cuts upon schools, work forces, and many other local programs. These enormous cuts amount to roughly 12.5 billion dollars in cuts while funds get shuffled around and divided up amongst local governments (Sabalow). Clearly, these immense cuts are bound to negatively affect Shasta County's schools; however, I believe that despite the recession, the government should not diminish school funding, since today's students will help determine tomorrow's future. These budget cuts will force students to suffer through increased class sizes and higher tuition rates. Instead of taking money from education, the government could cut funding from unnecessary roadwork.

2   Budget cuts throughout Shasta County are affecting all educational facilities including grammar schools, high schools, and community colleges. At a rally, nearly three hundred people gathered to protest budget cuts being made to Shasta county schools. At this rally, educators discussed how the budget cuts would result in a definite increase in class sizes; classroom sizes were said to increase up to thirty-four students (Winters). I have personally experienced this increase in class sizes and its negative effects at my previous high school. At Foothill High School, I was enrolled in the Calculus class, which was originally taught during two different class periods; however, due to insufficient funds, both periods were combined. My class went from having about 20 students, to having 38 students in one class. This increase of students meant that if everyone came to class, there were not enough seats. This increase also resulted in a different learning environment because the students were not focused. Also, our teacher did not have enough time to help all of us one-on-one. Hoxby, a Harvard student who did a study of the effects of class size on students, confirmed that larger class sizes result in a lack of student progress since teachers do not have enough time to spend with each student. Clearly, if budget cuts cause an increase in class size, student's grades and futures will suffer.

3   Not only are grammar schools and high schools feeling the scourge of budget cuts, but community colleges are also being affected. If these extreme budget cuts continue to be made to the educational system in Shasta County then tuition rates at Shasta College will increase. The budget cuts would force Shasta College to raise tuition by $10, making the cost of each class per unit rise from $26 to $36 (Sabalow). This seemingly small increase in money will add up for a student taking 20 units. Shasta College's Superintendant/President, Joe Wyse, stated that due to the $400 million in cuts to California community colleges, Shasta College funding would be cut approximately $1.5 million dollars, resulting in almost 400,000 dollars being backfilled through increased student fees (Sabalow). Clearly, since school is already expensive, an increase in tuition would prevent some students from pursuing school.

4   Clearly budget cuts are negatively affecting education; however, I think that we should prevent these changes. We can prevent these changes by diminishing funds from unnecessary roadwork. Some recent unnecessary roadwork was the construction of the roundabout at the intersection of Shasta View and Old Alturas, built

from August 19-29, 2011. This addition used roughly 2.24 million dollars of Shasta county's funds to create. This project was supposed to be finished before school started, but there was a delay due to the work costing almost 300,000 dollars more than what was expected (Mobley). What was the purpose for this roundabout? Nothing. It was completely unnecessary since nothing was wrong with the four way stop that previously occupied the area.

5   Overall, regardless of the recession in California, education should not suffer. School budgets should not be cut anymore because it would lead to increased class sizes and higher tuition costs. Also, we can reduce budget cuts in schools by reducing money wasted on unnecessary roadwork. After all, everyone in the community today affects the futures of our fellow citizens, so don't we want to prepare our future leaders?

Works Cited

Hoxby, Caroline M. "The Effects of Class Size on Student Achievement: New Evidence from Population Variation." *Quarterly Journal of Economics.* President and Fellows of Harvard College and the Massachusetts Institute of Technology 2000. Pg 1240. Web. 17 October 2011.

Mobley, Scott. "Roundabout work to shut Shasta View/Old Alturas intersection in Redding." Redding.com. 3 August 2011 at 11:17 p.m. n.p. n.d. Web. 18 October 2011.

Sabalow, Ryan. "Shasta County faces Cuts from Brown's Budget." Redding. com. 10 January 2011 at 11:56 pm. n.p. n.d. Web. 17 October 2011.

Winters, Amanda. "About 300 rally in Redding against school budget cuts." Redding.com. 4 March 2010 at midnight. n.p. n.d. Web. 17 October 2011.

ORGANIZATION AND IDEAS

1. What does the title suggest about the essay's subject? It's tone?
2. What paragraph or paragraphs supply the essay's introduction? In your own words and one sentence, what thesis does that introduction suggest?
3. Where in the essay does Magaña provide her first example? What is it? How well does it support her point?
4. Take another look at the opening sentences of paragraphs 2–4. How well does each one work as the topic sentence for the paragraph that follows?
5. Reread the last paragraph and then look at your response to question 1. How would you revise your statement of a working thesis? How well does the result suit the essay?

TECHNIQUE AND STYLE

1. Magaña deals with her personal experience and the larger contexts of California's budget cuts to education and the national recession. How well does she cover them? Which dominates? What examples support your opinion?
2. You'll notice that Magaña documents her claims by using sources from the Internet. How reliable do you find those sources? How varied?
3. The essay is aimed at the readers of *aNewsCafe.com*, a Web site that focuses on local news and opinions. How well does Magaña target that audience?
4. In journalism, Magaña's essay would be called an op-ed, a category for commentary, features, and opinion pieces, often placed on the page opposite the newspaper's editorials and letters to the editor. How well does it fit? If you were the local paper's editor, would you print it? Why or why not?
5. An argumentative essay aims to persuade the reader to accept the writer's thesis or at least to engage the reader with the issue. To what extent does Magaña make you aware of cuts to your own institution? To your city or state's system of education?

SUGGESTIONS FOR WRITING

Journal

1. Use your journal to record what your institution charges for tuition and your opinion of the value it returns.
2. To what extent does the essay persuade you? If you were to add to it, what would that be?

Essay

1. It's hard to listen to a political campaign, read a paper, or listen to the news without hearing about budget cuts, and a controversy often ensues. Often the argument focusses on why x should not be cut or why y should be cut instead. Choose one subject and write a letter to the editor arguing against the reduction. Possibilites:
   college or university budget
   state or municipal roads
   police or fire departments
   state supported hospitals
   garbage collection
   You might use your local paper to discover what the hottest topics are so you have a ready source of information.
2. Many students are only able to attend college because they can get a loan that helps pay for tuition, but the result can turn into a crippling burden. Use sources to investigate the dark side of student loans so that you can draft an essay arguing for reform.

Have Fun

Allison Silverman

If you have watched The Daily Show with Jon Stewart *or* The Colbert Report, *you have met Allison Silverman without knowing it. As one of the writers for* The Daily Show, *she won not only an Emmy but also a coveted Peabody Award, the latter given "for excellence in radio and television broadcasting." A graduate of Yale University, Silverman sharpened her sense of comedy and timing in Chicago doing improvisational skits before joining first* The Daily Show, *then* Late Night with Conan O'Brien, *and then* The Colbert Report, *where she was the head writer and executive producer. She left* The Colbert Report *in 2009, but you may have seen her work on the comedy television series* Portlandia. *Some of that wacky humor shows up in "Have Fun," her essay that appeared in* The New York Times Magazine *on April 8, 2007, as one of the magazine's "True-Life Tales."*

What to Look For   Although Silverman's essay has an informal tone, she has organized the essay carefully. As you read, mark the various places she echoes or ties events together. The result is a sense of seamlessness, coherence.

1   There's a particular tone of voice that mothers use when they watch their kids at the pool—a queasy combination of "have fun" and "don't die." It's how my mother sounded when I was leaving the country last year.

2   "Be safe," she said as I was packing. "Remember what happened to Jill Carroll." I did remember. Jill Carroll is the journalist held for 82 days by masked gunmen who ambushed her car in a notoriously dangerous district of Baghdad. I, on the other hand, was going to a friend's wedding on the Italian Riviera.

3   Like all mothers, mine worries. When I got my driver's license, she explained how to get wherever I wanted without taking a single left turn. When I said I might not have children, she expressed a disarming readiness to "harvest" my eggs against my will. There are times when my mother warns me of so many dangers that I find them irresistible. A few years ago, I had friends take

my picture in "hazardous" situations. In one, I am standing on a boulder by the sea, pointing to a road sign that reads: "Caution: Extremely Dangerous—People Have Been Swept From the Rocks and Drowned." The idea was to send them to my mother, but I never could bring myself to do it.

4   Before the wedding, I took a train to Trieste, which was empty except for the teenagers on the pier and the women in housecoats who fed chicken livers to stray cats. There, I caught a bus for Ljubljana, and then four trains and a taxi back west to the town of Lerici, where the wedding was held. After several nights of limoncello and rides home with new friends, I headed to Florence, all by myself.

5   My last morning there, I walked to the train station and checked the board that listed arrivals and departures. My train was 30 minutes late. When I checked again, it was 80 minutes late. Each time the numbers on the board fluttered, my train magically receded farther from the Florence station. It didn't make sense. Weren't the Florentines the first to master perspective?

6   I bought some Peanut M&M's and tried not to be annoyed. When I turned around, there was a woman walking toward me, a beggar. She had legs the color of butternut squash and a look that made you wonder if she'd ever baked children into pies. Her swinging bag hit a man square in the face—a tourist in a floppy hat who had been sitting on the platform—and she didn't even stop. My hands started to sweat; the Peanut M&M's slid around in my fist. Perhaps the worst time to be approached by a beggar is while you are eating Peanut M&M's. The way they tumble carelessly from their golden wrapper. Playful. Abundant. Incriminating.

7   She had set her sights specifically on me—a young woman alone, an easy mark. So when she asked for money, I said no.

8   She got louder. She talked faster.

9   I said no again.

10   She pulled out an empty baby bottle and waved it in my face, yelling.

11   But, I thought, this woman was in her 60s. She was no needy young mother. Instead, I suddenly felt she was an angry, older mother confronting an ungrateful child: me. I didn't understand what she was saying, but I got the unnerving sense that she was scolding me for taking last-minute trips in foreign countries, for hiking through forests alone, for hanging out at Internet cafes in the middle of the night, for making all those unnecessary left turns. How could I possibly do that to my mother?

12   And then she hit me. A hard, backhanded slap on the shoulder from a woman I had never met. I took a step back, and the postcard rack behind me teetered. She stared. I stared.

13   Then I hit her back. The tourist in the floppy hat applauded.

14   The woman shoved the baby bottle back in her bag. "*Tu sei cattiva*," she said. You are wicked. She pulled down the lower lid of her right eye. I was cursed. The train finally arrived. It took me to a bus, which took me to an airport terminal, where I was supposed to catch a shuttle to my hotel to sleep before an early-morning flight. But there was no shuttle. The terminal was empty except for a man in a business suit.

15   I waited. No one came. I showed the man in the business suit the address of my hotel. My Italian was too thin to explain much else. He left, and I sat in the terminal alone. Half an hour later, he reappeared, said nothing, picked up my bag and led me to his car.

16   I got in, trying not to think about Jill Carroll and being cursed. When curses are directed at other people, I absolutely know for a fact that they are complete hogwash. But I'm considerably more open-minded when it comes to curses directed at me.

17   Neither of us talked. We didn't even make eye contact. When we reached the hotel, he took my bag to the front desk and I kissed him on the cheek. By the time I found my room, I was in tears. I'd had fun. I didn't die. I wondered if I'd ever tell my mother.

Organization and Ideas

   1. Paragraphs 1–3 introduce the essay. What do they tell you about the mother? Silverman?
   2. What kind of example does what happened to Jill Carroll illustrate?
   3. How would you characterize Silverman? Her mother? Their relationship?
   4. Silverman uses description and narration to illustrate two events—one in the train station and the other in the airport. In what ways are those two events examples? What do they illustrate?
   5. Considering your responses to questions 1–4, what thesis does Silverman imply?

Technique and Style

   1. Consider all the negative details and the positive ones. Which group predominates? Why might Silverman have wanted that choice?
   2. How would you describe the atmosphere Silverman creates in paragraphs 4 and 14–16?

3. Reread the essay paying particular attention to tone. What different kinds of humor do you find? What effect do they achieve?

4. Silverman describes the incident with the old woman in considerable detail. Trace your emotional responses to each of paragraphs 4–14. How do your responses change and why?

5. Silverman's essay deals with personal experience centered on events that would be foreign to many readers. How does she try to link her experience to that of her readers? How well does she succeed?

SUGGESTIONS FOR WRITING

Journal

1. Reread paragraphs 4–14. To what extent are Silverman's reactions justified? Those of the old lady?

2. At the end of the essay, Silverman comments on her adventures, "I wondered if I'd ever tell my mother." Write up the version she might tell.

Essay

1. Think about the times you had an unexpected encounter. Where were you? What caused it? How did it affect you? Why? If nothing comes to mind, consider one of these suggestions:

seeing an old friend
visiting a once-familiar place
confronting an unfamiliar food
discovering a cultural difference
meeting up with a poisonous snake or wild animal

Use your ideas to write an essay in which you depend on examples to support your main point.

2. Think about your answers to question 3 in Technique and Style and use what you discovered to write an essay discussing Silverman's kind of humor. You may find it helpful to read about her work writing for Jon Stewart and Stephen Colbert, accounts that are readily available on the Web.

Baltimore Tales

Richard O'Mara

Baltimore is familiar territory for Richard O'Mara, for he spent much of his forty-year career working for the Baltimore Sun *as a reporter, columnist, and editor. O'Mara's time there included serving as Foreign Editor and resident correspondent in Europe and Latin America. Now retired, he continues to pursue his interests in the culture and history of Latin America and was named a Knight International Press Fellow. In addition to being a journalist, O'Mara is also a distinguished essayist whose work has been published in various literary journals such as* VQR (the Virginia Quarterly Review), *the* Antioch Review, *and the* Sewanee Review. *Twelve of his essays appear in his book* In The Street Where They Lived (2011), *an account of growing up poor and Irish-American during the Great Depression. The essay included here takes him back to Baltimore and an unusual experience.*

What to Look For   O'Mara's essay deals with an incident, an exchange, a puzzle and exemplifies how an object can become a symbol. As you read the essay, look for the ways he connects his unusual experience to the ordinary ones of the general reader.

1   There's a bullet in my car. It's in the compartment beside me where I put parking meter change. I hear it knocking around among the coins, a clunky bass amid a sprinkle of tinkling triangles.

2   I got it while stopped at a red light near Baltimore's downtown stadiums. A young man in a wheelchair rolled up and put his hand out. In these situations sometimes I give, sometimes not. I don't know why I give, or decline to, though it has little to do with how the beggar looks: sad, smiling, pathetic, rubbed raw and dirtied by life on the streets. The impulse for generosity is fickle and mysterious.

3   A lot of people disapprove of beggars. They don't just disapprove of giving to them, but of their very existence. They are afraid, and cultivate dubious notions. Don't roll down your window, they may have knives. Don't give them money, they take in hundreds every day; they have mansions in Florida.

4   The guy in the wheelchair was in his 30s, thin and shaved. There was nothing pathetic about him, the wheelchair notwithstanding. Because of his nimble ability to move around on it, I assumed he'd been at it for some time. I couldn't imagine him in a mansion anywhere. I gave him a dollar and he thanked me. Then, in the instant before the light changed, he put the bullet in my hand.

5   "Where'd this come from?"

6   "Around here," he said. "I picked it up a week ago. It's for you."

7   As I was trying to understand what he meant by that remark, so suggestive of a destiny, or to ask him what he thought I should do with the bullet, the car behind me barked and I had to move on. I plopped the thing in among the coins and thought no more of it.

8   Three days later, again while waiting for a light change, I took the slug out and held it in my hand. There are people in this world who believe that certain inanimate objects give off emanations, stones for instance. I wouldn't say what I felt was one of those, but I did detect a very faint sensation of comfort, though that might have been simple autosuggestion. I have memories of nervous young second lieutenants in the Army trying to draw confidence from their polished swagger sticks. And I'm sure the baton reinforces, to some degree, the symphony conductor's confidence in his authority.

9   As expected, the novelty of the bullet began to fade and it only reclaimed my attention when I came to a sudden stop: Then it unleashed an abrupt discordant rain of metallic noise, as if to complain for being awakened by my questionable driving skills.

10   I would never have thought this likely, but shortly after I came into possession of the bullet I learned there are people who collect them. These are not nearly so many as those who are attracted to rifles and handguns, but there are enough to form clubs and societies. And there are those who collect not only bullets, but the colorful metal boxes some of them come in. There are web sites attesting to these particular interests, sites such as "The Civil War Bullet," which describes itself as a "discussion community for serious bullet and relic collectors." Then there's the International Ammunition Association, Inc., which has assembled a "Cartridge Collector's Glossary": It displays drawings of a great variety of missiles that are shot from guns. I scrolled through this long list until my eyes were arrested by the Straight Case, a "cartridge case having no taper along its end and no abrupt change in diameter." There's my bullet! Blunt, inelegant, clothed in dirty copper and brass.

11   Still, not entirely certain of what I had in hand, I dropped by the Cop Shop on East Baltimore Street, where the police buy the

required tools of their trade. The man behind the counter, named Sam, seemed somewhat puzzled by what I showed him, but did determine that it wasn't an American cartridge; he said he could tell by its markings. He passed it to a customer, an off-duty officer, who immediately identified it as a German .45 caliber short round. It's only one inch and two sixteenths in length, seven sixteenths in diameter.

12   Eventually, I began to re-examine how I came by this stubby piece of ordnance. Did the peaceful passage of the bullet from one stranger to another have any significance? Was it symbolic or mere happenstance? I even revisited that most frustrating and meaningless argument of our time, as circular and permanent as the sun itself: Do guns kill people or do people kill people? Or do bullets kill people?

13   That was something to think about. Over the past decades there has been so much shot flying around Baltimore, more in some neighborhoods than others, that it occurred to me that removing just one of those projectiles from circulation might contribute to public safety, though admittedly insignificantly. This feeble notion was prompted by a flash of dialogue recalled from an old movie, the title of which is long gone from my mind. A dying thug, clutching a leaky hole in his chest, as his life drains out, gurgles: "Ya got me! But you'll get yours! There's a bullet out there waiting for every one of us."

14   Or words to that effect.

15   What a dark, sinister, and fanciful thought! Should that be so, would this mean that what I've been carrying around all these weeks has somebody's name on it? Maybe my wheel-chaired beggar believed that and cleverly recruited me to dispose of it. Well, if so, it's not exactly a mission impossible, nor something I take that seriously. One of these days, just to be sure, I intend to introduce Straight Case, or .45 short round, to the Patapsco River.

16   It's getting close to that time.

ORGANIZATION AND IDEAS

1. Although many essays have a straightforward organization, beginning at a certain point and moving on chronologically, O'Mara's is more complex. How would you describe it?

2. O'Mara spends paragraphs 2–7, almost half the essay, setting out the details of the incident with the beggar. What reasons can you think of for that choice?

3. What paragraphs deal with the meaning of the bullet? What ideas does O'Mara consider? What conclusion does he appear to reach?

4. What is the essay's subject: A mystery? Baltimore's crime rate? Gun control? Fate? Death? Something else, and if so what? What case can you make for your choice?

5. Is O'Mara's thesis implied or stated? State his thesis in your own words and explain the reasons for your ideas.

TECHNIQUE AND STYLE

1. Consider the difference between a dictionary definition of a word and the layers of meaning that are associated with it, known as its connotation. What are your associations with the word *bullet*? What does O'Mara imply in paragraph 8?

2. Paragraphs 10 and 11 deal with a literal description of the bullet. Why might O'Mara have included it?

3. How would you describe O'Mara's use of details? Which stand out and why? What do they add?

4. Why do you think O'Mara included paragraph 14? What does it add to paragraph 13?

5. What does O'Mara's last paragraph mean? Are you to take it literally or figuratively? Explain.

SUGGESTIONS FOR WRITING

Journal

1. O'Mara reveals a fair amount about himself in the essay. Use your journal to describe him: What sort of person is he?

2. Think about an object that holds special meaning for you. Perhaps it's a lucky charm, a particular gift, an old shirt or pair of jeans—anything you care a lot about. What does it mean to you and why?

Essay

1. You probably know someone who is a collector, or you may be one yourself. O'Mara mentions Web sites that designed for people who collect particular objects that can be almost anything—matchbooks, beer labels, bottle caps, dolls, china figures, even old ticket stubs. Choose something that strikes you as an unusual collectable and then consult the Web to research it. What are the collectors like? The collections? How expensive a hobby is it? How popular? What is unusual about it? The result will be an informative and researched essay.

2. Unusual incidents form the bases for the essays by Silverman and O'Mara, though the essays differ in many ways. What are they? What similarities can you find? How do the narrators compare? The tone? The settings? The description? The diction? Which essay do you prefer and why? Use examples from both narratives to support your thesis.

Define

Before even naming her subject, Diane Ackerman begins her essay with a question: "What food do you crave?" She then announces her subject—chocolate—and follows with a scattershot of short definitions:

> A wooer's gift. A child's reward. A jilted lover's solace. A cozy mug of slumber. Halloween manna. A gimme more that tantalizes young and old alike. Almost every candy bar. Chocolate.

The subject is one that readers know and have opinions about, so Ackerman's task is to define it in a way that interests her audience enough to keep reading. To do that she explores the central term's **connotations,** the word's associative or emotional meanings. A dictionary will provide the word's explicit meaning, its **denotation**—the different ways in which the word can be used and also its etymology—but none of that will convey the rich layers of meaning the word has accumulated through the years

How do you find a subject? Find a word that interests you. Perhaps it's an abstract one such as *freedom* or *honesty*. Think about some basic questions, such as "Whose freedom?" If it's your freedom you are writing about, who or what sets limits on your freedom? The law? The church? Parents? Family responsibilities? How does the concept of freedom touch your life? If your examples are specific, you can avoid the danger of slipping into clichés, which are images so familiar that they have lost any power they might have had, as in "free as a bird."

Perhaps it's a concrete word or term you want to write about, such as *tattoo* or *T-shirt*. Like Ackerman, you might begin with your reader's associations and then move on to the word's history, leading up to current use. The T-shirt, for instance, has progressed from undershirt to personal billboard. Throughout your essay, you'd want to include examples drawn both from your own experience and from outside sources.

What does your reader know? Unless the word you are defining is quite unusual, most readers will be familiar with its dictionary definition; your own definition and your speculations on the word's connotations

84

are of much greater interest. Jot down what you can assume your reader knows about your subject and then consider what effect you want to have. Are you primarily explaining, persuading, entertaining, or expressing your feelings to make a larger point? In the example quoted on page 89, for example, Ackerman uses positive images to express her own equally positive feelings, interest her readers, and persuade them to read on.

How do you explore your subject? You can start by jotting down your ideas and questions. If you were thinking of the general topic "college students," you might be struck by how they are portrayed in popular culture and how that differs from the reality. To write an essay that defines real college students, you might think of

> *Example* What films or TV shows portray college students?
> *Description* How can you describe them? What senses can you appeal to?
> *Narration* What are those students involved in? What conflicts do they face?
> *Comparison and contrast* How do these depictions differ from reality?
> *Division and classification* Who are the real college students? What types or categories can they be grouped into?
> *Process* How can you find out factual information? What steps are involved?
> *Cause and effect* What are the negative effects of the popular impression of "the college student"? The positive ones?
> *Analogy* What metaphor might contrast the popular to the real?

If you apply questions such as these to your word or concept, they will help develop your ideas and generate a rough draft.

If you don't find those probes useful or need to supplement them, you can draw on any number of outside sources. Check out Google and other search engines to find more information. For the preceding topic, a quick search will turn up a huge selection of movies that are set on college campuses. Checking out the plots of several recent ones will give you many examples of how college students are portrayed—more than you can use. And sites such as the National Center for Educational Statistics (*http://nces.ed.gov/*) will provide a different view based on reality, revealing facts such as that the average age of a college student is 27 and 38 percent of the college-age population is older than 30. Research such as this broadens the base of your information and adds to your credibility, your **persona**—the image of yourself that you create and then present through your writing.

What's your thesis and where do you put it?   Several of the essays in this chapter deal with the idea of identity: how one defines oneself or is defined by others. Thinking through the topic on your own, you might discover many ways one's identity can be defined: by age, race, nationality, religion, beliefs, and so on. Perhaps your thinking ends up as a question: What does it mean to be a _____? You can fill in the blank with anything that interests you—first-generation American, single father or mother, or Lakers fan. No matter what your topic, your answer could be developed into a draft of a definition essay, with your working thesis as a one-sentence assertion. You can tinker with the wording to make it as effective as possible, but you probably want to lead up to it and then place it at the end of your introduction. If you want to try a more unusual choice, place the thesis at the end of your essay and then check to make sure that everything that comes before it leads logically to that statement.

How do you organize the content?   You may want to use a roughly chronological pattern of organization, starting at one point in time and moving forward to another. Structuring an essay so that it moves from the least to the most important point is another obvious pattern, one used by several of the writers in this chapter. You might also consider organizing your paper by question and answer, the introduction posing a question and the body of the essay answering it. A variation on that pattern is one in which one part of the essay poses a problem that is then discussed and analyzed in terms of possible solutions. Or perhaps you'd prefer a more subtle structure that moves from the particular to the general. For that essay defining *college student*, for example, you might start with the particular—the popular stereotype you find in movies and television—and then discuss the general, the broader view you've discovered through your research.

Useful Terms

> **Connotation** The associations suggested by a word that add to its literal meaning. *Home* and *domicile* have similar dictionary meanings, but they differ radically in their connotation.
> **Denotation** The literal meaning of a word, its dictionary definition.
> **Persona** The character of the writer that comes through from the prose.

POINTERS FOR USING DEFINITION

Exploring the Topic

1. **What are the denotations of your term?** Consult an unabridged dictionary and perhaps a specialized one, such as the *Oxford English Dictionary* or a dictionary of slang.
2. **What are the connotations of your term?** What emotional reactions or associations does it elicit from people and why?
3. **What other words can be used for your term?** Which are similar?
4. **What are the characteristics, qualities, or components of your term?** Which are most important? Are some not worth mentioning?
5. **What other modes are appropriate?** What modes can you draw on to support your definition and organization of the essay? Where can you use description? Narration? What examples illustrate your term?
6. **Has your word been overused or misused?** If so, might that misuse be turned into an introductory narrative? A closing one?

Drafting the Paper

1. **Know your reader.** Review your lists of denotations and connotations together with the characteristics related to your term to see how familiar they are to your reader. Check to see if your reader may have particular associations that you need to redirect or change. Or if your reader is directly affected by your topic, make sure your definition does not offend.
2. **Know your purpose.** Unless your term is unusual, one of your biggest problems is to tell the reader something new about your term. Work on your first paragraph so that it will immediately engage the reader. From that point on, keep your primary purpose in mind. If you are writing a paper that is basically self-expressive or persuasive, make sure you have an audience other than yourself. If your aim is informative, consider narration, example, cause and effect, and analogy as possible ways of presenting familiar material in a fresh light.

(Continued)

POINTERS FOR USING DEFINITION *(Continued)*

3. Use evidence. Use examples as evidence to illustrate what your key term means. Also consider using negative examples and making distinctions between the meaning of your word and similar ones.

4. Draw on a variety of sources. Define your term from several perspectives. Perhaps a brief history of the word would be helpful, or maybe some statistical information is in order. See if a brief narrative might provide additional meaning for the term.

5. Make a point. Don't mistake your definition for your thesis. The two are certainly related, but one is an assertion; the other is not. Perhaps your definition is a jumping-off place for a larger point you wish to make or a key part of that point. Or perhaps your term evokes a single dominant impression you want to convey. Whatever purpose your definition serves, it needs to support your thesis.

Chocolate Equals Love

Diane Ackerman

At Boston University and then Pennsylvania State, Diane Ackerman studied both science and literature, interests she has pursued as a writer earning an MFA and PhD. Her books span many subjects: The Moon by Whale Light (1991) examines threats to endangered animals; A Slender Thread (1997), grew out of her volunteer work as a counselor at a suicide prevention and crisis center; and three volumes examine Natural Histor[ies]...of The Senses (1990), of Love (1995), and of My Garden (2001). One of her more recent nonfiction works has the descriptive title An Alchemy of Mind: The Marvel and Mystery of the Brain (2004), but Ackerman has also written The Zookeeper's Wife: A War Story (2007), a moving account of the director of the Warsaw Zoo and his wife who sheltered more than three hundred Jews and members of the resistance when the Nazis occupied Poland. One Hundred Names for Love: A Stroke, a Marriage, and the Language of Healing (2011), her most recent book, documents her husband's amazing recovery from a stroke. That's a long way from chocolate, the subject of her essay that follows, published in Parade Magazine on February 9, 2003. Reading it, you can tell Ackerman is also a well-published and respected poet, for in "Chocolate Equals Love" she combines the vivid detail and compression characteristic of poetry with the precise detail and keen observation associated with science.

What to Look For Good writers have a way of listening to words so that they are aware of a word's sound as well as sense. If you read Ackerman's second paragraph out loud, for instance, you'll hear a lot of *s* sounds that help make the prose flow smoothly. Reading your own work out loud will help you develop your own ear for the sound of good writing.

1 What food do you crave? Add a hint of mischief to your desire, and the answer is bound to be chocolate, Dark, divine, sense-bludgeoning chocolate. A wooer's gift. A child's reward. A jilted lover's solace. A cozy mug of slumber. Halloween manna. A gimmemore that tantalizes young and old alike. Almost every candy bar. Chocolate.

2 We can thank the Indians of Central and South America for chocolate's bewitching lusciousness. As the Spanish explorer Hernán

Cortés found, the Aztecs worshiped chocolate (which they named *cacahuatl*) as a gift from their wise god Quetzalcoatl. Aztec soldiers and male members of court drank as many as 2000 pitchers of chocolate every day. They spiked their drink with vanilla beans and spices, then drank it bubbly thick from golden cups. Adding chili peppers gave it bite. The Aztec leader Montezuma required a chocolate ice, made by pouring syrup over snow that runners brought to him from the nearest mountain.

3   Invigorating and dangerously sublime, chocolate dominated every facet of Aztec life, from sexuality to economy. Cocoa beans even served as currency: You could buy a rabbit for 10 beans, a slave for 100 beans.

4   At first, Cortés hated chocolate's shocking taste, which mingled bitter, spicy, pungent, silky, dank and dusty flavors. But in time its magic seduced him, and it is said that he introduced it to Spain, flavoring it with sugar instead of hot chili peppers.

5   By the 17th century, chocolate was thrilling Europeans with its sensory jolt—less devilish than liquor but still stimulating, luxurious and pleasantly addictive. Those who could afford it drank it thick and hot, as the Indians did, sometimes adding orange, vanilla or spices. Society ladies sipped several cups a day and even insisted on drinking it during church services. Doctors prescribed chocolate as a flesh-and-bone rejuvenator that could lift the spirits, hasten healing and raise a flagging libido.

6   Forget Viagra. Think bonbons.

7   Casanova, it is said, swore by chocolate and ate it as a prelude to lovemaking. The French King Louis XV's principal mistress Madame du Barry, served exquisitely refined but essentially drug-level chocolate to her various suitors. Unknowingly, they were following the custom of Montezuma, who was believed to have consumed extra chocolate before visiting his harem.

8   A liquid treasure until the 19th century, chocolate suddenly changed shape and personality when a Dutch chemist discovered how to separate cocoa butter, leaving powdered cocoa. The public clamored for portable, ever-ready chocolate, and confectioners obliged with pyramids of chocolate bars. Joining the chocolamania, the Cadbury brothers introduced chocolate in heart-shaped boxes in 1868. Milk chocolate appeared in Switzerland in 1875, thanks to Peter Daniel and Henri Nestlé. Then American mass-production provided cheap chocolates for the multitudes, thanks to the foresight of Milton Hershey. And the rest is history.

9   Is chocolate a health food? Chocolate is chemically active—a mind-altering drug that's good for you in moderation. The higher the cocoa content, the more antioxidants and other nutritious bonuses. Cocoa powder contains the most antioxidants, followed by dark chocolate and milk chocolate.

10   What delivers the chocolate buzz? Chocolate contains more than 300 chemicals, including tiny amounts of anandamide, which mimics the active ingredient in marijuana, plus such stimulants as theobromine and phenylethylamine. A 1.4-ounce bar of chocolate also can provide 20 milligrams of caffeine. That's jitters away from the 140 milligrams of an average cup of coffee, not to mention a thimbleful of espresso. But it's rousing enough, combined with the rest of chocolate's chemical bag of tricks. And the full sensory and nostalgic saga of eating chocolate—the mouth feel, the aroma, the taste, the memories—can calm the brain or lighten one's thoughts, for a while anyway.

11   If we luxuriate in a memory framed by the heaven of chocolate—say, eating s'mores around a campfire with a giggling Girl Scout troop or receiving a box of chocolates from a sappy beau and then sampling them with him—a small constellation of pleasure will attach itself to the idea of chocolate lifelong. That happens early on to nearly everyone.

12   For example, when I was a child, each year my mother and I would choose a colossal chocolate Easter rabbit with pink candy dot eyes. Together, we would sit on the floor in the aptly named "den" and devour most of the hollow rabbit—always starting with the ears and working our way down—until we went way beyond sated and started to feel a little sick. We would laugh with shared delight as we gobbled and afterward lounged about in a chocolate haze.

13   It was a cherished bonding ritual more visceral than verbal, reminding me how much we adore our senses. They're our houseguests, our explorers, our pets—and we love to give them treats. So how do you reward the sense of taste? For ages, the delicacy of choice has been rich, sensuously inviting chocolate.

ORGANIZATION AND IDEAS

1. Paragraph 1 announces the subject and describes it with quick images, all to interest the reader. How well does it succeed?
2. Ackerman chooses to begin the body of the essay (paragraphs 2–8) with a brief history of chocolate. How does that history help define it?
3. Paragraphs 9 and 10 provide a scientific view of chocolate. What information surprises you and why?

4. Think of the ideas Ackerman presents in paragraphs 2–10 and how chocolate can cause an emotional attachment, as described in paragraphs 11–13. State her thesis in one sentence.
5. To what extent does Ackerman's account of and appreciation for chocolate mesh with your own?

TECHNIQUE AND STYLE

1. Consult a handbook of grammar and usage for what it says about a sentence fragment, and then take another look at paragraph 1. To what extent, if any, are those fragments effective?
2. You are probably used to paragraphs as units that extend an idea, but Ackerman's sixth paragraph is quite different. What is its function?
3. In the last paragraph, Ackerman uses several metaphors for our senses. Which do you prefer and why?
4. In paragraphs 1, 9, 10, and 13, Ackerman uses questions. What purpose do they serve?
5. Most of the essay can be categorized as expository and objective, but in paragraphs 12 and 13, Ackerman switches to the personal. Why might she have chosen to do that and what effect does it have?

SUGGESTIONS FOR WRITING

Journal

1. Use your journal to explore how the senses can be viewed as pets.
2. Write a description that defines the kind of chocolate you like or dislike the most.

Essay

1. Think of the senses as possible topics for an essay that explains and defines the one you depend on the most: sight, smell, hearing, touch, or taste. Like Ackerman, you will want to include some scientific information, so you should do some research to be able to explain how that sense functions (a medical encyclopedia or medical Web page would be a good source). And, of course, use your own experience to explain why that sense is important to you.
2. Think about a kind of snack or food that you like a great deal, and write an essay that defines it. Like Ackerman, you can point out its history, how it is produced, the various forms it comes in, and your experiences with it. No matter what your topic, you can find a great deal of information about it from the Web by using a search engine.

I Was a Member of the Kung Fu Crew

Henry Han Xi Lau

> *The Chinatown that Henry Han Xi Lau writes about is one of the oldest of New York City's ethnic neighborhoods; you can still walk down the street and not hear a word of English. To Lau, its also home, even though he and his family had moved to Brooklyn, which, like Manhattan, is one of the city's five boroughs. A sophomore at Yale University at the time he wrote this essay, Lau describes the people and places of Chinatown, defining it as "ghetto." Lau went on to graduate with distinction in history and international studies and to earn a law degree from the University of California at Berkeley. He is now an associate in the law firm of Debevoise and Plimpton, working in Hong Kong. His essay was published in* The New York Times Magazine *on October 19, 1997. After it came out, Lau objected to the way it had been edited, and in a later piece he wrote for* Discourses, *an undergraduate journal at Yale, he called it a "warped presentation." If you'd like to read his critique, you can find it by typing his name into a search engine; it was reprinted in* Macrocosm, *a Web journal published by Rice University. What's missing in the* Times *version that follows, according to Lau, is the "resourcefulness and hard-working side of ghettoness." See if you agree.*

What to Look For   Lau relies heavily on definition to convey what it's like to be a member of the Kung Fu Crew and to be "ghetto." Many of the techniques he uses are ones that can carry over to your own writing, so be on the lookout for the details that define the Crew's physical prowess, hair, pants, attitudes, accessories, and language, all of which add up to being "cool."

1   Chinatown is ghetto, my friends are ghetto, I am ghetto. I went away to college last year, but I still have a long strand of hair that reaches past my chin. I need it when I go back home to hang with the K.F.C.—for Kung Fu Crew, not Kentucky Fried Chicken. We all met in a Northern Shaolin kung fu class years ago. Our *si-fu* was Rocky. He told us: "In the early 1900's in China, your grand master was walking in the streets when a foreigner riding on a

horse disrespected him. So then he felt the belly of the horse with his palms and left. Shortly thereafter, the horse buckled and died because our grand master had used *qi-gong* to mess up the horse's internal organs." Everyone said, "Cool, I would like to do that." Rocky emphasized, "You've got to practice really hard for a long time to reach that level."

2   By the time my friends and I were in the eighth grade, we were able to do 20-plus pushups on our knuckles and fingers. When we practiced our crescent, roundhouse and tornado kicks, we had 10-pound weights strapped to our legs. Someone once remarked, "Goddamn—that's a freaking mountain!" when he saw my thigh muscles in gym class.

3   Most Chinatown kids fall into a few general categories. There are pale-faced nerds who study all the time to get into the Ivies. There are the recent immigrants with uncombed hair and crooked teeth who sing karaoke in bars. There are the punks with highlighted hair who cut school, and the gangsters, whom everyone else avoids.

4   Then there is the K.F.C. We work hard like the nerds, but we identify with the punks. Now we are reunited, and just as in the old days we amble onto Canal Street, where we stick out above the older folks, elderly women bearing leaden bags of bok choy and oranges. As an opposing crew nears us, I assess them to determine whether to grill them or not. Grilling is the fine art of staring others down and trying to emerge victorious.

5   How the hair is worn is important in determining one's order on the streets. In the 80's, the dominant style was the mushroom cut, combed neatly or left wild in the front so that a person can appear menacing as he peers through his bangs. To gain an edge in grilling now, some kids have asymmetrical cuts, with long random strands sprouting in the front, sides or back. Some dye their hair blue or green, while blood red is usually reserved for gang members.

6   Only a few years ago, examination of the hair was sufficient. But now there is a second step: assessing pants. A couple of years ago, wide legs first appeared in New York City, and my friends and I switched from baggy pants. In the good old days, Merry-Go-Round in the Village sold wide legs for only $15 a pair. When Merry-Go-Round went bankrupt, Chinatown kids despaired. Wide-leg prices at other stores increased drastically as they became more popular. There are different ways of wearing wide legs. Some fold their pant legs inward and staple them at the hem. Some clip the back ends of their pants to their shoes with safety pins. Others simply cut the bottoms so that fuzzy strings hang out.

7   We grill the opposing punks. I untuck my long strand of hair so that it swings in front of my face. Nel used to have a strand, but he chewed it off one day in class by accident. Chu and Tom cut their strands off because it scared people at college. Jack has a patch of blond hair, while Tone's head is a ball of orange flame. Chi has gelled short hair, while Ken's head is a black mop. As a group, we have better hair than our rivals. But they beat us with their wide legs. In our year away at college, wide legs have gone beyond our 24-inch leg openings. Twenty-six- to 30-inch jeans are becoming the norm. If wide legs get any bigger, they will start flying up like a skirt in an updraft.

8   We have better accessories, though. Chi sports a red North Face that gives him a rugged mountain-climber look because of the jungle of straps sprouting in the back. Someone once asked Chi, "Why is the school bag so important to one's cool?" He responded, "Cuz it's the last thing others see when you walk away from them or when they turn back to look at you after you walk past them." But the other crew has female members, which augments their points. The encounter between us ends in a stalemate. But at least the K.F.C. members are in college and are not true punks.

9   In the afternoon, we decide to eat at the Chinatown McDonald's for a change instead of the Chinese bakery Maria's, our dear old hangout spot. "Mickey D's is good sit," Nel says. I answer: "But the Whopper gots more fat and meat. It's even got more bun." Nel agrees. "True that," he says. I want the Big Mac, but I buy the two-cheeseburger meal because it has the same amount of meat but costs less.

10   We sit and talk about ghettoness again. We can never exactly articulate what being ghetto entails, but we know the spirit of it. In Chinatown toilet facilities we sometimes find footprints on the seats because F.O.B.'s (fresh off the boats) squat on them as they do over the holes in China. We see alternative brand names in stores like Dolo instead of Polo, and Mike instead of Nike.

11   We live by ghettoness. My friends and I walk from 80-some-thing Street in Manhattan to the tip of the island to save a token. We gorge ourselves at Gray's Papaya because the hot dogs are 50 cents each. But one cannot be stingy all the time. We leave good tips at Chinese restaurants because our parents are waiters and waitresses, too.

12   We sit for a long time in McDonald's, making sure that there is at least a half-inch of soda in our cups so that when the staff wants to kick us out, we can claim that we are not finished yet.

Jack positions a mouse bite of cheeseburger in the center of a wrapper to support our claim.

13   After a few hours, the K.F.C. prepares to disband. I get in one of the no-license commuter vans on Canal Street that will take me to Sunset Park in Brooklyn, where my family lives now. All of my friends will leave Chinatown, for the Upper East Side and the Lower East Side, Forest Hills in Queens and Bensonhurst in Brooklyn. We live far apart, but we always come back together in Chinatown. For most of us, our homes used to be here and our world was here.

ORGANIZATION AND IDEAS

1. The essay is set out in chronological order. What paragraphs cover what times?

2. What categories of kids does Lau describe? Where does the Crew fit?

3. Lau describes "grilling" in paragraphs 4–8. What is his point?

4. Lau may have moved away from Chinatown, but he is still very much a part of its community. How would you characterize that community and its values?

5. Is Lau's thesis explicit or implicit? How can you phrase it in your own words?

TECHNIQUE AND STYLE

1. Look up the term *comma splice* in a handbook of grammar and usage, and check what you find against Lau's first sentence. Why is it a legitimate comma splice?

2. Lau uses dialogue in paragraphs 8 and 9. What does it add to the essay?

3. The essay piles on details and information that lead up to a definition of *ghetto*. State that definition in your own words.

4. *Ghetto* usually has a negative connotation. How does Lau make it positive?

5. The essay is written in standard American English. Why might Lau have chosen to write it that way instead of in "ghetto"?

SUGGESTIONS FOR WRITING

Journal

1. If you met the Kung Fu Crew on the street, you might find yourself ignoring them, "grilling" them, admiring them, but no matter what, you'd have some sort of reaction. Describe how you would react.

2. Look up the word *intimidation* in an unabridged dictionary, and think about times in your experience when you were intimidated or when you intimidated someone else. Use your journal to define how you felt.

Essay

1. People spend a lot of time analyzing what's in and what's out. For some, those in advertising or fashion, for instance, it's a business, but all of us are affected by it. Perhaps you would find a lot to say in an essay about what it means to be "in" or "cool" or the opposite. Think about a category (some suggestions are listed here), choose a subject, and then start jotting down details such as the particulars of language (spoken and body), appearance, attitudes, and likes and dislikes that define your central term.

   music

   films or television shows

   dates

   schools

   cars

   As you draft your essay, try to keep your focus on definition. It's natural to lean toward comparisons, but, like Lau, make sure you use them to support what you are defining.

2. Each generation usually ends up with at least one label or tag—the Baby Boomers, Gen X, or some such. What label works for your generation? Write an essay that explains your choice, providing examples to prove your point.

The Handicap of Definition

William Raspberry

William Raspberry left the small and segregated town in Mississippi where he grew up to take a summer job with the Indianapolis Reporter, *moving on in 1962 to* The Washington Post. *Although now the Knight Chair in Communications and Journalism at Duke University, he is better known as a writer for* The Washington Post *and as the author of a syndicated column that ran in more than 200 newspapers. His commentary on issues such as rap music, crime, and AIDS earned him a Pulitzer Prize in 1994. Raspberry retired from the* Post *in 2005, but in 2008 he contributed one more piece for the paper when Barack Obama was elected president. In the essay that follows, he writes about the terms* black *and* white, *showing us that if we stop to think about* black, *we'll see that it has so narrow a definition that it is "one of the heaviest burdens black Americans— and black children in particular—have to bear." Ask yourself if much has changed since 1982, when this essay first appeared in Raspberry's syndicated column.*

What to Look For Somewhere along the line, we've all been warned never to begin a sentence with a conjunction such as *and, but,* and the like. But as long as you know how to avoid the trap of a sentence fragment, beginning a sentence with a conjunction can lend a conversational tone to your essay. As you read Raspberry's essay, notice how often he uses this technique.

1   I know all about bad schools, mean politicians, economic deprivation and racism. Still, it occurs to me that one of the heaviest burdens black Americans—and black children in particular—have to bear is the handicap of definition: the question of what it means to be black.

2   Let me explain quickly what I mean. If a basketball fan says that the Boston Celtics' Larry Bird plays "black," the fan intends it—and Bird probably accepts it—as a compliment. Tell pop singer Tom Jones he moves "black" and he might grin in appreciation. Say to Teena Marie or The Average White Band that they sound "black" and they'll thank you.

3   But name one pursuit, aside from athletics, entertainment or sexual performance in which a white practitioner will feel complimented to be told he does it "black." Tell a white broadcaster he talks "black," and he'll sign up for diction lessons. Tell a white reporter he writes "black" and he'll take a writing course. Tell a white lawyer he reasons "black" and he might sue you for slander.

4   What we have here is a tragically limited definition of blackness, and it isn't only white people who buy it.

5   Think of all the ways black children can put one another down with charges of "whiteness." For many of these children, hard study and hard work are "white." Trying to please a teacher might be criticized as acting "white." Speaking correct English is "white." Scrimping today in the interest of tomorrow's goals is "white." Educational toys and games are "white."

6   An incredible array of habits and attitudes that are conducive to success in business, in academia, in the nonentertainment professions are likely to be thought of as somehow "white." Even economic success, unless it involves such "black" undertakings as numbers banking, is defined as "white."

7   And the results are devastating. I wouldn't deny that blacks often are better entertainers and athletes. My point is the harm that comes from too narrow a definition of what is black.

8   One reason black youngsters tend to do better at basketball, for instance, is that they assume they can learn to do it well, and so they practice constantly to prove themselves right.

9   Wouldn't it be wonderful if we could infect black children with the notion that excellence in math is "black" rather than white, or possibly Chinese? Wouldn't it be of enormous value if we could create the myth that morality, strong families, determination, courage and love of learning are traits brought by slaves from Mother Africa and therefore quintessentially black?

10   There is no doubt in my mind that most black youngsters could develop their mathematical reasoning, their elocution and their attitudes the way they develop their jump shots and their dance steps: by the combination of sustained, enthusiastic practice and the unquestioned belief that they can do it.

11   In one sense, what I am talking about is the importance of developing positive ethnic traditions. Maybe Jews have an innate talent for communication; maybe Chinese are born with a gift for mathematical reasoning; maybe blacks are naturally blessed with athletic grace. I doubt it. What is at work, I suspect, is assumption, inculcated early in their lives, that this is a thing our people do well.

12   Unfortunately, many of the things about which blacks make this assumption are things that do not contribute to their career success—except for that handful of the truly gifted who can make it as entertainers and athletes. And many of the things we concede to whites are the things that are essential to economic security.

13   So it is with a number of assumptions black youngsters make about what it is to be a "man": physical aggressiveness, sexual prowess, the refusal to submit to authority. The prisons are full of people who, by this perverted definition, are unmistakably men.

14   But the real problem is not so much that the things defined as "black" are negative. The problem is that the definition is much too narrow.

15   Somehow, we have to make our children understand that they are intelligent, competent people, capable of doing whatever they put their minds to and making it in the American mainstream, not just in a black subculture.

16   What we seem to be doing, instead, is raising up yet another generation of young blacks who will be failures—by definition.

ORGANIZATION AND IDEAS

1. Examine paragraphs 1–4, 5–7, and 8–11. Each functions as a unit. What sentence is the major assertion for each group of paragraphs?
2. Examine paragraphs 12–16 as a concluding paragraph block. What is the relationship between paragraph 12 and the preceding paragraphs?
3. Consider the controlling ideas that guide the paragraph blocks and the conclusions Raspberry draws from the examples that support those assertions. Stated fully, what is Raspberry's thesis?
4. A militant who reads this essay would argue that Raspberry is trying to make blacks "better" by making them white. Is there any evidence to support this view? Explain.
5. A feminist who reads the essay might argue that it is sexist. Is there any evidence to support this view? Explain.

TECHNIQUE AND STYLE

1. This essay was one of Raspberry's syndicated columns; as a result, it appeared in a large number of newspapers with equally large readerships, mostly white. What evidence can you find that Raspberry is trying to inform his white audience and persuade his black readers?
2. How and where does Raspberry establish his credibility as a writer on this subject? What grammatical point of view does he use?
3. Where in the essay does he qualify or modulate his statements? What is the effect of that technique?
4. Paragraphs 3, 7, 13, and 14 all begin with a conjunction. What effect does this technique achieve? Consult a handbook of grammar and usage for a discussion of this device. To what extent does Raspberry's usage conform to the handbook's advice?
5. Paragraph 16 is an example of a rhetorical paragraph, a one-sentence paragraph that gives dramatic emphasis to a point. If you eliminate the dash or substitute a comma for it, what happens to the dramatic effect? What does the pun add?

SUGGESTIONS FOR WRITING

Journal

1. Raspberry's essay was published in 1982. Write a journal entry explaining whether his point holds true today.
2. Write down any examples you can think of that can substitute for those Raspberry uses, but focus on women. In a paragraph or two, explain how the substitutions would add to or detract from his point.

Essay

1. Find a word that has accumulated broad connotations and then see what definitions have evolved and their effect. Like Raspberry, you may want to consider two terms but emphasize only one. Possibilities:
man
hero
student
woman
worker
lover
politician

2. Raspberry says "we have to make our children understand that they are intelligent, competent people, capable of doing whatever they put their minds to..." (paragraph 15). But *intelligent* and *competent* mean different things to different people. Select one of the words and write an essay in which you define what the word means to you. As you think about your topic, remember that it can be useful to define something by what it is not, by comparisons.

High on Progress

Derrick Jensen

Derrick Jensen has been called many things—doomster, farmer, philosopher, anarchist, teacher, bee-keeper, activist, writer (and you may have seen him in one of several documentaries)—but he certainly is prolific: a coauthor of nine and sole author of eleven books, many of which question our modern world and its values. His titles declare his attitudes: A Language Older Than Words (2000) on domestic violence; The Culture of Make Believe (2002) on racism and misogyny; Walking on Water (2005) on education; Endgame (2006) about civilization's dim future; and Dreams (2011) on hope for a better world through the ideas of indigenous cultures and progressive philosophers. Jensen holds a BA in Mineral Engineering Physics from the Colorado School of Mines as well as an MFA in Creative Writing from Eastern Washington University. The essay reprinted here is from the May/June 2010 issue of Orion, a magazine, according to its Web site, "devoted to creating a stronger bond between people and nature."

1   WHY HAVE WE come to assume that "progress" is always good? The Nazis' treatment of Jews progressed toward their final solution. And many individual Jews followed a line of progress: get an ID card, move to a ghetto, get on a cattle car, arrive at a camp, work at the camp, go to a gas chamber, get put in an oven, rise as smoke, fall as ashes.

2   A stalker can progress from one stage to another, beginning with e-mails, then phone calls, then moving to the victim's community, then haunting places the victim might go, then showing up at the victim's home. Cancer can and usually does progress. Addictions, including cultural addictions, can and often do progress.

3   That's not to say that progress can't be good. A friendship or romantic relationship can progress as surely as can an abusive relationship—the affection you feel growing with time, leading to a deep familiarity and comfort as the relationship matures.

4   In a lot of cases, progress is good for some and bad for others. For the perpetrators of the Nazi Holocaust, the technological progress that made possible more efficient ways to kill large numbers of human beings was "good," or "useful," or "helpful" from the perspective of the victims, not so good. For the perpetrators of the United States Holocaust, the development of railroads to move men and machines was "good" and "useful" and "helpful" from the perspective of the Dakota, Navajo, Hopi, Modoc, Squamish, and others, not so good. From the perspective of bison, prairie dogs, timber wolves, redwoods, Douglas firs, and others, not so good.

5   In 1970 Lewis Mumford wrote, "The chief premise common to both technology and science is the notion that there are no desirable limits to the increase of knowledge, of material goods, of environmental control; that quantitative productivity is an end in itself, and that every means should be used to further expansion." Mumford asked the same question that so many of us ask, which is, "Why on earth would a culture do so many crazy, stupid, destructive things?" His answer cuts through the typical cornucopian garbage: "The desired reward of this magic is not just abundance but absolute control." Mumford knew—as we all do—that there was no hope in proceeding "on the terms imposed by technocratic society."

He didn't think change would be easy, saying that it might take "an all-out fatal shock treatment, close to catastrophe, to break the hold of civilized man's chronic psychosis." He was not optimistic: "Even such a belated awakening would be a miracle."

6   Most people today have not awakened from the Cult of Progress. Even with the world being dismembered before their eyes, nearly all public figures continue to be members of this cult. The same is true for many nonpublic figures—for most of us—as we seem unquestioningly to presume that tomorrow's progress will bring more good things to life, and will simultaneously solve the problems created by yesterday's and today's progress (without then creating yet more problems, as "progress" always seems to do).

7   For those who benefit from it, progress is about improving their material lifestyle at the expense of those they enslave, steal from, or otherwise exploit. For everyone else, it is about loss.

8   Progress. In vast stretches of the Pacific Ocean, there is forty-eight times as much plastic as phytoplankton.

9   Progress. One million migratory songbirds die every day because of skyscrapers, cell-phone towers, domesticated cats, and other trappings of modern civilized life.

10   Progress. A half million human children die every year as a direct result of so-called debt repayment from so-called third-world countries (the colonies) to so-called first-world countries (the nations that have undergone progress).

11   Progress is polar bears swimming hundreds of miles to ice floes that have melted away, till finally they can swim no more. Progress is nuclear weapons, depleted uranium, and "drones" piloted from an office in Florida to kill people in Pakistan. Progress is the ability of fewer and fewer people to control more and more people, and to destroy more and more of the world. Progress is a god. Progress is God. Progress is killing the world.

12   The evolutionary biologist Richard Dawkins said that science's claim to truth is based on its "spectacular ability to make matter and energy jump through hoops on command." Anthropologist Leslie White stated that "the primary function of culture" is to "harness and control energy." Quite simply, this culture is about enslaving everyone and everything its members can get their hands (or machines) on. What is another word for making someone jump through hoops? Enslavement. In this culture, progress is measured by the ability to enslave, to control, and to do so with ever-increasing efficiency. The ultimate goal is to control everyone and everything.

13   I know, I know, I can hear the cry of the cult members now: "If progress is so bad, why does everyone want it?" Well, they don't. Nonhumans certainly don't. But they don't count. They're only there for you to use. Many humans don't want progress, either. Or at least they didn't, when they still had intact social structures. That's why so many indigenous peoples have taken up arms in defense of their ways of life. I often think of a line by Samuel Huntington: "The West won the world not by the superiority of its ideas or values or religion (to which few members of other civilizations were converted) but rather by its superiority in applying organized violence. Westerners often forget this fact, non-Westerners never do."

14   Part of the problem is that progress can be not merely seductive, but addictive. My compact *OED* defines the verb *addict* as "to bind, devote, or attach oneself as a servant, disciple, or adherent." In Roman law, an addiction was "a formal giving over or delivery by sentence of court. Hence, a surrender, or dedication, of any one to a master." To be addicted is to be a slave. To be a slave is to be addicted. The heroin ceases to serve the addict, and the addict begins to serve the heroin. We can say the same for progress: it does not serve us, but rather we serve it.

15   Every addiction has its allure. I recently had some extended conversations with people who'd used a lot of crack. Their descriptions of the drug's effects were consistent with what I'd heard from students when I taught at a supermaximum-security prison. The people who've used crack uniformly say that crack makes them feel extremely good, and powerful, and invincible. Their descriptions of the high make crack seem pretty damn appealing. Unfortunately the high doesn't last all that long, and when you come down you not only feel wretched, but you immediately start looking for another hit.

16   Severe addicts may give up everything else for their addiction. My students had lost their freedom, in some cases for the rest of their lives. Their addictions had cost many of them their families. Yet even after that, a fair number said that if you put that rock in front of them, they'd still find a way to smoke it. This culture's addiction to progress runs far deeper than any individual's chemical addiction. It is more powerful than many people's desire for a living planet.

17   Progress is hot showers (which require mining, manufacturing, and energy infrastructures). Progress is computers (which require mining, manufacturing, and energy infrastructures, and are used far more effectively by those in power than by us). Progress is the Internet, which allows for instantaneous communication with distant loved ones (and which requires mining, manufacturing, and

energy infrastructures, and is used far more effectively by those in power than by us). Progress is supermarkets, which require industrial food production (which in turn requires mining, manufacturing, and agricultural, chemical, and energy infrastructures, and is controlled by ever fewer giant corporations).

18　　All other things being equal, I'd rather have a nice space heater to keep my toes toasty warm. But all other things aren't equal, and I'd rather have a living planet.

ORGANIZATION AND IDEAS

1. The essay opens with a question that rests on an assumption. How accurate is that assumption?
2. What paragraph or paragraphs introduce the essay? Explain your choice.
3. What is the controlling idea for paragraphs 8–12?
4. Where in the essay does Jensen use *progress* as a noun? As a verb? Check a dictionary to clarify the definitions. What differences in meaning do you note? Is Jensen being fair in his use?
5. Jensen points out all that is negative about progress, but is he arguing against all progress? For a redefinition? For a balance? For the planet? Or is he being an alarmist? Explain your choice.

TECHNIQUE AND STYLE

1. How effective is the repetition in paragraphs 8–11? What effect do they achieve?
2. Jensen quotes a number of authorities in paragraphs 5, 12, 13, and 14. How reliable are they? What do they add to the essay?
3. According to Jensen, we are addicted to progress, an idea he emphasizes with his comparisons in paragraphs 14–16. How effective are those comparisons? How accurate?
4. Where in the essay does Jensen recognize objections to his argument? How well does he counter them?
5. Most readers may find Jensen's view extreme, but given that *Orion*—where the essay appeared—is "devoted to creating a stronger bond between people and nature," it fits those readers. How might the essay be changed for a more general audience?

SUGGESTIONS FOR WRITING

Journal

1. Choose one statement from Jensen's essay and explain your reaction to it.
2. Jensen has been called a doomster, philosopher, and activist. What adjective best fits him and why?

Essay

1. In paragraph 4, Jensen states "progress is good for some and bad for others," but it is also true that what's bad may take time to discover. The scientific and technological world is full of discoveries that failed and some that were successful and then took years to backfire. Think about a backfire and use the Web to research it. Suggestions:

   oleo
   plastic bags
   disposable diapers
   thalidomide
   laudanum

   Be careful about definitions and check out your sources to make sure they're reliable.

2. Reread Jensen's essay looking for holes in his argument and ways you can refute his points. Construct your own essay in response to his but try not to be extreme. You might imagine *Orion* is your audience and come up with a thesis that's some place between Jensen's and the idea that all progress is good.

Baby Blues

Rick Kirkman

If you have ever seen the cartoon strip Baby Blues, *you know Rick Kirkman. His interest in drawing started in kindergarten although his professional career began in junior high: "I drew a parody of* Mad Magazine *and, having only one copy, charged my friends to read it—until all the other parents found out." Since that time, he spent his time in advertising and drawing cartoons until just after the birth of his second child. At that point, he joined up with Jerry Scott and* Baby Blues *was the result. Now syndicated by King Features Syndicate, the strip runs in more than 850 newspapers and eighteen different countries. In 1995, the National Cartoonists Society honored Kirkman for "Best Newspaper Comic Strip," later shared with Jerry Scott, and now the strip has been published in more than thirty books. You can check them out on Amazon.*

FOR DISCUSSION

1. In what ways does Kirkman's cartoon relate to Jensen's essay?

2. Why might Kirkman have chosen the two figures he uses in the cartoon? Who are they?

3. What does Kirkman achieve by delaying dialogue till the last panel?

4. The older brother sees what's about to happen but doesn't try to stop it. How does that inaction relate to Jensen's essay? To Raspberry's?

5. What is Wren standing on in the last panel? What does that suggest about the difficulty of making Raspberry and Jensen's ideas a reality?

SUGGESTIONS FOR WRITING

Journal

The general subject of Kirkman's cartoon can be said to be progress. What other subjects does the cartoon suggest? Which has the greatest impact and why?

Essay

If you have any brothers or sisters, you probably know something about sibling rivalry. Think about your own experiences and write an essay that defines how that sort of rivalry operated in your family. What were or are the points of contention? Who fought for what? What were the results? How did the rivalry affect you? Your siblings?

Compare and Contrast

1   It's fair to say that Japanese people are unbelievably busy. Working 10 hours a day, and often coming in on days off, they rarely take a vacation of more than three or four days. A straight week is a hedonistic luxury. Students have less than a month for summer vacation, and even then they have all kinds of assignments to do.

2   Watching people live like this, with almost no time for themselves, makes an American like me wonder why more of them don't throw themselves under subway trains. But I seem to have far more anxiety about free time than my Japanese friends do—even though, compared to them, I have much more of it. Why doesn't this cradle-to-grave, manic scheduling bother them?

Right away, you know Lynnika Butler is an American who has spent a fair amount of time in Japan, where she was struck by the differences between the two cultures, time being one of the major ones. The introduction to her essay first uses details to describe ways in which the Japanese are "unbelievably busy," then shifts to what strikes her as odd, that "I seem to have far more anxiety about free time than my Japanese friends do—even though, compared to them, I have much more of it." She then poses a question that she answers in the rest of her essay by comparing how the two cultures treat the concept of time.

Butler's comparison is both narrow and fair, essential qualities whether you stress differences or similarities. Deciding where to go out to dinner often depends on how much you are willing to spend, so comparing a fast-food place to an elegant French restaurant doesn't have a point unless you want to treat the comparison humorously. If neither is worth the money, however, you've established a similarity that gives you a working assertion.

If Butler had examined how more than two cultures regard the concept of time, then she would have been using division and classification to analyze her topic. But because division and classification are extentions of comparison and contrast, it's best to look at the simpler structure first.

How can you shape comparison and contrast for your readers? Often you may want only to inform your reader; that gives you at least three possible theses:

> *x* is better or worse than *y*.
> *x* has a lot in common with *y*, though not obviously so.
> *x* is quite different from *y*, though superficially similar.

Butler doesn't take a stand in her first two paragraphs, but when you read the rest of the essay, you can decide which of the three directions she takes. Her introductory two paragraphs, however, make clear that the two cultures' use of time differs radically.

How can you use analogy? An analogy is an extended **metaphor** or **simile** in which a primary term is equated with another quite dissimilar term. An **analogy** can emphasize a point or illuminate an idea. If you are writing about an abstraction, for example, you can make it more familiar by using an analogy to make it concrete and, therefore, more understandable. For Butler, free time may be like being in a foreign country where she's glad to be, but it makes her nervous; for the Japanese, free time may be like money one has to spend for the good of the community. Extend those similes and you'd have an analogy.

How can you organize your draft? Comparison and contrast essays group information so that the comparison is made by **blocks** or **point by point** or by a combination of the two. If you were to write an essay explaining the differences between an American feast, such as Thanksgiving, and a Chinese one, here is what the two major types of organization would look like in outline form:

Type	Structure	Content
Block	Paragraph 1	Introduction
	Block A, Paragraphs 2–4	American culture
	Point 1	Preparation
	Point 2	Courses and types of food
	Point 3	Manners
	Block B, Paragraphs 5–7	Chinese culture
	Point 1	Preparation
	Point 2	Courses and types of food
	Point 3	Manners
	Paragraph 8	Conclusion

Type	Structure	Content
Point by point	Paragraph 1	Introduction
	Point 1, paragraph 2	Preparation
		Chinese
		American
	Point 2, paragraph 3	Courses and types of food
		Chinese
		American

And so on. As you can see, sticking rigorously to one type of structure can become boring or predictable, so writers often mix the two.

How can you apply what you've learned from previous chapters? A close look at any of the essays that follow will show how you can use other modes, such as description, narration, and cause and effect, to help flesh out your draft. A brief narrative or anecdote is often a good way to begin an essay, as it usually sets a conversational tone and establishes a link between writer and reader. Examples can clarify your points and description can make them memorable, while exploring why the differences or similarities exist or what effect they may have will lead you into pondering cause-and-effect relationships.

Where should you place your thesis? The one-sentence thesis placed at the end of an introductory paragraph certainly informs your readers of your subject and stance, but you might find your paper more effective if you treat your thesis more subtly, trying it out in different forms and positions. Although some of the essays in this chapter save their major assertion until last, others combine ideas from various points in the essay to form a thesis. And, of course, not all theses are explicit; but if you want to imply yours, you have to be sure your implication is clear or the reader may miss the point.

Some writers begin the writing process with a thesis clearly set out, but many find that it is easier to write their way into one. As a result, you may find that the last paragraph in your draft will make a good introductory one; by the time you have written it, you have refined your thesis. At that point, you'll find coming up with a new introduction isn't the task it was to begin with—you already know where you ended up and how you got there.

How do the essays in this chapter illustrate comparison and contrast? Lynnika Butler examines U.S. and Japanese concepts of time; Denise Leight focuses on living together and marriage; Frank Deford analyzes the popularity of sports and reality television; John

Abell explains why book books are better than E-books, and Steve Kelley and Jeff Parker's cartoon questions the labeling used by fast food franchises.

Useful Terms

Analogy An analogy examines a subject by comparing it point by point to something seemingly unlike but more commonplace and less complex. An analogy is also an extended metaphor.

Block comparison A comparison of x to y by grouping all that is to be compared under x and then following with the same information under y.

Comparison and contrast An examination of two subjects by exploring their similarities and differences that are usually developed through literal and logical comparisons within like categories.

Metaphor An implied but direct comparison in which the primary term is made more vivid by associating it with a quite dissimilar term. "Life is no bed of roses" is a familiar metaphor. Link the two elements being compared with *like* or *as* and the result is a **simile.**

Point-by-point comparison A comparison that examines one or more elements by stating them, then comparing subject x to subject y, and then continuing to the next point.

POINTERS FOR COMPARING AND CONTRASTING

Exploring the Topic

1. **What are the similarities and differences?** Are the similarities so similar that little distinguishes them? So different that the contrast isn't fair? If so, try another subject; if not, pare down your list to the most important ones.

2. **Should you emphasize similarities or differences?** Which pattern of organization best fits your material? Block? Point by point? A combination of the two? Might a chart or table be appropriate?

3. **What examples will work best?** If your reader isn't familiar with your topic, what examples might be familiar? What
examples will make clear what may be unfamiliar?
4. **What other modes are appropriate?** What modes can you
draw on to help support your comparison and the organization of the essay? Do you need to define? Where can you use
description? Narration? Example? Do any of your comparisons
involve cause and effect?
5. **What is your point? Your purpose?** Do you want to entertain,
inform, or persuade? Given your point as a tentative thesis, should
you spell it out in the essay or imply it? If you are writing to
inform, what information do you want to present? If you are writing to persuade, what do you want your reader to believe or do?
6. **What persona do you want to create?** Is it best for you to be
a part of the comparison and contrast or to be an observer? Do
you have a strongly held conviction about your subject? Do you
want it to show? Does your persona fit your audience, purpose,
and material?

Drafting the Paper

1. **Know your reader.** Use your first paragraph to set out your
major terms and your general focus and to prepare the reader for
the pattern of organization and tone that will follow. Reexamine
your examples to see which ones may be unfamiliar to your
reader. What does your audience know about your topic? Not
know? Your audience might be biased toward or against your
subject and perspective. How can you best foster or combat
the bias?
2. **Know your purpose.** Writing to inform is probably the easiest
here, because although your subject may be familiar, your
comparisons are probably new. If your primary purpose is to
express your feelings, make sure that you are not just writing to yourself and that you are not putting off your audience.
Similarly, if you are writing to persuade, make sure you are
not convincing only yourself. Check to see that you are using
material that may convince someone who disagrees with you
or is either sitting on the fence or hasn't given the matter much
thought. On the other hand, writing to entertain is difficult and
requires a deft use of persona.

(Continued)

POINTERS FOR COMPARING
AND CONTRASTING *(Continued)*

3. **Use other modes to support your comparisons.** Description and example are probably the most obvious modes to use, but consider narration, cause and effect, definition, and analogy as well. A short narrative may add interest to your paper, or perhaps cause and effect enters into your comparisons. Definition may be vital to your thesis, and analogy may help clarify or expand a point.

4. **Check your pattern of organization.** If you are using block comparison, make sure you have introduced your two subjects and that your conclusion brings them back together. In the body of the paper, make sure that what you cover for one, you also cover for the other. In point-by-point comparison, check to see that your points are clearly set out. You may want to use both types of organization, though one will probably predominate.

5. **Make a point.** Perhaps you want to use your comparisons to make a comment on the way we live, perhaps to clarify two items that people easily confuse, perhaps to argue that one thing is better than the other. Whatever your point, check it to make sure it is an assertion, not a mere fact. Whether your purpose is to inform or to persuade, take a stand and make sure that your thesis clearly implies or states it.

Living on Tokyo Time

Lynnika Butler

During the five years Lynnika Butler spent in Japan, she taught English, worked as a coordinator for international relations, and volunteered as an interpreter—an experience that made her an astute observer of how the Japanese treat time. That experience, together with her BA in English and Spanish, may have also contributed to her decision to pursue a graduate degree in linguistics, earning a PhD from the University of Arizona. Her goal is "to use what I am learning about the science of language to help communities who are trying to preserve or revitalize their native languages." She is now engaged in research on dormant American Indian languages. Butler's essay was first published in the Salt Journal, *Fall 2001, and then reprinted in the* Utne Reader's January–February 2003 *issue.*

What to Look For The concept of time is a slippery one, but Butler explains it clearly. As you read her essay, be aware of how she leads into it and then explains how the two cultures view it.

1   It's fair to say that Japanese people are unbelievably busy. Working 10 hours a day, and often coming in on days off, they rarely take a vacation of more than three or four days. A straight week is a hedonistic luxury. Students have less than a month for summer vacation, and even then they have all kinds of assignments to do.

2   Watching people live like this, with almost no time for themselves, makes an American like me wonder why more of them don't throw themselves under subway trains. But I seem to have far more anxiety about free time than my Japanese friends do—even though, compared to them, I have much more of it. Why doesn't this cradle-to-grave, manic scheduling bother them?

3   A lot of Westerners make the glib assumption that Japanese people are simply submissive, unoriginal, or masochistic enough to put up with such a punishing system. I don't think that's it. In Japan, time is measured in the same hours and minutes and days as anywhere else, but it is experienced as a fundamentally different phenomenon. In the West, we save time, spend time, invest time,

even kill time—all of which implies that it belongs to us in the first place. We might find ourselves obliged to trade huge chunks of our time for a steady salary, but most of us resent this as something stolen from us, and we take it for granted that our spare hours are none of our teachers' or bosses' business.

4   The Japanese grow up with a sense of time as a communal resource, like the company motor pool. If you get permission, you can borrow a little for your own use, but the main priority is to serve the institution—in this case, society as a whole. Club activities, overtime, drinks with the boss, and invitations to the boring weddings of people you hardly know are not seen as intruding on your free time—they are the *shikata ga nai* (nothing you can do about it) duties that turn the wheels of society. "Free" time (*hima*) is something that only comes into existence when these obligations have all been fulfilled. This is nicely borne out by an expression my boss uses whenever he leaves work a little early: *chotto hima morau* ("I'm going to receive a little free time").

5   Though I can't pretend I like living on a Japanese schedule, I try hard not to make judgments. *Oku ga fukai*—things are more complicated than they appear. The Japanese sacrifice their private time to society, but in return they get national health insurance, a wonderful train system, sushi, the two thousand temples of Kyoto, and traditional culture so rich that every back-water village seems to have its own unique festivals, seasonal dishes, legends, and even dialect. All of which are invaluable social goods that I would not trade for a lifetime of free hours.

ORGANIZATION AND IDEAS

1. Butler opens by stating that the Japanese are "busy." How effective are the examples that support her statement?
2. In paragraph 2, Butler poses a question. What is the answer?
3. Sum up the Japanese attitude toward time. What is the American one?
4. Of the two views of time, which does Butler prefer and why?
5. Butler says that Americans treat time as though "it belongs to us" (paragraph 3). How accurate do you find that statement?

TECHNIQUE AND STYLE

1. Butler states a paradox in paragraph 2. How would you state it in your own words?
2. The essay opens with a description of Japanese "busyness" and follows it with a paragraph that gives Butler's reaction to it. To what extent is her response similar to the reader's?

3. Think about the simile Butler uses in paragraph 4. How effective is it?
4. Butler occasionally uses a Japanese term that she then translates. What does her use of Japanese add to the essay?
5. Reread the last paragraph. Given your sense of what a conclusion should do, how well does it fit?

SUGGESTIONS FOR WRITING

Journal

1. To what extent do you share the U.S. sense of time being a personal possession?
2. How difficult would it be for you to adapt to the Japanese sense of time? Explain.

Essay

1. You can use Butler's essay as a model for your own, one in which you compare and contrast two groups' attitudes toward something. Think, for instance, of the difference between how you and your parents view vacations. For your own topic, consider first two different groups and then think your way into their attitudes toward *x*, with *x* standing for what they differ about. Suggestions for different categories:
generations
regions, for example, North and South
city and country residents
males and females
teachers and students
2. Butler contrasts the various intrusions on what Americans would think of as their free time to what Japanese see as "duties that turn the wheels of society" (paragraph 4). Think about your own sense of obligation and those things you do and do not feel a sense of duty toward. Write an essay in which you define your sense of duty by contrasting examples of where it does and does not apply.

Who's Watching?
Reality TV and Sports

Frank Deford

It's hard to find something Frank Deford doesn't do and do well: If you read Sports Illustrated, *you've probably seen his byline; if you listen to National Public Radio's "Morning Edition," you've heard his commentary; if you watch Bryant Gumbel's "Real Sports" on HBO, you've even seen him. Deford taught at Princeton University before he took up journalism as his career, and he has won almost every prize for sports writing there is to win: the National Magazine Award, the U.S. Sportswriter of the Year (six times), the Christopher Award, and the Peabody Award. The author of several screenplays and sixteen books, he has had two books made into films and one into a Broadway musical. His latest work is a novel,* Bliss, Remembered *(2011), written as a memoir and unlikely love story that started at the 1936 Olympics. Hailed by* GQ *as "the world's greatest sportswriter," Deford read the piece that follows on NPR on June 2, 2004.*

What to Look For   Though Deford depends on comparison and contrast to examine his subject, be on the lookout for how he also uses examples and explains causal relationships—why *x* happened and the results. Note how these other modes support the main one.

1   It would seem to me that reality TV is nothing more than a form of sport. It's a competition, a game, but on a coast-to-coast basis it's more emotionally appealing than many of our sports. So I have to believe that as many people get more interested in the reality shows, they lose some interest in the old-fashioned sports.

2   The constant problem that sports in this country suffers from is that there are just too many teams playing too many games. People, especially local fans, can follow their teams, but only the hard-core zealots monitor a whole sport. As a consequence, especially in the team sports with myriad games—baseball, basketball and hockey— home attendance may remain high, while at the same time ratings for national games decrease. That may sound contradictory, but it makes sense.

3   Let's just take one city as example. The good people in Dallas may have cared passionately about their basketball and hockey teams, but as soon as the Stars and the Mavericks were eliminated in the playoffs, I would suspect that a goodly number of the Dallas fans dropped their interest altogether in the NBA and NHL playoffs and started devoting their attention to the local baseball team, the Texas Rangers.

4   Reality TV focuses. There are only a small number of competitors and we get to meet them and know them well, a whole lot better than our friends in Dallas ever got to know the Calgary Flames or the Milwaukee Bucks during the regular season. In many respects, in fact, reality TV shows essentially start with the elimination playoffs, which concentrate the mind without having to bother us with the long, boring regular season. Reality television shows also are scheduled for just once a week. Every competition becomes important, in TV language, "appointment viewing."

5   Football has become the one traditional team sport that continues to have a growing national audience, and a large reason for that is that there are only a limited number of games, with the vast majority taking place on the weekends. It's no coincidence, I think, that the one sport which has shown great ratings gains in the last few years is NASCAR, which follows the once-a-week NFL model. NASCAR is like an all-star reality show every week. Everybody who follows the sport knows all the major drivers. Contrast NASCAR, say, to the PGA, where each week there are different contenders. The casual fan can't keep them all straight, so he only stays tuned when Tiger Woods has a chance.

6   Familiarity is so important when we are watching any kind of game. If we know the contestants, we can decide whether we want to root for them or against them. That's why the NFL and the NBA drafts are more interesting to more people than most actual games. We become familiar with the prospects before the draft and get involved.

7   Anyway, with all the competition from the new once-a-week television competitions, maybe major-league baseball, the NBA and the NHL are just going to have to settle for having intense local followings with declining national impact, and the hero that a nation turns its lonely eyes to is not going to be a great star who hits home runs or scores baskets, but some guy who sings songs or picks a bride or gets a job with Donald Trump. Yes, indeed, your new American idol, but that's reality.

ORGANIZATION AND IDEAS

1. What paragraph or paragraphs function as the introduction? How much information does it give you?
2. Deford cites examples in paragraphs 3 and 4. How apt are they?
3. In what ways are reality shows and sports similar? Different? What kind of organizational pattern does Deford use?
4. Reread the essay to see how many examples of sports Deford provides and how many of reality shows. How fair is his comparison?
5. Think about what Deford says about NASCAR (paragraph 5). Is that also true of the World Series? The Super Bowl? Why or why not?

TECHNIQUE AND STYLE

1. How important is Deford's use of cause and effect in supporting his points? Explain what it adds to or detracts from the essay.
2. What is Deford's purpose? Is he writing to argue, explain, speculate, lament, complain, or what?
3. Consider the examples Deford draws from sports. What definition can you deduce for his concept of what is covered by the word *sports*?
4. Deford's essay was written to be heard on radio. What can you spot that shows he was aware of how his essay would sound?
5. How would you describe Deford's persona? What examples can you cite to support your view?

SUGGESTIONS FOR WRITING

Journal

1. What are your least and most favorite sports and why?
2. What are your least and most favorite television shows and why?

Essay

1. "Reality show" is a broad label, but Deford does bring out some of the shows' characteristics. Think about them and think also of the various kinds of shows that appear on television:
   quiz shows
   major sports events (Indy 500, Kentucky Derby)
   survival shows
   talent shows
   talk shows (such as Oprah, Conan O'Brien, Jay Leno, David Letterman)
   Select two programs within a category and compare them, analyzing the kind of "reality" that is being presented. What conclusion can you draw? State it as an assertion and you have your thesis.
2. If you think about the word *sports*, you'll find it covers a large group of activities. Aside from the obvious ones, the term can also be applied to

many that are less obvious, such as fencing, synchronized swimming, logrolling, and fox hunting. Take your own favorite sport and compare it to one that you don't think deserves the name. The essay that results will use comparison and contrast to explain what you mean by *sport.*

Playing House

Denise Leight Comeau

As a student at Middlesex County College in Edison, New Jersey, Denise Comeau wrote "Playing House" in response to Daniel Zimmerman's research assignment for his English class. The essay was then published in the Spring 2001 issue of Becoming Writers, *one of the English Department's three journals. The collection, according to its editors, "celebrates the achievements of our students, who worked hard over the past semester to translate the insights and responses of full and busy lives into the well-crafted and thoughtfully imagined essays reprinted here. As writers we know it is never easy to find the words and form that most accurately communicate what we know, and the finished piece almost never emerges in the shape we originally imagined it. But it is in the struggle to express ourselves that our thoughts become fully ours, and the battle is always a richly rewarding process."* Becoming Writers *is an appropriate title for such a collection.*

What to Look For   As you read Denise Comeau's essay, figure out if she is explaining her subject or arguing for a specific position or something in between.

1   More and more couples today live together or "play house" before taking the matrimonial plunge. Living together before marriage has become so popular that approximately half the couples in America participate in this activity (Gorrell 16). Some couples choose to live together to test their compatibility and possibly avoid an unsuccessful marriage. With the number of marriages ending in divorce these days, it sounds reasonable that many couples want to give marriage a trial run before making any formal commitment. But do the chances of a successful marriage actually improve by cohabiting?

2   "Cohabitation isn't marriage," says sociology professor Linda Waite of the University of Chicago (qtd. in Jabusch 14). Married and cohabiting couples do not have the same characteristics. According to Professor Waite, cohabiting couples lack both specialization and commitment in their relationships (Jabusch 14). Unwed cohabitants generally live more financially and emotionally independent of one another to allow themselves the freedom to leave. This often results in less monogamous, short-term relationships.

3   Married couples specialize—while one partner might take over the cooking, the other might specialize in cleaning. They pool their money, time, and other resources, creating a higher quality lifestyle. Unmarried couples find it much harder to trust each other financially without the legal bond and, therefore, do not move quickly to pool those resources. While marriage does not ensure monogamy, married couples have more invested in their relationship and think longer before acting on their impulses and stepping outside of the relationship. Unmarried couples do not operate as a partnership, says Waite: "they are being two separate people—it is trading off freedom and low levels of commitment for fewer benefits than you get from commitment" (qtd. in Jabusch 15).

4   Many singles believe that by practicing marriage they will receive the commitment they desire. With this in mind, they move in together intending to tie the knot eventually. Time passes and the couple rarely talks seriously about finalizing the commitment. And so, they often end up cohabiting for a few years until eventually someone gets tired of waiting and leaves. Cohabitation can suppress the development of a higher level of commitment.

5   Sometimes, one or both of the people involved become complacent in the relationship, and without any pressure to move forward, they won't. As social psychologist Dr. Julia Hare puts it, "Why would you go to the store to buy some milk with the cow standing in the living room?" (qtd. in "Why...Marriage?" 53). Certainly, to call a marriage successful, it must actually take place.

6   A study conducted by an assistant professor of human development and family studies at Pennsylvania State University, Catherine Cohan, Ph.D., found that those who had lived together before marriage "displayed more negative and fewer positive problem solving and support behaviors than couples that had not cohabitated prior to marriage" (Gorrell 16). For example, if one partner of a cohabiting couple diagnosed a particular topic as a problem, the other would express more negative behaviors such as forcefulness and attempts to control. Women who had lived with their partners

before marriage generally exhibited more verbal aggressiveness than those in the couples without premarital cohabitation.

7   One cannot ignore the possibility that cohabitants as a group may have certain distinguishable characteristics that make them more likely to divorce. The type of people who would choose to cohabit before marriage may simply be less willing to put the full amount of effort required into a relationship. However, a recent study determined that "the cohabitor selectivity reflected in four sociodemographic variables—parental divorce, marital status homogamy, age homogamy, and stepchildren—is unable to materially account for the cohabitation effect" (Hall and Zhao 424). In other words, the study did not show that these predisposing factors contributed greatly to the marriage dissolution of cohabiting couples.

8   Cohabiting does not necessarily equal the tragic end of a relationship, but couples who do marry after living together have higher rates of separation and divorce (Gorrell 16). The lack of commitment in such a relationship plays a large role in this scenario. If a couple wishes to have a successful marriage, they should show their commitment to each other from the beginning. If they trust each other enough not to cohabit before marriage, their marriage already has a higher probability of success.

Works Cited

Gorrell, Carin. "Live-in and Learn." *Psychology Today*. Nov. 2000: 16.

Hall, David R., and John Z. Zhao. "Cohabitation and Divorce in Canada: Testing the Selectivity Hypothesis." *Journal of Marriage & the Family* 57.2 (1995): 421–27.

Jabusch, Willard F. "The Myth of Cohabitation." *America* 7 Oct. 2000: 14–16.

"Why Are So Many Couples Living Together Before Marriage?" *Jet* 3 Aug. 1998: 52–55.

ORGANIZATION AND IDEAS

1. Comeau poses a question in paragraph 1. What is it and what is her answer?
2. What are the characteristics of a cohabiting couple? A married couple?
3. What is Comeau's view of cohabitation versus marriage? What evidence supports your opinion?
4. As expected in a research paper, you find Comeau cites evidence throughout. Is it sufficient? Why or why not?
5. What arguments or loopholes can you think of that Comeau does not mention?

TECHNIQUE AND STYLE

1. In what ways is the title a pun?
2. What is the function of paragraph 7, and how necessary is it?
3. How would you describe Comeau's level of diction? How appropriate is it for the assignment?
4. Think about what Comeau lists as works cited. What conclusions can you draw from her list?
5. What is the essay's aim—to explain, argue, or both? What evidence can you find to back up your view?

SUGGESTIONS FOR WRITING

Journal

1. Set a timer for 15 minutes and use your journal to explore the extent to which you are convinced by Comeau's essay.
2. How would you describe Comeau's persona, the person behind the writing? Quote from the essay to illustrate your impressions.

Essay

1. Comeau's essay focuses on an important decision that many people face. Think about the decisions you have made between two choices, choose one, and write an essay in which you explain the choice and analyze whether it was the correct one. Suggestions:
   to go to college
   to take a particular job
   to pick a major
   to stand up for a friend
   to take a risk
2. Write your own version of "Playing House," using your library or the Web to research the subject, then selecting your own sources, using Comeau's essay as an additional source. Argue for your own point of view.

5 Reasons Why E-Books Aren't There Yet

John C. Abell

In the course of his twenty-six years working at Reuters, the global news agency, John C. Abell has experienced and written about two worlds, the one that existed before the Internet and the one after. Starting as a reporter and editor, he then became the founding editor of reuters.com *and now writes a weekly column for the service. Firmly attached to the Internet, Abell is also the New York Bureau Chief for* Wired *and has his own blog,* planetabell.blogspot.com, *though his actual whereabouts may be hard to find: "I won't leave home without my iPhone or iPad—which I use to write, record, photograph and publish from pretty much anywhere." Whether the medium is print or electronic, Abell subscribes to three principles: "Good journalism has nothing to do with the medium; If the medium is the message, you're not doing it right; and Nothing is more important than aspiring to be correct." This essay was published in* Wired *in June of 2011.*

What to Look For   Abell depends on comparison and contrast to develop his ideas, but you can also find he uses a problem–solution pattern, a choice that lends variety to his essay and can work for you.

1   There are no two ways about it: E-books are here to stay. Unless something as remarkable as Japan's reversion to the sword occurs, digital books are the 21st century successor to print. And yet the e-book is fundamentally flawed. There are some aspects to print book culture that e-books can't replicate (at least not easily)—yet.

2   Let's put this into some context first. Amazon sparked the e-reader revolution with the first Kindle a mere three-and-a-half years ago, and it now already sells more e-books than all print books combined. Barnes & Noble, the century-old bricks-and-mortar bookseller, is being pursued by Liberty Media not because it has stores all over the place but because its Nook e-reader is the Kindle's biggest competitor.

3   Reasonable arguments that the iPad would kill the e-reader seem laughable now, as both thrive and many people own one of each.

One thing E-books and books are equally good at: In their own ways, they're both platform agnostic.

4   But for all of the benefit they clearly bring, e-books are still falling short of a promise to make us forget their paper analogs. For now, you still lose something by moving on.

5   It isn't always that way with tech: We rejoice at cutting the phone cord, we don't fret that texting causes lousy penmanship and we are ecstatic that our computers, tablets and phones are replacing the TV set.

6   I'm not resorting to variations on the ambiguous tactile argument ("The feel and smell of paper is an integral part of the reading experience....") that one hears from some late-to-never adopters. And—full disclosure—I have never owned an e-book reader, because I have an ingrained opposition to single-purpose devices. But since getting an iPad on day one, I haven't purchased a print edition of anything for myself.

7   I am hooked—completely one with the idea that books are legacy items that may never go away, but have been forever marginalized as a niche medium. With that in mind, however, here are five things about e-books that might give you pause about saying good riddance to the printed page.

8   Fix these problems, and there really will be no limits to the e-book's growth.

9   **1) An unfinished e-book isn't a constant reminder to finish reading it.**

10   Two months into 2011, *The New York Times* tech reporter (and former *Wired* reporter Jenna Wortham) wrote excitedly that she had finally finished her first e-book—how is such technological tardiness possible for someone so plugged in? Wortham had an excellent explanation: She kept forgetting to pick up any e-book she had started reading. It took the solemn determination of a New Year's resolution to break that spell.

11   E-books don't exist in your peripheral vision. They do not taunt you to finish what you started. They do not serve as constant, embarrassing reminders to your poor reading habits. Even 1,001 digital books are out of sight, and thus out of mind. A possible solution? Notifications that pop up to remind you that you've been on page 47 of *A Shore Thing* for 17 days.

12   **2) You can't keep your books all in one place.**

13   Books arranged on your bookshelves don't care what store they came from. But on tablets and smartphones, the shelves are divided by app—you can't see all the e-books you own from various vendors,

all in one place. There is simply no app for that. (With e-readers, you are doubly punished, because you can't buy anything outside the company store anyway.)

14   Apple doesn't allow developers to tap into root information, which would be needed to create what would amount to a single library on an iOS device. If that restriction disappeared, there would still be the matter of individual vendors agreeing to cooperate—not a given since they are competitors and that kind of leveling could easily lead to price wars, for one thing.

15   But the way we e-read is the reverse of how we read. To pick up our next physical book, we peruse bookshelves we've arranged and pick something out. In the digital equivalent, we would see everything we own, tap on a book and it would invoke the app it requires—Kindle, Nook, Borders, etc. With the current sequence—open up a reader app, pick a book—you can easily forget what you own. Trivial? Try to imagine Borders dictating the size and shape of your bookshelf, and enforcing a rule that it hold only books you bought from them, and see if that thought offends you even a little bit.

16   **3) Notes in the margins help you think.**

17   It's not enough to be able to highlight something. A careful reader wants to argue with the author, or amplify a point, or jot down an insight inspired by something freshly read. And it has to be proximate to the original—a separate notebook is ridiculous, even with a clever indexing system that seems inventible but is yet to be invented.

18   Books don't offer much white space for readers to riff in, but e-books offer none. And what about the serendipity of sharing your thoughts, and being informed by the thoughts of others, from the messages in shared books?

19   Replicating this experience will take a new standard, adopted universally, among competitors whose book tech, unlike paper, is proprietary. For a notion of what this might look like, check out OpenMargin.

20   **4) E-books are positioned as disposable, but aren't priced that way.**

21   This one is simple, and also easy to oversimplify since people still have to get paid. But until e-books truly add new value, the way Hollywood did with DVD extras, it's just annoying to plunk down $13 for what amounts to a rental. E-books cost virtually nothing to produce, and yet the baseline cover price, set by publishers, is only fractionally below the discount price for the print version of new releases.

22   E-books can't be shared, donated to your local library shelter, or re-sold. They don't take up space, and thus coax conflicted feelings when it is time to weed some of them out. But because they aren't social, even in the limited way that requires some degree of human contact in the physical world, they will also never be an extension of your personality. Which brings me to...

23   **5) E-books can't be used for interior design.**

24   Before you roll your eyes at the shallowness of this gripe, consider this: When in your literate life you did not garnish your environment with books as a means of wordlessly introducing yourself to people in your circle? It probably began that time you toted *The Cat in the Hat,* trying not to be dispatched to bed during a grown-up dinner party.

25   It may be all about vanity, but books—how we arrange them, the ones we display in our public rooms, the ones we don't keep— say a lot about what we want the world to think about us. Probably more than any other object in our homes, books are our coats of arms, our ice breakers, our calling cards. Locked in the dungeon of your digital reader, nobody can hear them speak on your behalf.

26   It's a truism that no new medium kills the one that it eclipses— we still have radio, which pre-dates the internet, television and movies. So it would be foolish to predict the death of books anytime soon. And we haven't seen the end of creative business models—there is no "all access pass" in book publishing, as is the trend now for magazines and the newspapers which have put up paywalls. Getting an e-book along with your print edition (or, the other way around) could be the best of both worlds, or the worst.

27   It would certainly solve my unexpected home decor problem.

ORGANIZATION AND IDEAS

1. Paragraph 1 states Abell's subject and thesis. What does paragraph 4 add to that information?
2. Abell mentions the Kindle, Nook, and iPad. To what extent does he convince you he knows enough about e-books to be credible?
3. What is gained by comparing the e-book to other technological innovations?
4. Reread p. 110 on the two general patterns of comparison. Which does Abell follow? What does he achieve by delaying the comparisons till paragaphs 9–25?
5. Where in the essay does Abell present solutions to the problems he mentions? How does including solutions support or modify his overall thesis?

TECHNIQUE AND STYLE

1. Often a writer will use topic sentences that cover several paragraphs, but Abell opts instead for numbering and bold face. What would be gained or lost by incorporating the topic sentences into the paragraphs related to them?
2. Paragraphs 6, 7, and 24 give the reader a sense of Abell's personality. How would you describe him? What do those glimpses contribute to the essay?
3. What words does Abell use that mark him as techno savvy?
4. Why might Abell have positioned his fifth point last? What does he mean by his last paragraph?
5. Consider the tone of the essay. Does Abell seem reasonable? Biased against e-books? Biased in favor of print? How realistic is the future he predicts?

SUGGESTIONS FOR WRITING

Journal

1. Briefly explain why you would or would not prefer an e-book.
2. How well would an e-book work for text books? What advantages and disadvantages can you think of?

Essay

1. Technology advances so quickly that the old and new often appear side by side, and while the new may be tempting, the old always has some admirers. Write your own comparison and contrast similar to Abell's, opting for your own thesis. Suggestions:
   digital vs. analog watch
   movie in theater vs. DVD
   HD 3D vs. HD TV
   online vs. print newspapers or magazines
   satellite vs. cable televison
2. Abell points out the relative price of print and e-book versions and raises the possibility of rising e-book costs. One alternative is posed by The Gutenberg Project *(gutenberg.org)*, founded in 1971 and aimed at converting print books no longer under copyright to a digital format that can then be read as an e-book or on computer. Use the Web to research the pros and cons of the project, consider what you discover, form a tentative thesis, and then use your notes to write an essay that assesses and evaluates the project.

Dustin

Steve Kelley and Jeff Parker

*In 2010, Steve Kelley and Jeff Parker collaborated to create "Dustin,"
a comic strip particularly appropriate to our times: a son who can't
find the right job and his parents who are having a hard time
adjusting to the culture of young adults. The successful strip has been
syndicated by King Features and now runs in more than 100 newspapers. Both cartoonists started by drawing political cartoons for
newspapers; Kelley's home base is the New Orleans* Times-Picayune
and Parker's is Brevard, Florida's Today. *Their collaboration is an
equal one with Kelly doing most of the writing and Parker most of the
drawing. Though Dustin, the son, is the main character, his parents
also figure largely in the strip as they are often confounded by the
world they live in. The panels below first appeared in October 2011.*

For Discussion

1. To what extent are the characters "typical" Americans?
2. To what extent is the setting typical? Stereotypical?
3. How would you interpret the look on the face of the young man in
   each of the panels?
4. What does the strip imply about working in a fast food outlet?
5. What does the strip imply about products and their advertising?

SUGGESTIONS FOR WRITING

Journal

Faulty comparisons come to life in packaging and on supermarket aisles. Describe a time when you noticed one and your reaction to it.

Essay

"Buyer beware" is a warning that too often needs to be taken seriously. Flip through a national magazine looking for an ad or think about a product you purchased recently and analyze how it compares to a rival ad or product. Break down the features of each, describe them, and compare the two to determine which is better and why. Consider who the ad or product is aimed at as well as the accuracy of the advertisement or labeling. You can use what you have discovered to write an essay with what you concluded as your thesis.

Divide and Classify

5

Baseball romantics always make such a fuss about how there is no clock in baseball, so the game is eternal or something and the team behind always has a chance.

This is literally true, of course, but, hey, if you're behind 11 runs with two outs in the ninth, you haven't got any more chance than if you're down three touchdowns with 28 seconds left. But it sounds good in baseball Shangri-La.

Maybe this anti-clock phobia is why umpires never punish a pitcher when he takes too long to throw the bloody ball. There is, you know, that one clock in baseball—a pitcher has to pitch the ball in 20 seconds. Of course, he seldom does. But baseball umpires don't know from clocks.

The sports that have clocks are all different, too. I've never understood why they stop the clock in football after an incomplete pass but not a completed one or a run. What's the logic in that?

So begins Frank Deford's **division and classification**, and his title declares his twin subjects, clocks and sports: "Watching the Clock: A Sport All Its Own." From the start, you know what he's setting out to do. Starting with baseball, Deford explains how the clock does or does not operate in the game and then goes on to say: "The sports that have clocks are all different too." His tone is informal, his humor playful. What follows is his humorous analysis of the different ways time is treated by different sports.

How do division and classification extend comparison and contrast? Instead of focussing on two points of comparison, division and classification examine several. You might begin by first dividing the subject into a system of classification, then moving on to focus on one of the classes. Say you chose as a topic the electronic objects we often take for granted. You might have found yourself making notes that include a huge list. Thinking through that list you might have noticed that you can divide it into machines that can be controlled with a remote device

132

and those that cannot, or at least not yet. In one category are items such as microwaves and computers, and in the other you've lumped together CD players, television sets, and DVDs.

You sketch out notes that may look like this:

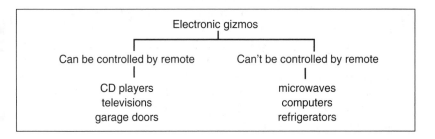

Electronic gizmos

Can be controlled by remote | Can't be controlled by remote

CD players | microwaves
televisions | computers
garage doors | refrigerators

The more you think about it, the longer the list for remote-controlled objects becomes; so instead of writing about both categories, you stick to one, perhaps ordering it by ease of use.

On the other hand, you may find your central question so intriguing that you want to get right to it, in which case you wouldn't need to discuss the division at all; instead, like Pierce, you can dive straight in. Perhaps the greatest trap in writing an essay that uses division and classification is having a string of examples that don't lead anywhere. All your examples are well developed, yes, but they don't support an assertion. It's the cardinal sin—an essay without a thesis.

If you find yourself headed in that direction, try answering your own questions. In the course of thinking about your subject, you may well have come up with a solid, focused, central query, such as "What kind of life will the American consumer have in a remote-controlled world?" Your one-sentence answer to that question can be your thesis.

In structuring an essay by division and classification, you may do best to use a straightforward pattern of organization, devoting the body of the paper to developing the category or categories involved. Your reader can then follow your reasoning and understand how it supports your thesis. Because readers can get lost in a tangle of examples, you might opt for an explicit thesis in an obvious place, such as at the end of your introduction.

What is your purpose? Knowing the effect you want to have on your readers will help you devise your system of classification and sharpen your thesis. If, like Deford, you want to amuse and inform your audience, you may need to explain some of your terms. Deford's audience knows the major American sports—baseball, football, basketball—but may be far less familiar with soccer, so he's careful to describe just enough about the game. And even if the sport is familiar, Deford includes some information many readers may not know.

If, like Deford, you want to tackle a topic using a humorous tone, you will not only be informing your audience but entertaining them as well. But humor comes in many shapes, evoking everything from belly laughs to giggles to knowing smiles. When you see Russell Baker's title "The Plot Against People" and read his first sentence, you know you will be reading a satire. Like Deford and Baker, you may find yourself using exaggeration (also known as **hyperbole**), **irony**, **sarcasm**, or a combination of all three and more. Your title can tip off your readers to your tone: an essay on difficulty of finding the right kind of electronic tablet might be titled "Too Much for Too Little" (irony); "Tablets No Longer Clay" (exaggeration); "The Tablet is a Bitter Pill" (sarcasm).

You can also use division and classification to explore a topic and then argue a point. Thinking of ways in which a driver can be distracted, you might first divide the subject into people and gadgets. Under gadgets, you come up with cell phones, mp3 players, and navigation systems, as well as the car's standard dials and gauges. Perhaps you want to argue technology has made driving a hazard.

How do the essays in this chapter illustrate division and classification? Frank Deford examines different sports' use of the clock; Wise Geek focusses on varous social networks; and Russell Baker satirizes everyday annoyances (dividing familiar objects into animate and inanimate and then focusing on the inanimate ones and the ways they frustrate us); and Richard Rodriguez analyses what unites and divides Judaism, Christianity, and Islam, "the three great desert religions."

Useful Terms

Division and classification An extension of comparison and contrast. Division first divides the subject into groups so that they can be sorted—classified—into categories; classification focuses on characteristics, placing items that share like features into categories.
Hyperbole Obvious overstatement, exaggeration.
Irony A statement or action in which the intended meaning or occurrence is the opposite of the surface one.
Sarcasm A caustic or sneering remark or tone that is usually ironic as well.

POINTERS FOR DIVIDING AND CLASSIFYING

Exploring the Topic

1. **How can your topic be divided?** What is your principle for division? Have you applied it consistently?
2. **Are your categories for classification appropriate?** Are the categories parallel? Do they cover the topic? Do they contain enough examples? Do they overlap? Do you need to make any adjustments? How can your categories be sequenced? From simple to complex? Least to most important? Least to most effective?
3. **Set out your system of classification early in the paper.** You may find that a definition is needed or that some background information is necessary.
4. **What is your point?** What assertion are you making? Does your system of classification support it? Are your examples appropriate?
5. **What is your purpose?** Are you primarily making your point to express your feelings, to inform, to persuade, or to entertain?

Drafting the Paper

1. **Know your reader.** Is the reader part of your system of classification? If so, how? If the reader is not part of your system, is he or she on your side, say a fellow student looking at teachers? What does your audience know and not know about your topic? Your system of classification?
2. **Check your persona.** How would you describe it? Do you have a strongly held conviction about your subject? Do you want it to show? Does your persona fit your audience purpose and material?
3. **Check your categories of comparison.** Are they complete? Do you need to define any terms? Would a chart be appropriate?
4. **Reread your first and last paragraphs.** What does your first paragraph introduce? What does your last paragraph conclude? What is your thesis?

Watching the Clock: A Sport All Its Own

Frank Deford

If you read Frank Deford's brief biography in Chapter 4 (pp. 118–119), you know that he is one of the most versatile and popular sports writers in the country, and he has numerous awards to prove it. And if you've heard him read one of his essays on NPR's "Morning Edition," you also have a good sense of what he's like as a person: easy-going, knowledgeable, and humorous. Whether he's writing about mainstream sports such as baseball, football, basketball, soccer, or more unusual sports such as the roller derby leagues, he's always worth reading. His essay on the eccentricities of clocks in various sports aired on March 4, 2009.

What to Look For   As a way to organize an essay, division and classification can become too predictable and list-like—first A, then B, C, D and so on. As you read Deford's essay look for the ways he avoids that pitfall.

1   Baseball romantics always make such a fuss about how there is no clock in baseball, so the game is eternal or something and the team behind always has a chance.

2   This is literally true, of course, but, hey, if you're behind 11 runs with two outs in the ninth, you haven't got any more chance than if you're down three touchdowns with 28 seconds left. But it sounds good in baseball Shangri-La.

3   Maybe this anti-clock phobia is why umpires never punish a pitcher when he takes too long to throw the bloody ball. There is, you know, that one clock in baseball—a pitcher has to pitch the ball in 20 seconds. Of course, he seldom does. But baseball umpires don't know from clocks.

4   The sports that have clocks are all different, too. I've never understood why they stop the clock in football after an incomplete pass but not a completed one or a run. What's the logic in that?

5   Basketball was saved by the 24-second clock, which was dreamed up in 1954 by Danny Biasone, who owned the Syracuse Nationals of the NBA. Danny also owned a bowling alley, where

136

you can't make any money if the bowlers hang onto the ball. Pro basketball was being destroyed because teams froze the ball. One game ended 19–18.

6   You know how Danny decided on 24 seconds? He just took the average total number of shots in a game and divided them into the total number of seconds. Today, they'd spend four years testing stuff out with computers, and at the end of the day, it wouldn't work as well as what Danny dreamed up on a scratch pad.

7   If a team in any sport, in the vernacular, sits on the clock, it's a bad game—bad for the game. I hate it when somebody says that some football coach exhibits good "clock management." Basically that means he just knows how to waste time.

8   Soccer, of course, has the goofiest clock...well, at least from our American point of view. The soccer clock rarely stops, but the soccer referee keeps the official tally himself and calculates what's called stoppage time. Then he adds this on to the end of the game—only nobody but the referee knows how much extra time it is, so of course, you miss all that wonderful suspense about there only being 38 seconds or 5.9 seconds or whatever it is left in the game.

9   Of course, nobody ever scores in soccer, so it really doesn't matter that much. And ties are very common in soccer.

10   We've created overtimes in sports because we Americans hate ties. As someone once said, snarling: A tie is like kissing your sister. There used to be lots of ties in American football and hockey, but they added overtimes to the clocks so there would be no sister-kissing in the United States of America!

11   And you know what I like best about clocks in sports? When time runs out, there's a buzzer.

ORGANIZATION AND IDEAS

1. Aside from the subject of the essay, what else does Deford's title tip you off to?
2. Which paragraphs mention what sports? How does Deford weave them together?
3. Why might Deford begin his essay with baseball?
4. Given the number of sports Deford mentions, which does he seem to favor? Why?
5. Consider Deford's examples of the various sports and their use of clocks. In your own words state what you find to be his thesis and explain your choice.

TECHNIQUE AND STYLE

1. The essay was written to be read over the radio. What examples can you find to show Deford shapes his prose to be heard?
2. How would you describe Deford's tone? What examples support your view?
3. How would you describe Deford's attitude toward sports? Toward how sports use the clock?
4. What is the effect of the last paragraph? Why does Deford like the buzzer?
5. Deford mixes his opinion with facts. What information surprises you? What does his use of facts contribute to the essay?

SUGGESTIONS FOR WRITING

Journal

1. Deford uses a simile in paragraph 10. What point is he making about ties? Explain the degree you do or don't agree with him.
2. In paragraph 1, Deford accuses some baseball fans of being "romantics." Why might he have chosen that word?

Essay

1. Deford writes about how the idea of "the clock" differs among sports, but different sports appeal to different kinds of people. Think about a particular sport you enjoy watching, whether live or on television and take a good look at the fans and their behavior. See if you can identify different groups and if you can draw some conclusions based on what you find. You might consider how they express themselves by what they wear (or don't wear), how they act, their cheers (or boos), their pregame activities, what they contribute to the game. The result will be an essay controlled by classification and your thesis.
2. It's hard to think of professional sports and not also think of injuries. Choose your favorite sport and team and then consult the Web to research the injuries that took place in a given season. Which ones occur most frequently? How bad are they? What toll do they take on the individual? The team? What conclusions can you draw and which seems the most important?

What Are the Different Types of Social Network Applications?

Wise Geek

Wise Geek is a Web site (wisegeek.com) *"dedicated to providing short, clear and concise answers to common questions." It was started in 2003 by Denis Grosz when armed with a degree in philosophy from the University of California, Berkeley, curiosity, frustration, and techological savvy, he solved a problem that had bothered many: the answer to a simple question is often scattered among many Web sites. Wise Geek is the result and now has a large team of researchers, writers, and editors as well as more than two hundred active contributors. The accuracy of the answers is assured by the "wiseGeek features" menu on every page along with an option to "comment on this article." Needless to say the home page has a search feature, so you can ask almost anything and get a reliable answer. The answer in this essay came from the Internet section, one of the five headings on the home page.*

What to Look For   The article that follows contains a lot of information about social networking Web sites, so be on the lookout for the ways the author tries to clarify a complicated answer.

1   There are many different types of social network applications and attempting to list them all would be nearly impossible. Some specific types of applications, however, include social networking websites, programs that allow people to chat through instant messaging, and Internet forums designed to encourage the exchange of ideas and the establishment of a community. There are also .a number of social network applications that can run with other types of social networking sites, such as games, polls, quizzes, and horoscope programs.

2   In general, social network applications are programs or websites that allow or encourage social interactions and virtual community building through the Internet. These can consist of anything from websites that promote social interaction, such as

forums, social networking sites, and blogs to programs that allow electronic communications between individuals, such as instant messengers, chat programs, and online games. Social network applications allow people in different places to communicate, exchange ideas, work together to achieve tasks and goals, and generally create virtual communities.

3   Some of these social network applications are created to enable people in different places to work on a project together. These include programs that can allow users in separate geographic regions to work on a file together, such as a spreadsheet, allowing each of them to view the file and see changes others make in real time. There are also simpler types of applications that allow communication through instant messaging or by allowing access to chat rooms. These are not always created for work, but are commonly used for recreation and instant communication over great distances.

4   There are many Internet websites designed as social network applications, such as social networking sites like MySpace® or Facebook®. While these sites themselves may be seen as social applications, they can also include a variety of other programs that enhance social interactions even more. These include simple games that people can play together or competitively, quizzes and polls that allow thousands of users to compare ideas, and daily horoscope and news posts that can connect events across the world.

5   Some social network applications can also consist of virtual worlds inhabited by digital avatars that represent people in the real world. These can consist of online games such as massively multiplayer online role-playing games (MMORPGs), or non-game environments that enable social interactions through avatars without any objectives beyond the social aspects. In many ways, these latter types of programs are similar to chat rooms, but they incorporate a digital world for people to communicate within. These types of social network applications have been used by businesses, helped law enforcement officers find criminal suspects, and even connected people in romantic relationships that have led to weddings and families.

ORGANIZATION AND IDEAS

1. The first paragraph divides the subject into types of social network applications. What are they?
2. Paragraph 2 defines the article's central term and explains the uses to which these applications can be put. How well does the paragraph's last sentence adequately cover those uses?
3. What is the main division in paragraph 3?

4. The Wise Geek points out the other uses of Web sites such as MySpace. In your experience do those other uses "enhance social interactions even more"?
5. Definition and division also occur in paragraph 5. Why might the author have put this information last? Assuming the article has an implied thesis, state it in your own words.

TECHNIQUE AND STYLE

1. Take another look at the idea of tone as defined on page 19 in Chapter 1. How would you describe the tone of the article?
2. Wise Geek uses division, classification, definition, and example to answer to the title's question. How would you assess the answer's comprehensiveness? Clarity? Interest?
3. At no point does the article include a personal pronoun. What is gained or lost by that decision?
4. Even though there is no narrator as such in the article, some sense of the person or persons behind the words comes through. How would you describe it?
5. Assuming you have some experience with social networking sites, how effective do you find the answer to the question? What would you change and why?

SUGGESTIONS FOR WRITING

Journal

1. Briefly explain why you do or do not use a social networking application.
2. The Wise Geek mentions "simple games that people can play together or competitively, quizzes and polls that allow thousands of users to compare ideas." If you participated in any of these, how would you describe your experience?

Essay

1. Ways to communicate have come a long way since the days of Alexander Bell. Think about your experiences with some of those methods: telex, fax, telegram, e-mail, land line, cell phone, chat rooms, or Skype. You can probably add to the list. Pick three or more and write your own classification essay.
2. Cell phones, tablets, and computers also lend themselves to playing video games. Use the Web to find recent lists of the more popular ones, choose several, and then research them, noting what they have in common and how they differ. What conclusions can you draw? Would a chart be helpful? Use what you discover to write an essay using division and classification.

The Plot Against People

Russell Baker

Russell Baker grew up in poverty, enlisted in the U.S. Navy for pilot training in World War II, then returned to finish his degree at Johns Hopkins University and take up a career as a journalist. He is best known for his light tone, one that many readers enjoyed during the thirty-six years he was a regular columnist for The New York Times. *Winner of two Pulitzer Prizes, one for biography and another for commentary, Baker is the author of several collections of essays and autobiographical books, among them* So This Is Depravity *(1980),* Growing Up *(1982),* The Good Times *(1989),* There's a Country in My Cellar: The Best of Russell Baker *(1991). Baker is also the editor of* The Norton Book of Light Verse *(1986) and* Russell Baker's Book of American Humor *(1993). The essay that follows typifies the humorous side of Baker's style: his analysis of the principles behind the continuing battle between humans and inanimate objects. He discusses these principles as he neatly divides things into three categories and then places objects into his classifications.*

What to Look For   Transitions between paragraphs can be wooden, so obvious that they leap off the page to say "Look at me! I'm a transition." The more effective variety is subtle, and one way to bring that about is to pick up a key word from the previous sentence and repeat it in the first sentence of the paragraph that follows. After you've read Baker's essay, go back over it searching for his transitions between paragraphs.

1   Inanimate objects are classified into three major categories—those that don't work, those that break down and those that get lost.

2   The goal of all inanimate objects is to resist man and ultimately to defeat him, and the three major classifications are based on the method each object uses to achieve its purpose. As a general rule, any object capable of breaking down at the moment when it is most needed will do so. The automobile is typical of the category.

3   With the cunning typical of its breed, the automobile never breaks down while entering a filling station with a large staff of idle mechanics. It waits until it reaches a downtown intersection in the middle of the rush hour, or until it is fully loaded with family and luggage on the Ohio Turnpike.

4   Thus it creates maximum misery, inconvenience, frustration and irritability among its human cargo, thereby reducing its owner's life span.

5   Washing machines, garbage disposals, lawn mowers, light bulbs, automatic laundry dryers, water pipes, furnaces, electrical fuses, television tubes, hose nozzles, tape recorders, slide projectors—all are in league with the automobile to take their turn at breaking down whenever life threatens to flow smoothly for their human enemies.

6   Many inanimate objects, of course, find it extremely difficult to break down. Pliers, for example, and gloves and keys are almost totally incapable of breaking down. Therefore, they have had to evolve a different technique for resisting man.

7   They get lost. Science has still not solved the mystery of how they do it, and no man has ever caught one of them in the act of getting lost. The most plausible theory is that they have developed a secret method of locomotion which they are able to conceal the instant a human eye falls upon them.

8   It is not uncommon for a pair of pliers to climb all the way from the cellar to the attic in its single-minded determination to raise its owner's blood pressure. Keys have been known to burrow three feet under mattresses. Women's purses, despite their great weight, frequently travel through six or seven rooms to find a hiding space under a couch.

9   Scientists have been struck by the fact that things that break down virtually never get lost, while things that get lost hardly ever break down.

10   A furnace, for example, will invariably break down at the depth of the first winter cold wave, but it will never get lost. A woman's purse, which after all does have some inherent capacity for breaking down, hardly ever does; it almost invariably chooses to get lost.

11   Some persons believe this constitutes evidence that inanimate objects are not entirely hostile to man, and that a negotiated peace is possible. After all, they point out, a furnace could infuriate a man even more thoroughly by getting lost than by breaking down, just as a glove could upset him far more by breaking down than by getting lost.

12   Not everyone agrees, however, that this indicates a conciliatory attitude among inanimate objects. Many say it merely proves that furnaces, gloves and pliers are incredibly stupid.

13   The third class of objects—those that don't work—is the most curious of all. These include such objects as barometers, car clocks,

cigarette lighters, flashlights, and toy train locomotives. It is inaccurate, of course, to say that they never work. They work once, usually for the first few hours after being brought home, and then quit. Thereafter, they never work again.

14   In fact, it is widely assumed that they are built for the purpose of not working. Some people have reached advanced ages without ever seeing some of these objects—barometers, for example—in working order.

15   Science is utterly baffled by the entire category. There are many theories about it. The most interesting holds that the things that don't work have attained the highest state possible for an inanimate object, the state to which things that break down and things that get lost can still only aspire.

16   They have truly defeated man by conditioning him never to expect anything of them, and in return they have given man the only peace he receives from inanimate society. He does not expect his barometer to work, his electric locomotive to run, his cigarette lighter to light or his flashlight to illuminate, and when they don't, it does not raise his blood pressure.

17   He cannot attain that peace with furnaces and keys and cars and women's purses as long as he demands that they work for their keep.

ORGANIZATION AND IDEAS

1. Paragraphs 3–6 explain the first category. What effects does the automobile achieve by breaking down? How do those effects support Baker's contention about "the goal of all inanimate objects"? What other examples does Baker put into his first category? What example does not fit?
2. Paragraphs 7–12 present the second classification. What causes, reasons, or motives are attributed to the examples in this group?
3. Paragraphs 13–16 describe the third group. What are its qualities? Why might Baker have chosen to list it last? What principle of organization can you discern beneath Baker's ordering of the three groups?
4. Consider how each group frustrates and defeats people together with the first sentence of paragraph 2. Combine this information into a sentence that states the author's thesis.
5. To what extent does Baker use the absurd in his essay? How is it appropriate?

TECHNIQUE AND STYLE

1. In part, the essay's humor arises from Baker's use of anthropomorphism, attributing human qualities to inanimate objects. How effectively does he use the technique?

2. Baker has a keen eye for the absurd, as illustrated by paragraph 10. What other examples can you find? What does this technique contribute to the essay?

3. Baker's stance, tone, and line of reasoning, although patently tongue-in-cheek, are also mock-scientific. Where can you find examples of Baker's explicit or implied "scientific" trappings?

4. The essay's transitions are carefully wrought. What links paragraph 3 to paragraph 2? Paragraph 7 to paragraph 6? Paragraph 10 to paragraph 9? Paragraph 12 to paragraph 11?

5. How an essay achieves unity is a more subtle thing. What links paragraph 8 to paragraph 6? Paragraph 9 to paragraphs 3–6? Paragraph 16 to paragraph 2? Paragraph 17 to paragraphs 10–12 and paragraphs 3–5?

SUGGESTIONS FOR WRITING

Journal

1. Describe a fight you have had with an inanimate object.

2. Of all the inanimate objects that can frustrate you, which one tops the list and why?

Essay

1. Write your own "plot" essay, imagining something else plotting against people. Like Baker, you can take a "scientific" stance or you may prefer your own humorous tone. Suggestions:
   clothes
   food
   pets
   the weather
   plants
   traffic

2. It's no news that we live in a highly technological society; it's also no news that at times that technology is frustrating. You may, for instance, have a number of objects that display the time—DVD, clock, stove, answering machine—but when the electricity goes off, getting them back in sync is a challenge. Choose a category and write an essay in which you explore whether that particular group of technological advances is good, bad, or somewhere in between.

Desert Religions

Richard Rodriguez

The son of Mexican immigrants, Richard Rodriguez did not learn English until he went to school, but he learned it well. He earned a BA from Stanford University and a PhD in English literature from the University of California at Berkeley. His public stands against bilingual education and affirmative action put him at odds with segments of the Chicano community, but he is best known for his writing, particularly his memoirs: Hunger of Memory *(1982),* Days of Obligation: An Argument with My Mexican Father *(1992), and* Brown: The Last Discovery of America *(2002). A contributing editor at* Harper's *and the* Los Angeles Times, *Rodriguez has been called the "best American essayist" by* The Village Voice. *You might have heard his own voice on* The News Hour with Jim Lehrer *where he is a regular contributor. For his "outstanding achievement" there he won a Peabody Award, the most coveted honor in television. The essay reprinted here was first aired on that show on July 8, 2002.*

What to Look For   When you think about placing items in categories, you are analyzing their shared characteristics, their similarities. That's exactly what Rodriguez does, so as you read, look for the ways he tracks what the three "desert religions" have in common.

1   The Catholic priest is under arrest, accused of raping altar boys. The Muslim shouts out the name of Allah as the jetliner plows into the skyscraper. The Jewish settler's biblical claim to build on the West Bank is supported by fundamentalist Protestants who dream of the last days.

2   These have been months of shame and violence among the three great desert religions—Judaism, Christianity, and Islam—the religions to which most Americans adhere. These desert religions are sister religions in fact, but more commonly they have been brother religions, united and divided by a masculine sense of faith. Mullahs, priests, rabbis—the business of religion was traditionally the male's. It was the male's task to understand how God exists in our lives.

3   Judaism gave Christianity and Islam a notion both astonishing and radical, the notion that God acts in history. The desert religions

became, in response to this idea, activist religions, ennobled at times by a sense of holy purpose, but also filled with a violence fed by the assumption that God is on my side and not yours. The history of the desert religions oft repeated by old men to boys, got told through stories of battles and crusades, sultans and emperors.

4 But within the three great desert faiths there was a feminine impulse, less strong but ever present, the tradition of absorption rather than assertion, service rather than authority, of play rather than dogmatic certitude. Think of the delicate poetry of the Song of Songs or the delicacy of the celebration of the maternal represented by the Renaissance Madonna or the architectural lines of the medieval mosques of Spain, light as music. And yet the louder, more persistent tradition has been male, concerned with power and blood and dogmatic points.

5 Now on the evening news, diplomats come and go speaking of [everything from] truces and terrorists to the price of oil. In truth, we are watching a religious war, Muslim versus Jew—a war disguised by the language of diplomacy. In decades and centuries past there have been Holocausts and crusades and violence as fierce among the members of a single religion, for example, Catholics contending with Protestant and Eastern Orthodox over heresies and questions of authority.

6 Yahweh, God, Allah—the desert Deity rarely expressed a feminine aspect as in Hinduism. The men who interpreted the Bible or Koran rarely allowed themselves a sense of unknowing or paradox as in Buddhism. And not coincidentally I know many Americans who are turning away from the desert religions or are seeking to moderate the certitude of the desert religions by turning to the contemplative physics of yoga and the play of the Zen koan.

7 Meanwhile, in my own Catholic Church, there is the squalor of sexual scandal—men forcing themselves on boys. One hears conservative Catholics who speak of ridding the seminaries and the rectories of homosexuals. As one gay Catholic, a single man in this vast world, I tell you pedophilia is no more an expression of homosexuality than rape is an expression of heterosexuality. Pedophilia and rape are assertions of power. Polls indicate that a majority of American Catholics are more forgiving of the fallen priests than they are forgiving of the bishops and cardinals who have treated us like children, with their secret meetings and their clutch on power, apologizing but assuming no penance.

8 Polls indicate also that Catholics continue to go to church. We go to church because of the sacramental consolation our religion gives.

9   All of us now in our churches and synagogues and mosques, what knowledge unites us in this terrible season? Are we watching the male face of the desert religions merely reassert itself? Or are we watching the collapse of the tradition and the birth of—what?

10   I think of the women of America who have become priests and rabbis. I think of the women of Afghanistan who came to the school door the first morning after the Taliban had disappeared. I think of Mother Teresa whose name will be remembered long after we have forgotten the names of the cardinals in their silk robes. I think that we may be at the beginning of a feminine moment in the history of the desert religions, even while the tanks rumble and the priest is arrested and the girl, unblinking, straps explosives onto her body.

ORGANIZATION AND IDEAS

1. Rodriguez divides desert religions into three groups and then traces the masculine and feminine impulses within them. How valid is his view of the masculine principle?
2. Paragraph 4 examines the feminine principle in the three religions. What other examples can you think of?
3. Reread the first and last paragraphs. In what ways do they frame the essay?
4. In paragraphs 8 and 9 Rodriguez speculates on why people still attend places of worship. What questions does he pose? What is his answer to those questions? How can you state it as a thesis?
5. The essay was aired in 2002, and many attitudes toward religion have changed since then. To what extent, if any, is it dated?

TECHNIQUE AND STYLE

1. In paragraph 4, Rodriguez defines what he means by the feminine impulse. How adequate is his definition?
2. The essay was written for television. What evidence can you find to show that Rodriguez shaped his prose to be heard instead of read?
3. Where in the essay does Rodriguez bring in his own experience? What does he achieve by doing so?
4. The details that Rodriguez uses, particularly those in paragraphs 1 and 9, are tied to the events of 2001 and 2002, times removed from that at which you are reading his essay. To what extent are those details still effective?
5. How would you describe the essay's overall tone: Pessimistic? Optimistic? Somewhere in between? What evidence supports your view?

SUGGESTIONS FOR WRITING

Journal

1. Think of your own religion or a religion you know well. Use your journal to write down examples of the masculine impulse.
2. Reread the essay, paying particular attention to Rodriguez's idea of the feminine impulse. To what extent does it apply to your religion or one that you know well?

Essay

1. Reread the essay, noting how Rodriguez defines the masculine and feminine impulses and the examples he uses to illustrate his definitions. Think about those impulses and consider how they operate in other areas or within other groups. If, for example, you were analyzing theme parks, you might think of all the kinds of rides, and then sort them into categories according to gender. Roller coasters would probably be masculine, ferris wheels feminine, and so on. Pick one of the suggestions below or one of your own and write an essay in which you analyze how masculine and feminine characteristics operate:
   musicians
   writers
   comics
   sports
   food
2. The terms *masculine* and *feminine* are very broad, encompassing a wide variety of behavior. Arnold Schwarzenegger and Jay Leno would both be called masculine, though they are very different. Choose one of the terms and write an essay in which you analyze the variations within the general category. You will find the Web a good source for researching the names that occur to you, but narrow your search by number of examples, genre, time, and achievement or some such or you will be overwhelmed by information.

That's Life

Mike Twohy

Cartoonist, illustrator, and artist, Mike Twohy has had his work appear in almost every kind of publication, starting in high school with a weekly sports cartoon for The Palo Alto Times *and moving on to the likes of* Ranger Rick *and* The New Yorker. *Working for years as a freelance cartoonist, he found that drawing for different publications with different readers gave him a welcome range of topics and characters. Many of his drawings appear in "Best Of" books such as* The Best of the Rejection Collection: 293 Cartoons That Were Too Dumb, Too Dark, or Too Naughty for the New Yorker (2011). *Twohy's* That's Life *series is represented by the Cartoonist Group and deals with everyday situations anyone can identify with. The cartoon here appeared on January 22, 2003.*

FOR DISCUSSION

1. What connections do you find between the title for Twohy's series and his drawing?
2. How would you describe the character in the drawing? What kind of job does he have? How old might he be? What does the expression on his face tell you?
3. What do you learn by looking at the background?
4. Given what you discovered from the previous questions, how appropriate are the labels for the sorting trays?
5. What does the cartoon say about communication? Social networks? Absurdity?

SUGGESTIONS FOR WRITING

Journal

How would you finish off each of the labels on the sorting trays? Use your journal to explain your choices.

Essay

Think about your own experiences at work, particularly if you have had several part-time jobs. How would you characterize them? How did the overall atmosphere affect you? What were your coworkers like? Did you find the pay sufficient? The job or jobs satisfying? These questions will probably lead to some of your own and together, they will generate enough material for you to come up with a tentative thesis and lots of examples.

Explain a Process

6

> *Even the best of revolutions can go awry when we internalize the attitudes we are fighting. The class of 1992 is graduating into a violent backlash against the advances women have made over the last 20 years. This backlash ranges from a senator using "The Exorcist" against Anita Hill, to beer commercials with the "Swedish bikini team." Today I want to give you a backlash survival kit, a four-step manual to keep the dragons from taking up residence inside your own heads.*

That is the opening paragraph of Naomi Wolf's address to the graduating class of women at Scripps College. She then relates an anecdote from the speech at her own commencement, one that made it a "Graduation from Hell," and presents her "backlash survival kit, a four-step manual." Wolf uses **process analysis** whereby a subject—for Wolf, women's "survival"—is analyzed and then broken down into steps or stages.

We deal with this practical, how-to kind of process analysis every day in recipes, user's manuals, instruction booklets, and essays. Process analysis calls for:

- dividing the topic into the necessary steps
- describing each step in sufficient detail
- sequencing the steps so they are easy to follow
- anticipating trouble spots

Although process analysis is usually associated with specialized subjects—how to do *x*, how *y* works, or how *z* came about—it also finds its way into less formal prose. If you were to write about how you got interested in a hobby, you would be using process analysis, as you would if you were writing an explanatory research paper on the history of Coca-Cola. Process analysis can also be a means of discovery. If you were to analyze the process you go through to revise a draft, you might find out that you overemphasize a particular stage or leave out a step. Because process analysis is often equated with the simpler forms of how-to writing, it's easy to underrate it as a way of thinking and expressing ideas. It can even be used to have fun with a subject; process analysis need not be dull.

152

How can you shape your subject for your reader? The concept of audience is crucial to process essays because you must know the reader's familiarity with the topic to know what you need to explain and how to explain it. Familiar topics challenge you; how can you interest your readers in a subject they already know about? The answer lies in what you have to say and how you say it. Naomi Wolf, for instance, addresses the class of 1992, but the "backlash" against the changes in women's roles is still with us. Although Wolf's examples may seem dated, her purpose is clear: "I want to give you a backlash survival kit, a four-step manual to keep the dragons from taking up residence inside your own heads." From that point on, she has the attention of her listeners and readers—at least women.

Like Wolf, your purpose is apt to be informative and persuasive, but if you want your essay to be read by people who don't have to read it, then you need to make your approach to your subject interesting as well. Wolf's audience at the time she gave the talk was the graduating class of women, but the audience also included parents, relatives, and friends. For some of them, Wolf's advice might have come as a surprise.

Whether a process is to inform or persuade, the writer has an assertion in mind and is trying to affect the reader. If, for example, you enjoy scuba diving and you're trying to describe the physiological effects the body is subject to when diving, you might first describe the necessary equipment and then take the reader on a dive, emphasizing the different levels of atmospheric pressure—the instant and constant need to equalize the air pressure in your ears, the initial tightness of your mask as you sink to ten feet, the gradual "shrinking" of your wet suit as the pressure increases with the depth of the dive. Then after a quick tour of the kinds of fish, sea creatures, and coral formations you see during the dive, you would return your reader to the surface, stopping at fifteen feet to release the buildup of nitrogen in the blood. The whole process may strike your reader as not worth the risk, so you would want to make sure not only that your thesis counters that opinion, but also that you describe what you see so the attractions outweigh the hazards and momentary discomfort.

How can process organize your essay? The sequencing of steps—**chronology**—is as crucial to process as it is to narration and it is inflexible. A quick safety check of the necessary equipment has to come before the dive. And then you must account for all the important steps. If time is crucial, you have to account for it.

Undergirding the concept of sequence, of course, is the pattern of cause and effect. Taking the previous example, you might want to explore the effects of long-term diving. Wolf, in her last paragraph, is careful to emphasize the positive effects of her plan. What's most important to process analysis, however, is neither cause nor effect, but the stages—the chronology of events.

To clarify the stages of the process, you will need to rely on logically placed transitions that lead the reader from one step to the next. Try to avoid depending only on obvious links, such as *first, next, then,* and instead use chronology, shifts in tense, and other indicators to spell out the sequence. The process itself may have markers that you can use as transitions. An essay explaining a historical event, for instance, will have specific dates or actions that you can use to indicate the next stage in the sequence.

The body of a process essay almost organizes itself because it is the sequence of the steps you have identified. Introductions and conclusions are trickier—as is the thesis—because you must not only set out a process but also make an assertion about it. Your thesis should confront the reader with a point, implicit or explicit, about the process involved, and in so doing, head off a "So what?"

How can you apply what you've learned from previous chapters? In writing a process analysis, you will draw on the same skills you use for description, narration, definition, and example papers because without supporting details and examples, a process essay can be tedious. An essay on scuba diving may need to define some terms and bring in examples from mathematics and physiology, as well as from scientific articles on the relative health of coral reefs in the Caribbean.

As you read Naomi Wolf's piece, you'll not only find narratives, but also comparisons (of gender roles and earnings), examples (in the form of quotations and allusions), and cause-and-effect relationships. And, throughout you'll find details and descriptions. Wolf ends by predicting what may happen if you face "the worst" and choose to speak "your truth." You might try a look into the future to end one of your own essays.

Useful Terms

Chronology The time sequence involved in events; what occurred when.

Process analysis An examination of a topic to discover the series of steps or acts that brought or will bring about a particular result. Whereas cause and effect analysis emphasizes *why*, process emphasizes *how*.

POINTERS FOR USING PROCESS

Exploring the Topic

1. **What kind of process are you presenting?** Is it a practical, "how-to" process? A historical one? A scientific one? Some mixture?
2. **What steps are involved?** Which are crucial? Can some be grouped together? Under what headings can they be grouped?
3. **What is the sequence of the steps?** Are you sure that each step logically follows the one before it?
4. **How familiar is your reader with your subject?** Within each step (or group of steps), what information does the reader need to know? What details can you use to make that information come alive? What examples? What connections can you make to what the reader already knows? Do you use any terms that need to be defined?
5. **Is setting or context important?** If so, what details of the setting or context do you want to emphasize?
6. **What is the point you want to make about the process?** Is your point an assertion? Will it interest the reader?

Drafting the Paper

1. **Know your reader.** List what your reader may and may not know about your topic. If you are writing about a practical process, figure out what pitfalls may be involved. If you are writing about a historical or scientific process, suit your diction to your audience. If your reader may have a bias, know what it is. If your topic is familiar, shape your first paragraph to enlist the reader's interest; if the topic is unfamiliar, use familiar images to explain it.
2. **Know your purpose.** If you are writing to inform, make sure you are presenting new information and that you are making an assertion about your topic. Try not to dwell on information that the reader already knows. If you are writing to persuade, remember that you do not know whether your audience agrees with you. Use your persona to lend credibility to what you say, and use detail to arouse your reader's sympathies.

(Continued)

POINTERS FOR USING PROCESS *(Continued)*

3. **Define your terms.** Think through the process you have chosen for your topic to make sure that your reader is familiar with all the terms associated with it. If any of those terms are technical or unusual ones, be sure you define them clearly.

4. **Present the steps in their correct sequence.** Make sure that you have accounted for all the important steps or stages in the process and that they are set out in order. If two or more steps occur at the same time, make sure you have made that clear. If time is crucial to your process, see that you have emphasized that point. If, on the other hand, the exact time at which an event occurred is less important than the event itself, make sure you have stressed the event and have subordinated the idea of time.

5. **Use details and examples.** Whether you are writing an informative or a persuasive essay, use details and examples that support your purpose. If you are explaining how to make your own ice cream, for example, draw on what the reader knows about various commercial brands and flavors to bolster the case for making your own. After all, your reader may not be interested in your subject and may have to be enticed into reading about it.

6. **Double-check your transitions.** If you have marked your stages with obvious transitions or with numbers, review and revise them, checking to see that they are clear and are not overly repetitious or obvious. Make sure each important stage (or group of stages) is set off by a transition. See if you can indicate shifts by using verb tense or words and phrases that don't call attention to themselves as transitions.

7. **Make a point.** Even if you are writing a practical process essay, make sure you have a point. A paper on "how to change a tire" becomes unbearable without a thesis. Given an assertion— "Changing my first flat was as horrible as I had expected it to be"—the paper at least has a chance.

A Woman's Place

Naomi Wolf

A graduate of Yale University and a Rhodes Scholar at Oxford University, Naomi Wolf was working on her PhD at Princeton University when she adapted her dissertation into The Beauty Myth: How Images of Beauty Are Used Against Women, *a best seller published in 1991. As the title implies, Wolf is concerned with issues that affect women, an interest that runs through all of her work as she tries to redefine feminism. She has explored the relationship between women and politics in* Fire with Fire: The New Female Power *(1993); girls, women, and sexuality in* Promiscuities: The Secret Struggle for Womanhood *(1997); women, childbirth, and the medical industry in* Misconceptions: Truth, Lies and the Unexpected on the Journey to Motherhood *(2001); and father/daughter relationships in* The Treehouse: Eccentric Wisdom from My Father on How to Live, Love, and See *(2005). Her essays have been published in print media as diverse as* Ms., Glamour, The Wall Street Journal, *and* The New Republic. The End of America: Letter of Warning to a Young Patriot *(2007), her latest book, reflects her concerns with progressive causes. The following essay was published in* The New York Times *on May 31, 1992, and is adapted from a commencement address she gave at Scripps College, a women's college in California.*

What to Look For   Many writers steer away from beginning a sentence with the word *and* because they are afraid of creating a sentence fragment. But as long as the sentence has a subject and main verb, it can begin with *and* (or, like this one, *but* or any other conjunction) and still be an independent clause, a complete sentence, with the conjunction serving as an informal transition. To see how effective that kind of sentence can be, notice Wolf's last paragraph.

1   Even the best of revolutions can go awry when we internalize the attitudes we are fighting. The class of 1992 is graduating into a violent backlash against the advances women have made over the last 20 years. This backlash ranges from a senator using "The Exorcist" against Anita Hill, to beer commercials with the "Swedish bikini team." Today I want to give you a backlash survival kit, a four-step manual to keep the dragons from taking up residence inside your own heads.

157

2   My own commencement, at Yale eight years ago, was the Graduation from Hell. The speaker was Dick Cavett, rumored to have been our president's "brother" in an all-male secret society.

3   Mr. Cavett took the microphone and paled at the sight of hundreds of female about-to-be Yale graduates. "When I was an undergraduate," I recall he said, "there were no women. The women went to Vassar. At Vassar, they had nude photographs taken of the women in gym class to check their posture. One year the photos were stolen, and turned up for sale in New Haven's redlight district." His punchline? "The photos found no buyers."

4   I'll never forget that moment. There we were, silent in our black gowns, our tassels, our brand new shoes. We dared not break the silence with hisses or boos, out of respect for our families, who'd come so far; and they kept still out of concern for us. Consciously or not, Mr. Cavett was using the beauty myth aspect of the backlash: when women come too close to masculine power, someone will draw critical attention to their bodies. We might be Elis, but we still wouldn't make pornography worth buying.

5   That afternoon, several hundred men were confirmed in the power of a powerful institution. But many of the women felt the shame of the powerless: the choking on silence, the complicity, the helplessness. We were orphaned from our institution.

6   I want to give you the commencement talk that was denied to me.

7   Message No. 1 in your survival kit: redefine "becoming a woman." Today you have "become women." But that sounds odd in ordinary usage. What is usually meant by "You're a real woman now"? You "become a woman" when you menstruate for the first time, or when you lose your virginity, or when you have a child.

8   These biological definitions are very different from how we say boys become men. One "becomes a man" when he undertakes responsibility, or completes a quest. But you, too, in some ways more than your male friends graduating today, have moved into maturity through a solitary quest for the adult self.

9   We lack archetypes for the questing young woman, her trials by fire; for how one "becomes a woman" through the chrysalis of education, the difficult passage from one book, one idea to the next. Let's refuse to have our scholarship and our gender pitted against each other. In our definition, the scholar learns womanhood and the woman learns scholarship; Plato and Djuna Barnes, mediated to their own enrichment through the eyes of the female body with its wisdoms and its gifts.

10   I say that you have already shown courage: Many of you graduate today in spite of the post-traumatic stress syndrome of acquain-
tance rape, which one-fourth of female students undergo. Many of
you were so weakened by anorexia and bulimia that it took every
ounce of your will to get your work in. You negotiated private
lives through a mine field of new strains of VD and the ascending
shadow of AIDS. Triumphant survivors, you have already "become
women."

11   Message No. 2 breaks the ultimate taboo for women: *Ask for
money in your lives.* Expect it. Own it. Learn to use it. Little girls
learn a debilitating fear of money—that it's not feminine to insure
we are fairly paid for honest work. Meanwhile, women make 68
cents for every male dollar and half of marriages end in divorce,
after which women's income drops precipitously.

12   Never choose a profession for material reasons. But whatever
field your heart decides on, for god's sake get the most specialized training in it you can and hold out hard for just compensation,
parental leave and child care. Resist your assignment to the class
of highly competent, grossly underpaid women who run the show
while others get the cash—and the credit.

13   Claim money not out of greed, but so you can tithe to women's
political organizations, shelters and educational institutions. Sexist
institutions won't yield power if we are just patient long enough.
The only language the status quo understands is money, votes and
public embarrassment.

14   When you have equity, you have influence—as sponsors, share-
holders and alumnae. Use it to open opportunities to women who
deserve the chances you've had. Your B.A. does not belong to you
alone, just as the earth does not belong to its present tenants alone.
Your education was lent to you by women of the past, and you will
give some back to living women, and to your daughters seven generations from now.

15   Message No. 3: Never cook for or sleep with anyone who routinely puts you down.

16   Message No. 4: Become goddesses of disobedience. Virginia
Woolf wrote that we must slay the Angel in the House, the censor within. Young women tell me of injustices, from campus rape
coverups to classroom sexism. But at the thought of confrontation,
they freeze into niceness. We are told that the worst thing we can
do is cause conflict, even in the service of doing right. Antigone is
imprisoned. Joan of Arc burns at the stake. And someone might call
us unfeminine!

17   When I wrote a book that caused controversy, I saw how big a dragon was this paralysis by niceness. *The Beauty Myth* argues that newly rigid ideals of beauty are instruments of a backlash against feminism, designed to lower women's self-esteem for a political purpose. Many positive changes followed the debate. But all that would dwindle away when someone yelled at me, for instance, cosmetic surgeons did on TV, when I raised questions about silicone implants. Oh, no, I'd quail, people are mad at me!

18   Then I read something by the poet Audre Lorde. She'd been diagnosed with breast cancer. "I was going to die," she wrote, "sooner or later, whether or not I had ever spoken myself. My silences had not protected me. Your silences will not protect you.... What are the words you do not yet have? What are the tyrannies you swallow day by day and attempt to make your own, until you will sicken and die of them, still in silence? We have been socialized to respect fear more than our own need for language."

19   I began to ask each time: "What's the worst that could happen to me if I tell this truth?" Unlike women in other countries, our breaking silence is unlikely to have us jailed, "disappeared" or run off the road at night. Our speaking out will irritate some people, get us called bitchy or hypersensitive and disrupt some dinner parties. And then our speaking out will permit other women to speak, until laws are changed and lives are saved and the world is altered forever.

20   Next time, ask: What's the worst that will happen? Then push yourself a little further than you dare. Once you start to speak, people *will* yell at you. They *will* interrupt, put you down and suggest it's personal. And the world won't end.

21   And the speaking will get easier and easier. And you will find you have fallen in love with your own vision, which you may never have realized you had. And you will lose some friends and lovers, and realize you don't miss them. And new ones will find you and cherish you. And you will still flirt and paint your nails, dress up and party, because as I think Emma Goldman said, "If I can't dance, I don't want to be part of your revolution." And at last you'll know with surpassing certainty that only one thing is more frightening than speaking your truth. And that is not speaking.

ORGANIZATION AND IDEAS

   1. Wolf's essay could easily be retitled "How to Survive the Backlash." What is the backlash?

   2. Why does Wolf include the anecdote about Dick Cavett? How is it related to the backlash?

3. What are the four steps for survival?
4. Wolf's essay gives advice and explains how to survive, but it also comments on women's place in society today. Combine those comments with her advice and the result will be the thesis.
5. The original audience for the essay was women, but it was republished for an audience that also includes men. Explain whether men would find the essay offensive. To what extent is it anti-male? Dated?

TECHNIQUE AND STYLE

1. What saying does Wolf's title refer to? How does her title set up her essay?
2. Throughout the essay, Wolf uses allusion—Anita Hill (paragraph 1), Plato and Djuna Barnes (paragraph 9), Virginia Woolf (paragraph 16), Audre Lorde (paragraph 18), and Emma Goldman (paragraph 21). Use a search engine to read about one of these allusions so that you can explain to the class how it is (or is not) appropriate.
3. To explore the effect of Wolf's repeated use of *and* in her last paragraph, try rewriting it. What is gained? Lost?
4. What can you find in the prose that suggests that "A Woman's Place" was written to be heard, not read?
5. Wolf is obviously a feminist, but think of feminism as a continuum ranging from conservative to radical. Based on this essay, what kind of feminist is Wolf? What evidence can you find for your opinion?

SUGGESTIONS FOR WRITING

Journal

1. Choose one of Wolf's "messages" and test it out against your own experience. Do you find the advice helpful? Necessary?
2. Relate an experience in which you ran into sexism, either antimale or anti-female. You could use this entry later as the basis for an essay in which you explain how to cope with sexism.

Essay

1. All of us at one time or another have played a role we didn't believe in or didn't like. Those roles vary greatly. Think about the parts you have had to play and how you broke out of them. Choose one and draft a paper explaining "How to Survive" or "How to Break Out." Some roles to think about:
dutiful daughter
responsible sibling
perfect husband (or wife)
brave man
happy homemaker
2. Write your own version of the essay but title it "A Student's Place" and create the advice and explanation to fit the title.

Runner

Laura McLaurin

Laura McLaurin has enjoyed running for more than ten years. When a junior at Valley City State University in Valley City, North Dakota, she wrote the essay that follows in a class taught by Noreen Braun, who reprinted the essay on a Web page devoted to "Some Fine Student Writing from Composition I, Fall Semester, 1997." After graduating, McLaurin spent "eight years teaching elementary students in both Idaho and North Dakota before changing paths a little to become an elementary school counselor. I currently spend at least an hour a day recording and writing up lessons and notes on my students, so writing has never gone away for me."

At the time she wrote the essay, McLaurin had thought about what she enjoyed and came up with the title of the essay. She notes that the idea "came naturally to me. I actually went out that day to run." Thinking about that experience, she had "tried to remember what it had been like; the feelings that I felt, the cold and the pictures in my mind, and I tried to incorporate them back into my writing. I think it really worked. I really just wrote about what I knew and how I really felt. Visualization was the key to my success with this essay." What worked for Laura may well work for you.

What to Look For Not everyone knows what it feels like to run for a fairly long distance, and even those who do may not know what it's like to do that on a cold North Dakota morning. To make her experience come alive and to make it immediate, McLaurin, therefore, chooses the present tense and descriptive details. The result is an essay that explains the process she goes through when she runs and makes the reader feel what McLaurin feels.

1 When I wake up this morning, I can feel the chill of the air in my joints. I am almost reluctant to give up the warmth of my bed, but I know I need to. Slowly, I step out of my bed and quickly throw on a sweatshirt and pants. Leaving my room, still tired, but slowly awakening, I yawn.

2 I stretch my tired limbs, first my arms, then my legs. Noticing a tightness in my right hip, I take a little extra time to stretch it. I am still moving slowly as if in a drugged stupor. Maybe I should just

go back to bed. Before I change my mind, I hurry outside into the brisk early morning air. I take three or four breaths to acclimate myself to the cold, cold air. I can see my breath on the air in little white puffs. I want to reach out as if I could float away with the rising mist. It is still dark outside. The sun hasn't quite poked his head out to greet the day. The blue black sky is waiting to engulf me as his arms extend as far as I can see.

3   Running on an October morning is so exhilarating! I think it is only about 20 degrees this morning. I am so cold!

4   My steps are slow to start. I feel my legs tighten and restrain me, not wanting to exert the effort to propel me forward, yet I know that it is mind over matter and I am going to win this battle! I tell myself that I need to get ready for the big meet that is coming up at the end of the month. My adrenaline is pumping and my mind is whirling at a mile a minute taking in the frosty scenery that is surrounding me. The trees are covered in a fine layer of crystals forming together to make a wintry scene unlike any other I have seen yet this season. My breathing is accelerating and my pulse is beating in my ears. The biting cold is gnawing at my skin. I refuse to give into the cold of the air and the gripping of my lungs.

5   As I slowly retreat into a solid pace, my body is more aware of my feet steadily pounding on the pavement and of the crunching of the leaves and twigs as they collapse under the weight of my body. The burning in my lungs is lessening as my pace is increasing. The steady flow of traffic helps keep my mind from wandering and keeps me focused. I only have a couple of miles to go. My nose is running just as fast as my feet. I feel the slight burning as if the air were actually freezing the breath entering and exiting my nostrils.

6   I can tell by the landmarks of the city that I am closing in on my destination: home. I pass the fenced-in yard with the barking dog who chooses to torment me each time I pass. I keep running, my pace not faltering. As I come within three blocks of my house, I pick up my pace as if in a race. I am feeling winded as my stride lengthens and my breathing becomes much more shallow. I am almost home. The scenery is changing as the sun has finally approached the horizon. The hues of the sky are changing rapidly with the approaching daylight.

7   My house is in sight. I slow my pace to a fast walk and slowly make my way to my driveway. I take deep breaths to get used to the different pace. I am done for another day. I feel refreshed and awakened. I am now ready to continue with another day.

ORGANIZATION AND IDEAS

1. Which paragraph or paragraphs make up the essay's introduction? What does it tell you?
2. Trace the process of the run itself. What paragraphs describe it?
3. One technique McLaurin uses to avoid the stilted *first-next-then* marking of the essay's chronology is to use the progress of the sunlight. Where in the essay does she note that progress?
4. Is McLaurin's thesis stated or implied? What evidence can you find to support your idea?
5. If you're a runner, how well does McLaurin describe the experience? If you're not, to what extent does she convince you that running is a pleasure?

TECHNIQUE AND STYLE

1. McLaurin gives the essay unity by frequently referring to the weather. What descriptive details does she use?
2. Throughout the essay, McLaurin uses the first person *I*. Does she avoid overusing it or not? How can you back up your opinion?
3. In paragraph 2, McLaurin personifies the sun and the sky by referring to them with the adjective *his*. What would be lost without that personification? What is gained?
4. The first sentence of paragraph 6 uses a colon. What other punctuation could be used? Which is the most effective and why?
5. Reread the last paragraph. How else might the essay have ended that would fit in with what has come before? Which is the more effective ending and why?

SUGGESTIONS FOR WRITING

Journal

1. Write your own last paragraph for the essay and then, briefly, explain why you think it is better or not as good as McLaurin's.
2. Briefly describe the feelings you have when you are involved in a sport, either as a spectator or a participant.

Essay

1. Like McLaurin, you might start by thinking about what you enjoy. Perhaps it's a sport or a hobby, but no matter what the subject, you can use McLaurin's essay as a model to write your own description of the process involved. You may find it easiest to start with the process, jotting down the steps or stages. Then once you have a rough draft, you can decide on the kind of introduction and conclusion that would

be most effective for the essay, and, of course, where best to put the thesis, if you want to state rather than imply it. Suggestions for a topic:
playing a sport
being involved with your hobby
playing a card game
cooking a favorite dish
enjoying a "do nothing" day
2. Even though many people participate in sports, even more watch games on television. During play-offs and championships, watching television has almost turned into a ritual. Choose a sport you like or a television show you are addicted to and describe the process you go through to watch it.

Independence Day

Dave Barry

It's a rare columnist who can claim both a Pulitzer Prize and a television sitcom, but few things aren't unusual about Dave Barry. Barry was the focus of the show "Dave's World," which ran from 1993 to 1997 and was based on two of his many books, and in 1988, he won a Pulitzer for Commentary "for his consistently effective use of humor as a device for presenting fresh insights into serious concerns." A humor writer for The Miami Herald, *his columns were carried by more than five hundred newspapers; now that his column has been retired, he continues to write humorous "Year in Review" surveys. A number of those surveys have been collected in* Dave Barry's History of the Millennium (So Far) *(2007), but Barry has also written novels:* Big Trouble *(1999),* Tricky Business *(2002), and with Alan Zweibel* Lunatic *(2012). His Web site (davebarry.com) notes that he "lives in Miami, Florida, with his wife, Michelle, a sportswriter. He has a son, Rob, and a daughter, Sophie, neither of whom thinks he's funny." "Independence Day" first appeared in* Tropic *magazine and was reprinted in* Mirth of a Nation, *Michael J. Rosen, editor.*

What to Look For   As you read Barry's essay, look for the ways he avoids using obvious markers as he takes his readers through a typical Fourth of July celebration.

1   This year, why not hold an old-fashioned Fourth of July picnic?

2   Food poisoning is one good reason. After a few hours in the sun, ordinary potato salad can develop bacteria the size of raccoons. But don't let the threat of agonizingly painful death prevent you from celebrating the birth of our nation, just as Americans have been doing ever since that historic first July Fourth when our Founding Fathers—George Washington, Benjamin Franklin, Thomas Jefferson, Bob Dole and Tony Bennett—landed on Plymouth Rock.

3   Step one in planning your picnic is to decide on a menu. Martha Stewart has loads of innovative suggestions for unique, imaginative and tasty summer meals. So you can forget about her. "If Martha Stewart comes anywhere near my picnic, she's risking a barbecue fork to the eyeball" should be your patriotic motto. Because you're having a *traditional* Fourth of July picnic, and that means a menu of hot dogs charred into cylinders of industrial-grade carbon, and hamburgers so undercooked that when people try to eat them, they leap off the plate and frolic on the lawn like otters.

4   Dad should be in charge of the cooking, because only Dad, being a male of the masculine gender, has the mechanical "know-how" to operate a piece of technology as complex as a barbecue grill. To be truly traditional, the grill should be constructed of the following materials:

- 4 percent "rust-resistant" steel;
- 58 percent rust;
- 23 percent hardened black grill scunge from food cooked as far back as 1987 (the scunge should never be scraped off, because it is what is actually holding the grill together);
- 15 percent spiders.

5   If the grill uses charcoal as a fuel, Dad should remember to start lighting the fire early (no later than April 10) because charcoal, in accordance with federal safety regulations, is a mineral that does not burn. The spiders get a huge kick out of watching Dad attempt to ignite it; they emit hearty spider chuckles and slap themselves on all eight knees. This is why many dads prefer the modern gas grill, which ignites at the press of a button and burns with a steady, even flame until you put food on it, at which time it runs out of gas.

6   While Dad is saying traditional bad words to the barbecue grill, Mom can organize the kids for a fun activity: making old-fashioned ice cream by hand, the way our grandparents' generation did.

You'll need a hand-cranked ice-cream maker, which you can pick up at any antique store for $1,875. All you do is put in the ingredients, and start cranking! It makes no difference what specific ingredients you put in, because—I speak from bitter experience here—no matter how long you crank them, they will never, ever turn into ice cream. Scientists laugh at the very concept. "Ice cream is not formed by cranking," they point out. "Ice cream is formed by freezers." Our grandparents' generation wasted millions of man-hours trying to produce ice cream by hand; this is what caused the Great Depression.

7   When the kids get tired of trying to make ice cream (allow about twenty-five seconds for this) it's time to play some traditional July Fourth games. One of the most popular is the "sack race." All you need is a bunch of old-fashioned burlap sacks, which you can obtain from the J. Peterman catalog for $227.50 apiece. Call the kids outside, have them line up on the lawn and give each one a sack to climb into; then shout "GO!" and watch the hilarious antics begin as, one by one, the kids sneak back indoors and resume trying to locate pornography on the Internet.

8   Come nightfall, though, everybody will be drawn back outside by the sound of loud, traditional Fourth of July explosions coming from all around the neighborhood. These are caused by the fact that various dads, after consuming a number of traditionally fermented beverages, have given up on conventional charcoal-lighting products and escalated to gasoline. As the spectacular pyrotechnic show lights up the night sky, you begin to truly appreciate the patriotic meaning of the words to *The Star-Spangled Banner*, written by Francis Scott Key to commemorate the fledgling nation's first barbecue:

> And the grill parts' red glare;
> Flaming spiders in air;
> Someone call 911;
> There's burning scunge in Dad's hair.

9   After the traditional visit to the hospital emergency room, it's time to gather 'round and watch Uncle Bill set off the fireworks that he purchased from a roadside stand operated by people who spend way more on tattoos than dental hygiene. As Uncle Bill lights the firework fuse and scurries away, everybody is on pins and needles until, suddenly and dramatically, the fuse goes out. So Uncle Bill

relights the fuse and scurries away again, and the fuse goes out again, and so on, with Uncle Bill scurrying back and forth with his Bic lighter like a deranged Olympic torchbearer until, finally, the fuse burns all the way down, and the firework, emitting a smoke puff the size of a grapefruit, makes a noise—"phut"—like a squirrel passing gas. Wow! What a fitting climax for your traditional old-fashioned July Fourth picnic!

10   Next year you'll go out for Chinese food.

Organization and Ideas

1. You could describe Barry's essay as a "how-to" guide for a traditional celebration on the Fourth of July, but his breaking down the event into steps is subtle. How does he do it?
2. It's possible to argue that the essay is organized by process (steps), chronology (time), drama (least to most effective), or some combination. Make a case for the way you read the organization.
3. How effective is Barry's last paragraph?
4. Barry's essay is obviously a satire, but of what: the Fourth of July, family gatherings, American values, the consumer culture, American sense of history, tradition, or some combination? What in the essay supports your view?
5. Take a look at the biographical information and note the reason Barry was awarded a Pulitzer Prize. In what ways does that statement apply to this essay?

Technique and Style

1. Look up *hyperbole* (p. 134). To what extent does Barry use the device? How effective is it?
2. Barry includes contemporary figures (paragraphs 2 and 3). Why might he have done that and what effect does he achieve?
3. What is the point of the fractured "facts" in paragraph 2?
4. Granted that the essay is humorous, but what kind of humor? How would you describe Barry's tone?
5. Reread the essay marking every use of *traditional*. To what extent is the repetition effective? What is Barry's point in using it?

Suggestions for Writing

Journal

1. In what ways is the title a pun?
2. What description do you find the most amusing and why? Quote from the essay to back up your view.

Essay

1. Write your own "how-to" essay on the preparations for a typical, traditional, or important time. Like Barry, you may want to remove yourself from the scene and generalize, or you may want to be part of it. Suggestions:

   Thanksgiving
   first date
   first day of classes
   looking cool
   dealing with a computer problem

2. Barry does an amusing job depicting the "typical" American family at play on a celebratory occasion. Think about the family gatherings you have attended, those of either your own family or someone else's, and write your own survivor's guide.

Becoming a Sanvicenteña: Five Stages

Kate Hopper

Kate Hopper describes herself as "a writer, teacher, editor, and mother (and wife and daughter and sister and friend...the list goes on and on). Primarily, I write about motherhood: the dark side, the humorous side, the places where these two intersect." That interest is reflected in the places where her work has been published: Literary Mama, Mamazine, Minnesota Parent, MotherVerse, Preemie Magazine, *and* Motherlode: Adventures in Parenting, *a New York Times* blog. *Hopper earned her MFA in creative writing from the University of Minnesota where she won the English Department's Outstanding Teacher Award for Graduate Assistants. She is the coeditor for "Literary Reflections" at* Literary Mama *and her first book,* Use Your Words: A Writing Guide for Mothers, *will be published in 2012. The essay included here is based on her experiences as a Fulbright Scholar in San Vicente, Costa Rica where she was working on a life history project with three generations of women. The essay was published in* Brevity's *thirty-second issue, January 2010.*

What to Look For   Hopper occasionally uses Spanish words but either translates them or makes their meaning clear through their context. Your own writing may contain an unusal word your readers may not know, so make sure the context is clear so the meaning will be understood.

1   Stage 1: Fear

2   The old highway to San Vicente is nothing more than a dirt road.
At the height of the dry season the landscape is leached of color, the
road pale as bone. We bump in and out of potholes, my American
advisor filling the Peugeot with 400 years of Costa Rican history: the
Chorotegan Indians, the Spanish conquistadors, ceramic arts, tourism.
Dust billows through the open windows, and I cough, struggle to
catch my breath. Against the vinyl seat, my legs are slick with sweat.

3   Stage 2: Uncertainty

4   I stare into the smiling faces of my host family and laugh when
I don't understand their rapid Spanish. *"¿Cómo?"* I ask, again and
again. The youngest boy is thirteen. He watches me eat my rice and
beans on the front porch, his dark eyes amused. "What?" I ask, but
he shakes his head. After two weeks he finally tells me: "You are as
white as a milk worm."

5   Stage 3: Enthusiasm

6   Behind the house, Betty fills the mouth of the metal grinder
with kernels of wet corn, and I turn the handle, my arm pumping in circles. Strings of dough spill into the wide bowl below, but
Betty says, *"Más rápido, hija."* Faster, daughter. I smile and crank
the handle as fast as I can. When I'm finished, I sit in the cracked
rocking chair, my shoulder aching, and watch as Betty kneads the
dough smooth, spinning a handful between her palms until it's a
disk. She rearranges the burning logs until flames engulf the lip of
the *comal,* and when she drops the tortilla into the concave plate, it
sizzles loudly. She motions to it with her lips. "Do you want to flip
it?" I nod, eager for an opportunity to earn the name *hija.* But the
fire is hot on my face and arms, and I pause too long. Smoke begins to curl from the *comal.* Betty gently pushes me aside and flips
the burning tortilla with her fingertips.

7   Stage 4: Withdrawal

8   In the late afternoon, I sit on the front porch with a cup of
sweetened coffee, hoping for a breeze as I wait for the *cañero*
truck to mark the end of another day. Before I see it, I hear it: the
rumble of its diesel engine, the clatter of wood and metal bouncing over pot holes, jostling the men in the tarp-covered *cajón.* As it
drives by, I can't make out the men's faces; all I see are hands and
arms, disembodied, jutting into the still-hot sun. These appendages
are dark and muscled from twelve hours a day slashing tall stalks
of sugar cane to the ground. Sometimes as the truck passes, someone raises a finger or two, and I raise my hand in response. But
mostly their hands stay where they are, holding tight to the wooden
planks, steady against the bucking of the truck.

9 Stage 5: Understanding

10 In the semi-darkness of the dance hall, I sit next to Sara, my host sister. The band has finished its set, and for the next fifteen minutes, the stereo will blare music: salsa, merengue, and piratiado, my favorite. I take a sip of beer, and when I look up, the lead singer of the band is standing before me, arm outstretched, palm open. I have watched this man dance with women between sets in San Lázaro, Guatíl, and Las Pozas. I have watched the way he twirls his partners, floats them across cement dance floors. Tonight, no one else is dancing. I swallow hard and resist the urge to shake my head. I take his hand, and when we step into the middle of the room, I hear a murmur: *la gringa*. I try to focus on his palm against my lower back, his fingers clasping my own, the old-fashioned music. I have practiced. I am ready when he turns me, our feet forward and back together. And as he spins me around and around, I catch Sara's eye and smile. She raises her eyebrows and nods approvingly. I recognize faces in the darkness outside, pressed against the chain-link fence. A thumb goes up. Someone yells, "Bravo, Katty!" When I sit back down at the table, I'm beaming. "Now I'm a real *sanvicenteña*," I say breathlessly. *"Sí,"* says Sara. "For now."

ORGANIZATIONS AND IDEAS

1. Hopper divides ther essay into five stages with each one followed by a descriptive paragraph. Does the numbering help? Hinder? Something in between?
2. Where in the essay does Hopper use comparisons? What function do they serve?
3. Evaluate how well Hopper makes unfamiliar scenes come to life.
4. Assuming Hopper's thesis is implied, how would you state it in your own words?
5. How would you describe Hopper? To what extent do you or can you identify with her?

TECHNIQUE AND STYLE

1. Choose one of the full paragraphs and explain whether it adequately supports its heading. What techniques does Hopper use?
2. What impression does the essay imply about Hopper's host family? The people of San Vicente?
3. What concrete details does Hopper use? What do they add to the essay?

4. Hopper labels stage 4 as "Withdrawal." Reread paragraph 8. What other words might she have used? Which is preferable and why?

5. The last words in the essay are "For now." What do you think those words imply? How many different meanings can you find?

SUGGESTIONS FOR WRITING

Journal

1. Would you trade places with Hopper? Use your journal to explain why or why not.

2. Reread the essay looking at Hopper's use of dialogue. Write a paragraph or two on what it adds to the essay.

Essay

1. Hopper's essay fits a classic genre, that of initiation: she details the emotional stages she undergoes to become a member of her host family and new community. It's likely that you have also had a number of similar experiences. Consider your own "initiation" into a:

college class or major
job
sport
club
foreign culture

2. Our educational system—K through college—is based on stages of development, and we go through a similar progression when learning a new subject or process. If you have tried to learn a foreign language, you can probably spot the different states of your progress. The same is probably true of learning to play a musical instrument or learning any other kind process. Choose a subject from your own experience and figure out the stages involved. The progression you spot can lead you to a working thesis.

Analyze Cause and Effect

7

1   My first victim was a woman—white, well-dressed, probably in her early twenties. I came upon her late one evening on a deserted street in Hyde Park, a relatively affluent neighborhood in an otherwise mean, impoverished section of Chicago. As I swung onto the avenue behind her, there seemed to be a discreet, uninflammatory distance between us. Not so. She cast back a worried glance. To her, the youngish black man—a broad 6 feet 2 inches with a beard and billowing hair, both hands shoved into the pockets of a bulky military jacket—seemed menacingly close. After a few more quick glimpses, she picked up her pace and was soon running in earnest. Within seconds she disappeared into a cross street.

That paragraph opens Brent Staples' essay "Black Men and Public Space" and shows how complex **cause-and-effect** relationships can be.

Cause	Effect
Staples's nighttime walk	Woman's fear
Woman's fear	Woman runs

You can see how causal analysis can be confusing in that a cause leads to an effect, which can then become another cause. Staples' sleeplessness causes his walk that then becomes the cause of the woman's fear.

Chapter 6 explains how process analysis focuses on *how*; causal analysis emphasizes *why*. Though some writers examine both cause and effect, most will stress one or the other. Causal analysis looks below the surface of the steps in a process and examines why they occur: why *x* happens and what results from *x*. As a way of thinking, causal analysis is a natural one. In this chapter, you'll see how it works with various topics—a nighttime walk, lack of sleep, music, prejudice and iPods.

173

How can you explore a subject?   To avoid a confused causal analysis apply some of the skills used in division and classification and in process analysis:

1. Divide your subject into two categories—causes and effects.
2. Think about the steps or stages that are involved and identify them as possible causes or effects.
3. List an example or two for each possible cause or effect.
4. Sort out each list by dividing the items into primary or secondary causes and effects—that is, those that are relatively important and those that are relatively unimportant.

If you were writing a paper on cheating in college, your notes might resemble these:

	Possibilities	**Examples**	**Importance**
Causes	Academic pressure	Student needs an A	Primary
	Peer pressure	Everybody does it	Primary
	System	Teachers tolerate it	Secondary
		No real penalty	
	Moral climate	Cheating on taxes	Secondary
		False insurance claims	
		Infidelity	
		Breakup of family unit	
Effects	Academic	Grades meaningless	Primary
	Peers	Degree meaningless	Primary
	System	Erodes system	Secondary
	Moral climate	Weakens moral climate	Secondary

The train of thought behind these notes chugs along nicely. Looking at them, you can see how thinking about the moral climate might lead to speculation about the cheating that goes undetected on tax and insurance forms, and for that matter, the cheating that occurs in a different context—that of marriage. The idea of infidelity then sets off a causal chain: Infidelity causes divorce, which causes the breakup of families. Pause there. If recent statistics show that a majority of students have cheated, and if recent statistics also reveal a large number of single-parent households, is it safe to conclude that one caused the other? No. The relationship is one of time, not cause. Mistaking a **temporal relationship** for a causal one is a **logical fallacy,** technically called **post hoc reasoning.**

It is also easy to mistake a **primary cause** or effect for a **secondary** one. If the notes above are for an essay that uses a narrative framework, and if the essay begins by relating an example of a student who was worried about having high enough grades to get into law school, the principle behind how the items are listed according to importance makes sense. To bring up his average, the student cheats on a math exam, justifying the action by thinking, "Everybody does it." The essay might then go on to speculate about the less apparent reasons behind the action—the system and the moral climate. For the student who cheated, the grade and peer pressure are the more immediate or primary causes; the system and climate are the more remote or secondary causes.

How can you shape cause and effect for your readers?   Staples, for instance, may have made several assumptions about his readers: that most are white and might react the same way as the woman; that crime is an urban problem and creates fear. His first paragraph is a narrative that sets a scene those readers can identify with. His second paragraph, however, explores the event from the perspective of a black man, a perspective these readers have never experienced. To make them understand it, Staples uses precise diction: The only thing he was "stalking" was sleep; he's a "softy"; he was "surprised, embarrassed, and dismayed…an accomplice in tyranny," branded as "mugger." He then generalizes about his experience, concluding that "being perceived as dangerous is a hazard in itself."

An awareness of your readers and their possible preconceptions can also guide your approach to a topic. If, for example, your focus is the single-parent family, and you want to dispel some ideas about it that you think are misconceptions, you might assume that your audience regards single-parent families as at best incomplete and at worst irresponsible. It's obvious that you won't win your argument by suggesting that anyone with such ideas is a fool; it's also obvious that making your point while not offending some readers requires a subtle approach. You can avoid offense by putting yourself in the shoes of the reader who has the negative associations. Then, just as you learned more about the topic and became enlightened, so, with any luck, may your reader.

How can you use examples?   As noted earlier, it is ea~~ to mistake a temporal relationship for a causal relationship and to ass   ~~e to something relatively unimportant. That's another wa evidence and logical reasoning are essential to cause-a If, for instance, you find yourself drawn to one exam think about how to avoid resting your entire argumen

Writing about collegiate sports, for instance, you mig by the story of a high school basketball star who war but wasn't good enough to go straight to the pros;

the admission requirements for an NCAA Division I basketball school. After playing at several junior colleges, he finally transferred to an NCAA I institution. There, he was tutored and received a lot of individual attention, so he was able to maintain his academic eligibility. Then, one year short of graduation, all that support vanished because he had used up his time limit and was no longer eligible to play. The effect—no degree, little education, and few chances for review by pro scouts—was devastating. You want to write about it. You want to argue that college sports take advantage of high school athletes, but you have only one example. What to do?

You can use your one example as a narrative framework, one that is sure to interest your reader. But to make that example more than an attention-getting device that enlists the reader's emotions, you have a number of alternatives. If your research shows that a fair number of athletes have a similar story, then you have multiple examples to support your point. If only a few share the experience, you'll need to modify your thesis to argue that even a few is too many. And if you can't find any other examples, then you must narrow your focus to fit what you have, arguing that this particular individual was victimized. While you can ask how many more like him there may be, you cannot state that they exist.

Should your thesis emphasize cause or effect?   Although a cause can lead to an effect that then becomes a cause leading to another effect and so on, most essays are organized around either one or the other: why high school students drop out, why a person returns to college, what happens if a college takes advantage of an athlete, what effect does a one-parent household have on children. That's not to say that if your essay focuses on cause, you have to avoid effect and vice versa; think of the complex interrelationships Staples sets out in his introduction. In your own writing, whichever one you don't emphasize can make a good conclusion. Your introduction, however, is a good place for your thesis; the reader can then follow the logical relationships between ideas as you develop your main point.

Useful Terms

Cause and effect An analysis of a topic to discover, explain, or argue why a particular action, event, situation, or condition occurred.

Logical fallacy An error in reasoning such assigning a causal relationship to a temporal one or reaching a general conclusion based on only one example.

Post hoc reasoning A logical fallacy in which a temporal relationship is mistaken for a causal one.

Primary cause The most important cause or causes.

Secondary cause The less important cause or causes.

Temporal relationship Two or more events related primarily by time.

POINTERS FOR USING CAUSE AND EFFECT

Exploring the Topic

1. **Have you stated the topic as a question that asks why *x* happened or what results from x?** What are the possible causes or effects? The probable ones? Rank them by priority.

2. **Is a temporal relationship involved?** Review your lists of causes and effects, ruling out any only related by time.

3. **Which do you want to emphasize—cause or effect?** Check to make sure your focus is clear.

4. **What is your point?** Are you trying to show that something is so or to explore your topic? Are you making an argument?

5. **What evidence can you use to support your point?** Do you need to cite authorities or quote statistics? If you depend on personal experience, are you sure it represents general experience?

6. **What does your reader think?** Does your audience have any preconceived ideas about your topic? What? How can you counter them?

7. **Do you need to define any terms?** What words are crucial to your point? Are any of them abstract and, therefore, need to be defined? Have you used any technical terms that need definition?

8. **What role do you want to play in the essay?** Are you an observer or a participant? Do you intend to inform, persuade, or entertain? What point of view best serves your purpose?

Drafting the Paper

1. **Know your reader.** Figure out what attitudes your reader may have about your topic. If the causal relationship you are discussing is unusual, you might want to shape your initial attitude so that it is as skeptical as your reader's. On the other hand, you may want to start with a short narrative that immediately puts

(Continued)

POINTERS FOR USING CAUSE AND EFFECT *(Continued)*

the reader on your side. If you are the expert, make sure you explain everything that needs to be explained without being condescending.

2. **Know your purpose.** Adjust your tone and persona to your purpose. If you are writing a persuasive paper, make sure your persona is credible and that you focus your ideas to change the mind of a reader or at least rethink a position. If you are writing an informative paper, choose a persona and tone that will interest the reader. Tone and persona are even more crucial to essays written to entertain, in which the tone can range from ironic to lighthearted.

3. **Emphasize a cause or effect.** Essays that focus on cause probably cover a variety of reasons that explain the result. Though there may be only one effect or result, your conclusion may want to consider other possible effects. For instance, an essay that explores the causes of violence may examine a number of causes but then conclude by speculating on the possible effects of a rising crime rate. On the other hand, essays that focus on effect will more than likely cover a number of possible effects that are produced by a single cause, though again you may want to speculate on other causes.

4. **Check for validity.** Don't hesitate to include quotations, allusions, statistics, and studies. Choose your examples carefully to buttress the relationship you are trying to establish, and be sure you don't mistake a temporal relationship for a causal one.

5. **Make a point.** The cause-and-effect relationship you examine should support an assertion: video games not only entertain, they also stimulate the mind and improve coordination; video games are not only habit-forming, they are also addictive.

6. **Proofread.** Check to make sure you are using *affect* and *effect* correctly. While a handbook will provide a longer explanation, the short one is to think of *affect* as a verb and *effect* as a noun. That's true most of the time.

Black Men and Public Space

Brent Staples

> *Born in Chester, Pennsylvania, Staples was one of nine children in a blue-collar family that watched Chester slide into poverty and crime with the closing of city's major industries. Though he hadn't thought of going to college, he was encouraged to do so by Eugene Sparrow, a black college professor, and was chosen for Project Prepare, a program aimed at providing bright undereducated students with the skills needed for college. Staples went on to graduate with honors from Widener University and then to earn an MA and PhD in psychology from the University of Chicago. A former reporter for the* Chicago Sun-Times, *Staples became the assistant metropolitan editor of* The New York Times, *then editor of* The New York Times Book Review, *and now writer on education, race, and culture for* The New York Times *editorial board. Hailed as one of the best coming-of-age books in recent years,* Parallel Time: Growing Up in Black and White, *his memoir, was published in 1994.*
>
> *The essay reprinted here was first published in Harper's Magazine in 1986. Any woman who walks along city streets at night knows the fear Brent Staples speaks of, but this essay shows us how fear can also affect the innocent. We see and feel what it is like to be a tall, strong, young black man who enjoys walking at night but innocently terrifies any lone woman. His solution to his night walking problems gives a nice twist to nonviolent resistance.*

What to Look For Before you read the essay, look up the dash in a handbook of usage so you'll be on the lookout for Staples' use of it. He uses it in two different ways, but always appropriately.

1   My first victim was a woman—white, well-dressed, probably in her early twenties. I came upon her late one evening on a deserted street in Hyde Park, a relatively affluent neighborhood in an otherwise mean, impoverished section of Chicago. As I swung onto the avenue behind her, there seemed to be a discreet, uninflammatory distance between us. Not so. She cast back a worried glance. To her, the youngish black man—a broad 6 feet 2 inches with a beard and billowing hair, both hands shoved into

the pockets of a bulky military jacket—seemed menacingly close. After a few more quick glimpses, she picked up her pace and was soon running in earnest. Within seconds she disappeared into a cross street.

2   That was more than a decade ago. I was 22 years old, a graduate student newly arrived at the University of Chicago. It was in the echo of that terrified woman's footfalls that I first began to know the unwieldy inheritance I'd come into—the ability to alter public space in ugly ways. It was clear that she thought herself the quarry of a mugger, a rapist, or worse. Suffering a bout of insomnia, however, I was stalking sleep, not defenseless wayfarers. As a softy who is scarcely able to take a knife to a raw chicken—let alone hold one to a person's throat—I was surprised, embarrassed, and dismayed all at once. Her flight made me feel like an accomplice in tyranny. It also made it clear that I was indistinguishable from the muggers who occasionally seeped into the area from the surrounding ghetto. That first encounter, and those that followed, signified that a vast, unnerving gulf lay between nighttime pedestrians—particularly women—and me. And I soon gathered that being perceived as dangerous is a hazard in itself. I only needed to turn a corner into a dicey situation, or crowd some frightened, armed person in a foyer somewhere, or make an errant move after being pulled over by a policeman. Where fear and weapons meet—and they often do in urban America— there is always the possibility of death.

3   In that first year, my first away from my hometown, I was to become thoroughly familiar with the language of fear. At dark, shadowy intersections, I could cross in front of a car stopped at a traffic light and elicit the *thunk, thunk, thunk, thunk* of the driver— black, white, male, or female—hammering down the door locks. On less traveled streets after dark, I grew accustomed to but never comfortable with people crossing to the other side of the street rather than pass me. Then there were the standard unpleasantries with policemen, doormen, bouncers, cabdrivers, and others whose business it is to screen out troublesome individuals *before* there is any nastiness.

4   I moved to New York nearly two years ago and I have remained an avid night walker. In central Manhattan, the near-constant crowd cover minimizes tense one-on-one street encounters. Elsewhere—in SoHo, for example, where sidewalks are narrow and tightly spaced buildings shut out the sky—things can get very taut indeed.

5   After dark, on the warrenlike streets of Brooklyn where I live, I often see women who fear the worst from me. They seem to have set their faces on neutral, and with their purse straps strung across their chests bandolier-style, they forge ahead as though bracing themselves against being tackled. I understand, of course, that the danger they perceive is not a hallucination. Women are particularly vulnerable to street violence, and young black males are drastically overrepresented among the perpetrators of that violence. Yet these truths are no solace against the kind of alienation that comes of being ever the suspect, a fearsome entity with whom pedestrians avoid making eye contact.

6   It is not altogether clear to me how I reached the ripe old age of 22 without being conscious of the lethality nighttime pedestrians attributed to me. Perhaps it was because in Chester, Pennsylvania, the small, angry industrial town where I came of age in the 1960s, I was scarcely noticeable against a backdrop of gang warfare, street knifings, and murders. I grew up one of the good boys, had perhaps a half-dozen fistfights. In retrospect, my shyness of combat has clear sources.

7   As a boy, I saw countless tough guys locked away; I have since buried several, too. They were babies, really—a teenage cousin, a brother of 22, a childhood friend in his mid-twenties—all gone down in episodes of bravado played out in the streets. I came to doubt the virtues of intimidation early on. I chose, perhaps unconsciously, to remain a shadow—timid, but a survivor.

8   The fearsomeness mistakenly attributed to me in public places often has a perilous flavor. The most frightening of these confusions occurred in the late 1970s and early 1980s, when I worked as a journalist in Chicago. One day, rushing into the office of a magazine I was writing for with a deadline story in hand, I was mistaken for a burglar. The office manager called security and, with an ad hoc posse, pursued me through the labyrinthine halls, nearly to my editor's door. I had no way of proving who I was. I could only move briskly toward the company of someone who knew me.

9   Another time I was on assignment for a local paper and killing time before an interview. I entered a jewelry store on the city's affluent Near North Side. The proprietor excused herself and returned with an enormous red Doberman pinscher straining at the end of a leash. She stood, the dog extended toward me, silent to my questions, her eyes bulging nearly out of her head. I took a cursory look around, nodded, and bade her good night.

10   Relatively speaking, however, I never fared as badly as another black male journalist. He went to nearby Waukegan, Illinois, a couple of summers ago to work on a story about a murderer who was born there. Mistaking the reporter for the killer, police officers hauled him from his car at gunpoint and but for his press credentials would probably have tried to book him. Such episodes are not uncommon. Black men trade tales like this all the time.

11   Over the years, I learned to smother the rage I felt at so often being taken for a criminal. Not to do so would surely have led to madness. I now take precautions to make myself less threatening. I move about with care, particularly late in the evening. I give a wide berth to nervous people on subway platforms during the wee hours, particularly when I have exchanged business clothes for jeans. If I happen to be entering a building behind some people who appear skittish, I may walk by, letting them clear the lobby before I return, so as not to seem to be following them. I have been calm and extremely congenial on those rare occasions when I've been pulled over by the police.

12   And on late-evening constitutionals I employ what has proved to be an excellent tension-reducing measure: I whistle melodies from Beethoven and Vivaldi and the more popular classical composers. Even steely New Yorkers hunching toward nighttime destinations seem to relax, and occasionally they even join in the tune. Virtually everybody seems to sense that a mugger wouldn't be warbling bright, sunny selections from Vivaldi's *Four Seasons*. It is my equivalent of the cowbell that hikers wear when they know they are in bear country.

ORGANIZATION AND IDEAS

1. Reread paragraph 1. What expectations does it evoke in the reader? For paragraph 2, state in your own words what Staples means by "unwieldy inheritance." What effects does that inheritance have?

2. The body of the essay breaks into three paragraph blocks. In paragraphs 3–5, what effects does the author's walking at night have on others? On himself?

3. In paragraphs 6 and 7, Staples refers to his childhood. Why had he been unaware of his effect on others? What effect did the streets he grew up on have on him?

4. Summarize the causes and effects Staples brings out in paragraphs 11 and 12, and in one sentence, make a general statement about them. What does that statement imply about being a black male? About urban life? About American culture? Consider your answers to those questions, and in one sentence state the thesis of the essay.

5. Who are the "victims" in Staples' essay? What are they victims of?

TECHNIQUE AND STYLE

1. A large part of the essay's impact lies in the ironic contrast between appearance and reality. What details does Staples bring out about himself that contrast with the stereotype of the mugger?
2. In paragraph 1, Staples illustrates the two uses of the dash. What function do they perform? Rewrite either of the two sentences so that you avoid the dash. Which sentence is better and why?
3. Trace Staples' use of time. Why does he start where he does? Try placing the time period mentioned in paragraphs 6 and 7 elsewhere in the essay. What advantages does their present placement have? What is the effect of ending the essay in the present?
4. Examine Staples' choice of verbs in the second sentence of paragraph 5. Rewrite the sentence using as many forms of the verb *to be* as possible. What differences do you note?
5. Staples concludes the essay with an analogy. In what ways is it ironic? How does the irony tie into the essay's thesis?

SUGGESTIONS FOR WRITING

Journal

1. To what extent do you identify with the women in the essay? With Staples? With both? Explain.
2. Think about a time when, intentionally or unintentionally, you threatened or intimidated someone. Describe either the causes or effects.

Essay

1. You can develop either of the journal ideas above into a full-fledged essay. Or, if you prefer, think about a situation in which you have been stereotyped and that stereotype determined your effect on others. Among the physical characteristics that can spawn a stereotype are
   age
   race
   gender
   physique
   clothing
2. All of us have been in a situation in which we felt threatened. Select an incident that occurred to you and describe its effect on you.

Forget A's, B's, and C's—What Students Need Is More Zzzz's

Mary A. Carskadon

If you were to Google Mary A. Carskadon, you would discover that in many ways her life has been devoted to sleep. She earned her PhD from Stanford University in neuro and behavioral sciences, studying sleep patterns and disorders. Now a Professor at Brown University's Warren Alpert Medical School, she also directs the Chronobiology and Sleep Research Laboratory at Bradley Hospital in Providence, Rhode Island. Author of numerous publications on sleep and sleeplessness, she also is the editor of Adolescent Sleep Patterns: Biological, Social, and Psychological Influences *(2002). Among her many honors are the Lifetime Achievement Award of the National Sleep Foundation (2003) and the Mark O. Hatfield Public Policy Award of the American Academy of Sleep Medicine (2003). But the essay that follows will not put you to sleep; you'll discover that she knows a lot about college students as well. The article appeared under Opinion and Ideas in the Commentary section of* The Chronicle of Higher Education, *November 20, 2011.*

> **What to Look For**   What's tricky about cause and effect relationships is the way they interweave. Sometimes it's a good idea to deal with both, which is what Carskadon does in this essay. Be on the lookout for where she switches from one to the other.

1   Some advertisers routinely entreat us to undermine our health, but rarely through overt attacks on healthy behavior. When one such unhealthful message assaulting sleep reached my university's campus this fall, I began to hear about it from offended and sympathetic colleagues. One saw it in her freshman daughter's dorm. Another saw it in a campus convenience store. The makers of the energy drink Red Bull advised students that "Nobody ever wishes they'd slept more during college."

2   Decades of studies about the neurological and psychiatric importance of sleep in teens and young adults indicate that this "advice" is rubbish. Unlike the drink maker's aluminum cans, it should never be recycled.

3   In adolescents—and younger college students, according to recent data from my lab—sleep is a neurologically important process during which the fast-growing brain becomes better organized. Many neural connections forged earlier in life during rapid growth are pruned away if they are no longer needed, and new pathways are established to the parts of the brain that are responsible for such things as planning, organizing, and abstract thinking.

4   Adequate sleep has implications not only for proper brain development but also for immediate behavior and safety. The list of negative outcomes associated with insufficient sleep goes well beyond merely feeling tired. A recent study of college students in Texas indicated that 16 percent of the participants reported falling asleep at the wheel. A study published by a researcher in my lab, Kathryn Orzech, found that college students who report inadequate sleep also report lower grades and more trouble with coursework. Still other studies have found an association between poor sleep and elevated alcohol use. The literature also supports associations between poor sleep and depressed mood and poorer physical health.

5   Any one of those outcomes should be enough to make a student wish he or she had slept more in college.

6   To be fair to the advertiser and its fun-loving sentiment, there really are a lot of opportunities for college students to have a good time. If students were getting enough sleep, they probably *would* miss out on some fun. But many studies, including Orzech's, have found that on average, young college students are not within shouting distance of the amount of sleep clinicians believe to be healthy. I tell my students that they should get about eight and a half hours of sleep every night, but a recent study found that students on average are getting nearly an hour less than that. I'll make that more explicit: College students should sleep more.

7   The well-substantiated finding that adolescents go to bed later and later as they age is not the fault of advertising. In fact, it is quite natural for older teens to stay up later—about 90 minutes or so—than younger ones. But the need for sleep doesn't change. Unfortunately, because many high schools start too early and assign a lot of homework, teens lose sleep simply because they are caught between two immutable forces: biology and the school schedule. That's probably why one lesson that college students learn quickly is to avoid early classes.

8   Other activities limit sleep as well, including texting, tweeting, and Facebooking in bed, which can keep students awake by producing light and causing social stimulation. (Studying late at night

also involves light, although it is surely not as stimulating as is social networking.) Once teens get to college, whatever help their parents still provided to set a bedtime, or at least to encourage sleep, is no longer available. Students are left to exercise their judgment about when to sleep, and their decisions are based more on what to do while awake than when to sleep.

9   Advertising slogans that mock the choice for healthy sleep, and then deliver on that message with such chemical stimulants as caffeine, are certainly not helping. Caffeine is no more a substitute for sleep than are CliffsNotes for reading original works of literature.

10   What will help, though, is education. Working with her former colleagues at the University of Arizona, Orzech found that a campus advertising campaign costing a mere $2,500 helped improve the sleep of about 10 percent of the students who saw it. It is also important to staff health- and psychological-services offices with people who are aware of the importance of sleep.

11   Although they suffer because of it, many students can at least get by with not getting enough sleep. But it is especially important that those who are struggling academically, medically, or psychologically receive guidance on how to improve their sleeping habits.

12   Students (and parents and educators) who think that sleep is directly related to mental health, academic performance, and personal safety will be better armed when faced with competing pressures, such as advertising.

13   Perhaps we'll someday hear of students referring to an "all nighter" to describe their sleep rather than their lack of it.

ORGANIZATION AND IDEAS

1. What paragraph or paragraphs introduce the essay? What reasons do you have for your choice?
2. Where in the essay does Carskadon analyze the effects of not enough sleep? What are those effects?
3. How does Carskadon recognize objections to her advice? How does she counter them?
4. Paragraphs 7 and 8 analyze the causes behind inadequate sleep. What are they? How well chosen are Carskadon's examples?
5. Reconsider the essay from the perspective of problem/solution. Write out the problems and their solutions as fully as you can and then summarize the information in one sentence. The result is the essay's thesis.

TECHNIQUE AND STYLE

1. To what extent does Carskadon appear to sympathize with students? What evidence supports your conclusion?
2. Carskadon uses the familiar—Red Bull and its slogan—as a jumping off place for her subject. Where else does she mention advertising? What do those references contribute to the essay?
3. Why is Carskadon's choice of the word *help* crucial to her point about education? To her thesis?
4. Paragraph 5 consists of one sentence. What function does it serve? What effect does it have?
5. How effective a conclusion is paragraph 13? Carskadon's choice of "all nighter"?

SUGGESTIONS FOR WRITING

Journal

1. Carskadon's research shows that college students "should get about eight and a half hours of sleep every night." Use your journal to explain whether that is realistic.
2. What experience have you had with Red Bull and similar stimulants? What conclusions do you reach about their negative and positive qualities?

Essay

1. Hollywood has portrayed the life of a college student as fun and games, but any student and anyone who has worked with students know that's not so. Consider your own experience with the pressures of college life and analyze their effects. Think about the stress caused by:

   time
   money
   deadlines
   parents/spouses
   grades
   competition

   You can probably add a few more to the list. You may want to do some research on the subject to set your experiences in a larger context.

   Carskadon states, "Some advertisers routinely entreat us to undermine our health, but rarely through overt attacks on healthy behavior." Spend some time viewing television ads aimed at young people so you can assess the accuracy of some or all of Carskadon's claim.

When Music Heals Body and Soul

Oliver Sacks

For Oliver Sacks, medicine is a family tradition. Born in England to parents who were both physicians, he is one of three sons who became doctors. Armed with a medical degree from Oxford University, Sacks moved to the United States for his internship and residency and is now Professor of Neurology and Psychiatry at Columbia University Medical Center. Sacks is probably best known for his book Awakenings *(1974), an account of his work with "frozen" patients that was made into a film in 1990, starring Robin Williams and Robert De Niro. Part of another of his clinical studies,* An Anthropologist on Mars *(1995), was made into* At First Sight, *starring Val Kilmer (1999). Other medical works include* The Man Who Mistook His Wife for a Hat *(1985),* The Island of the Colorblind *(1998), and* The Mind's Eye *(2010), on the relationship between vision and perception. Sacks' autobiographical books are* A Leg to Stand On *(1989) (where he recounts the accident he refers to in his essay that follows),* Uncle Tungsten: Memories of a Chemical Boyhood *(2001), and* Oaxaca Journal *(2002). Though Sacks calls himself a "lonely person, not at ease socially," it's obvious that he cares deeply about people in general and the link between "body and soul" in particular. He also emphasizes that link in* Musicophilia: Tales of Music and the Brain *(2008). The essay reprinted here was published in* Parade Magazine *on March 31, 2002.*

What to Look For   It's often difficult for someone in a highly technical field to write in a way that is understood by ordinary readers. That's the problem Sacks faces when he describes a number of medical cases and neurological symptoms. As you read his essay, check to see if his prose is clear and comprehensible.

1   All of us have all sorts of personal experiences with music. We find ourselves calmed by it, excited by it, comforted by it, mystified by it and often haunted by it. It can lift us out of depression or move us to tears. I am no different. I need music to start the day

and as company when I drive. I need it, propulsively, when I go for swims and runs. I need it, finally, to still my thoughts when I retire, to usher me into the world of dreams.

2   But it was only when I became a patient myself that I experienced a *physical* need for music. A bad fall while climbing a mountain in Norway had left me incapacitated by damage to the nerves and muscles of one leg. After surgery to repair the torn tendons in my leg, I settled down to await some return of function in the torn nerves.

3   With the leg effectively paralyzed, I lost all sense of its existence—indeed, I seemed to lose the very *idea* of moving it. The leg stayed nonfunctional for the longest 15 days of my life. These days were made longer and grimmer because there was no music in the hospital. Radio reception was bad. Finally, a friend brought me a tape recorder along with a tape of one of my favorite pieces: the Mendelssohn *Violin Concerto.*

4   Playing this over and over gave me great pleasure and a general sense of being alive and well. But the nerves in my damaged leg were still healing. Two weeks later, I began to get small twitches in the previously flaccid muscle and larger sudden, involuntary movements.

5   Strangely, however, I had no impulse to walk. I could barely remember how one would go about walking—until, unexpectedly, a day or two later, the *Violin Concerto* played itself in my mind. It seemed, suddenly, to lend me its own energy, and I recovered the lost rhythm of walking—like remembering a once-familiar but long-forgotten time. Only then did walking regain its natural, unconscious, kinetic melody and grace.

6   Music can have the same effect on the neurologically impaired. It may have a power beyond anything else to restore them to themselves—at least in the precious few minutes that it lasts.

7   For reasons we do not yet understand, musical abilities often are among the last to be lost, even in cases of widespread brain damage. Thus, someone who is disabled by a stroke or by Alzheimer's or another form of dementia may still be able to respond to music in ways that can seem almost miraculous.

8   After a stroke, patients may suffer from *aphasia,* the inability to use or comprehend words. But the ability to sing words is rarely affected, even if an aphasic cannot speak them. Some patients can even be "reminded" in this way of words and grammatical constructions they have "forgotten." This, in turn, may help them start to regain old neural pathways for accessing language or to build new pathways in their place. Music becomes a crucial first step in a sequence followed by spontaneous improvement and speech therapy.

9   Some of my patients with strokes or Alzheimer's are unable to carry out a complex chain of actions: to dress, for example. Here, music can work as a mnemonic—a series of promptings in the form of verse or song, as in the childhood rhyme "One, two, buckle my shoe."

10   My patient Dr. P. had lost the ability to recognize or identify even common objects, though he could see perfectly well. He was unable to recognize a glove or a flower when I handed it to him, and he once mistook his own wife for a hat. This condition was almost totally disabling—but he discovered that he could perform the needs and tasks of the day if they were organized in song. And so he had songs for dressing, songs for eating, songs for bathing, songs for everything.

11   As a result of a brain tumor, my patient Greg has not been able to retain any new memories since the 1970s. But if we talk about or play his favorite Grateful Dead songs, his amnesia is bypassed. He becomes vividly animated and can reminisce about their early concerts.

12   I first saw the immense therapeutic powers of music 30 years ago, in the postencephalitic patients I later wrote about in *Awakenings.* These 80 individuals all were victims of *encephalitis lethargica,* the viral sleeping sickness that swept the globe just after World War I. When I came to Beth Abraham Hospital in the Bronx in 1966, most of them had been "frozen," absolutely motionless, for decades.

13   Their voices, if they could speak, lacked tone and force; they were almost spectral. Yet these patients were able to *sing* loudly and clearly, with a normal range of expressiveness and tone. Among those who could walk and talk—though only in a jerky, broken way—music gave their movement or speech the steadiness and control it usually lacked.

14   We could observe this effect on the patients' electroencephalograms. If we found music that worked, their EEGs—often exceedingly slow, reflecting their frozen states—would become faster and more regular. We noted this when patients listened to music or sang it or played it—even when they imagined it.

15   Take Rosalie B., a patient who had a severe form of parkinsonism. She tended to remain transfixed for hours a day, completely motionless, stuck, usually with one finger on her spectacles. But she knew all of Chopin's works by heart, and we had only to say "Opus 49" to see her whole body, posture and expression change. Her parkinsonism would vanish as soon as she even imagined Chopin's *Fantaisie in F minor.* Her EEG would become normal at the same instant the Chopin played itself in her mind.

16   Clearly, human brains are able to tenaciously hold and replay musical stimuli. This is why tunes may repeat themselves endlessly, sometimes maddeningly, in the mind. Musical hallucinations are far more common than visual hallucinations. There even seems to be a sort of normal "reminiscence" or "recycling" of early musical memories, especially in the aging brain.

17   To help, however, the music must be the right kind for each patient—music that has meaning and evokes feeling for that individual. Music therapists who work with a geriatric population often find that only old popular songs can bring such patients to life. While singing them, these patients are able to find a brief but intense sense of community and connectedness with their past lives—and perhaps a deep emotional catharsis.

18   This almost universal responsiveness to music is an essential part of our neural nature. Though analogies often are made to birdsong or animal cries, music in its full sense—including complexities of rhythm and harmony, of pace, timbre and tonality no less than of melody—seems to be confined to our own species, like language. Why this should be so is still a mystery. Our research is only now beginning to unlock those secrets.

ORGANIZATION AND IDEAS

1. What kind of music do you enjoy? How does it affect you?
2. To what extent are your responses similar to those Sacks describes in paragraph 1?
3. Trace the pattern of general and particular through the essay. How would you describe it?
4. How does music affect Sacks' recovery? Those who are neurologically damaged?
5. Consider all the effects Sacks shows that music can have on people and in one sentence state what you find to be his thesis.

TECHNIQUE AND STYLE

1. Paragraphs 10–15 set out a number of examples. What do they add to the essay?
2. You may be familiar with *Parade Magazine,* for it accompanies many a Sunday newspaper. Its readership is about as general as one can be, yet Sacks is very much a specialist. How well does he tailor his knowledge to his audience?
3. Sacks blends personal narrative with examples from his medical practice. How effective is his use of the subjective and the objective?

4. Sacks focuses on the effects of music. To what extent does he bring in causal analysis?

5. Paragraphs 16–18 provide the essay's conclusion. How satisfactory is it? Explain.

SUGGESTIONS FOR WRITING

Journal

1. In what ways is the title of the essay appropriate? What others can you think of?

2. What surprises you most in Sacks' essay? Explain why.

Essay

1. Almost everyone uses leisure time to relax by pursuing some form of pleasure. Think about what you do for day-to-day fun and make a list of what you come up with. Choose one subject and consider why you do it as well as its effects on you. Then draft an essay in which you explain what you do and why. You may want to emphasize cause rather than effect or vice versa. Suggestions:

  talking to friends
  playing a sport
  watching television
  pursuing a hobby
  exercising

2. Think about the ways in which music affects you and explore that subject in an essay. You might begin by defining the kind of music you like and then go on to analyze its effect.

Retreat into the iWorld

Andrew Sullivan

Andrew Sullivan was born in England, where he graduated from Oxford University and then won a fellowship to the John F. Kennedy School of Government at Harvard. There he received an MA in public administration and, later, a PhD in political science. His career in journalism, however, started by interning for The Daily Telegraph *and at the conservative Centre for Policy Studies, both in London, and then in Washington, D.C., at* The New Republic, *where at the age of 27 he rose to editor. A frequent guest on radio and TV news and talk shows, Sullivan has written four books:* Virtually Normal *(1996),* Love Undetectable: Notes on Friendship, Sex, and Survival *(1999),* Same-Sex Marriage: Pro and Con *(2004), and* The Conservative Soul: How We Lost It, How to Get It Back *(2006). His blog—the Daily Dish—appears on* The Daily Beast, *and his print journalism has appeared in* The Wall Street Journal, The Washington Post, *and* Esquire. *You may have seen him on one of many television shows, among them* Nightline, Meet the Press, Hardball, The O'Reilly Factor, *and* Hannity and Colmes. *Though he is still a senior editor at* The New Republic, *he also writes for* Time, The New York Times Book Review, *and the* Sunday Times *of London, where this essay appeared on February 20, 2005.*

What to Look For If Sullivan is right, then most cities are full of iPod people, which means they are part of the audience for his essay. As you read it, keep track of how he tries not to alienate them.

1   I was visiting New York last week and noticed something I'd never thought I'd say about the city. Yes, nightlife is pretty much dead (and I'm in no way the first to notice that). But daylife—that insane mishmash of yells, chatter, clatter, hustle and chutzpah that makes New York the urban equivalent of methamphetamine—was also a little different. It was quieter.

2   Manhattan's downtown is now a Disney-like string of malls, riverside parks and pretty upper-middle-class villages. But there was something else. And as I looked across the throngs on the pavements, I began to see why.

3   There were little white wires hanging down from their ears, or tucked into pockets, purses or jackets. The eyes were a little vacant. Each was in his or her own musical world, walking to their soundtrack, stars in their own music video, almost oblivious to the world around them. These are the iPod people.

4   Even without the white wires you can tell who they are. They walk down the street in their own MP3 cocoon, bumping into others, deaf to small social cues, shutting out anyone not in their bubble.

5   Every now and again some start unconsciously emitting strange tuneless squawks, like a badly tuned radio, and their fingers snap or their arms twitch to some strange soundless rhythm. When others say "Excuse me" there's no response. "Hi", ditto. It's strange to be among so many people and hear so little. Except that each one is hearing so much.

6   Yes, I might as well own up. I'm one of them. I witnessed the glazed New York looks through my own glazed pupils, my white wires peeping out of my ears. I joined the cult a few years ago: the sect of the little white box worshippers.

7   Every now and again I go to church—those huge, luminous Apple stores, pews in the rear, the clerics in their monastic uniforms all bustling around or sitting behind the "Genius Bars", like priests waiting to hear confessions.

8   Others began, as I did, with a Walkman—and then a kind of clunkier MP3 player. But the sleekness of the iPod won me over. Unlike other models it gave me my entire music collection to rearrange as I saw fit—on the fly, in my pocket.

9   What was once an occasional musical diversion became a compulsive obsession. Now I have my iTunes in my iMac for my iPod in my iWorld. It's Narcissus heaven: we've finally put the "i" into Me.

10   And, like all addictive cults, it's spreading. There are now 22m iPod owners in the United States and Apple is becoming a mass-market company for the first time.

11   Walk through any airport in the United States these days and you will see person after person gliding through the social ether as if on autopilot. Get on a subway and you're surrounded by a bunch of Stepford commuters staring into mid-space as if anaesthetised by technology. Don't ask, don't tell, don't overhear, don't observe. Just tune in and tune out.

12   It wouldn't be so worrying if it weren't part of something even bigger. Americans are beginning to narrow their lives.

13   You get your news from your favourite blogs, the ones that won't challenge your view of the world. You tune into a satellite radio service that also aims directly at a small market—for new age fanatics, liberal talk or Christian rock. Television is all cable. Culture is all subculture. Your cell phones can receive e-mail feeds of your favourite blogger's latest thoughts—seconds after he has posted them—get sports scores for your team or stock quotes of your portfolio.

14   Technology has given us a universe entirely for ourselves— where the serendipity of meeting a new stranger, hearing a piece of music we would never choose for ourselves or an opinion that might force us to change our mind about something are all effectively banished.

15   Atomisation by little white boxes and cell phones. Society without the social. Others who are chosen—not met at random. Human beings have never lived like this before. Yes, we have always had homes, retreats or places where we went to relax, unwind or shut out the world.

16   But we didn't walk around the world like hermit crabs with our isolation surgically attached.

17   Music was once the preserve of the living room or the concert hall. It was sometimes solitary but it was primarily a shared experience, something that brought people together, gave them the comfort of knowing that others too understood the pleasure of a Brahms symphony or that Beatles album.

18   But music is as atomised now as living is. And it's secret. That bloke next to you on the bus could be listening to heavy metal or a Gregorian chant. You'll never know. And so, bit by bit, you'll never really know him. And by his white wires, he is indicating he doesn't really want to know you.

19   What do we get from this? The awareness of more music, more often. The chance to slip away for a while from everydayness, to give our lives its own soundtrack, to still the monotony of the commute, to listen more closely and carefully to music that can lift you up and keep you going.

20   We become masters of our own interests, more connected to people like us over the internet, more instantly in touch with anything we want, need or think we want and think we need. Ever tried a Stairmaster in silence? But what are we missing? That hilarious shard of an overheard conversation that stays with you all day; the child whose chatter on the pavement takes you back

to your early memories; birdsong; weather; accents; the laughter of others. And those thoughts that come not by filling your head with selected diversion, but by allowing your mind to wander aimlessly through the regular background noise of human and mechanical life.

21   External stimulation can crowd out the interior mind. Even the boredom that we flee has its uses. We are forced to find our own means to overcome it.

22   And so we enrich our life from within, rather than from white wires. It's hard to give up, though, isn't it.

23   Not so long ago I was on a trip and realised I had left my iPod behind. Panic. But then something else. I noticed the rhythms of others again, the sound of the airplane, the opinions of the taxi driver, the small social cues that had been obscured before. I noticed how others related to each other. And I felt just a little bit connected again and a little more aware.

24   Try it. There's a world out there. And it has a soundtrack all its own.

ORGANIZATION AND IDEAS

   1. Sullivan begins with a personal narrative. Where else in the essay does he return to that mode? What effects does it achieve?
   2. Reread Sullivan's essay, marking each instance of cause and of effect. Which predominates?
   3. In paragraphs 17 and 18, Sullivan uses comparison and contrast. In what ways does that mode contribute to the primary one of cause and effect?
   4. Sullivan states a bare-bones thesis in paragraph 12. Given the essay as a whole, how can you flesh it out?
   5. Test Sullivan's thesis against your own experience. How valid is it?

TECHNIQUE AND STYLE

   1. Sullivan refers to "Narcissus heaven" (paragraph 9) and "Stepford commuters" (paragraph 11). What does he mean by these allusions?
   2. Reread the essay looking for unusual or striking words. How would you characterize Sullivan's diction? What does he achieve by using it?
   3. In paragraph 7, Sullivan sets out an analogy. What is being compared? How effective is the comparison?
   4. Sullivan begins paragraph 15 with three incomplete sentences that amount to a short list. Rewrite them to make one or more complete sentences. What is gained? Lost?
   5. Where in the essay does Sullivan use metaphor? Choose the one you like best and explain what it adds to the essay.

SUGGESTIONS FOR WRITING

Journal

1. If you have an iPod, how accurate do you find Sullivan's essay? If you don't have one, explain why you would or would not want one.

2. In paragraph 20, Sullivan argues for "allowing your mind to wander aimlessly through the regular background noise of human and mechanical life." Explain to what extent you agree or disagree with the value of letting your mind wander.

Essay

1. It's a rare invention or technical advance that doesn't have some drawbacks, major or minor. Think about the electronic or mechanical innovations that are now available, choose one, and analyze its effects, both positive and negative. Once you've weighed those effects, you can form your thesis for an essay. Suggestions:
   camera phones
   chat rooms
   blogs
   digital cameras
   DVDs
   cell phone ring tones

2. Analyze Sullivan's essay to determine the extent to which he takes a stand. Is he arguing, explaining, speculating, musing, analyzing, what? Back up your interpretation with quotations and examples from the essay.

Candorville

Darrin Bell

Darrin Bell is best known for Candorville, *an aptly named comic strip featuring a diverse inner-city cast. Writing as an African American, he depicts tough issues—race and poverty among them—in a way that is both honest and upbeat, and as a result the strip has a wide appeal. Now syndicated by the Washington Post Writers Group,* Candorville *is carried by newspapers such as the* Los Angeles Times, *the* Chicago Tribune, *and the* Detroit Free Press, *as well as* Al Dia, *a Spanish language paper published in Dallas. Bell grew up in Los Angeles, earned a degree in Political Science at the University of California, Berkeley, and now lives and works in Berkeley. His work has been published in several collections:* Thank God for Culture Clash *(2005),* Another Stereotype Bites the Dust *(2006),* Katrina's Ghost *(2011), and* The Starbucks at the End of the World *(2011). Working with the writer Theorn Heir, Bell also draws the comic strip* Rudy Park. *The cartoon below appeared on September 9, 2006.*

FOR DISCUSSION

1. Describe the setting in detail. What kind of restaurant is it? What sort of neighborhood?
2. To what extent are Bell's characters typical? Stereotypical?
3. What does each character assume about the other? How do those assumptions relate to cause and effect?
4. In what ways does the cartoon relate to the essay by Brent Staples?
5. What connections can you find between Bell's cartoon and the essay by Andrew Sullivan?

SUGGESTIONS FOR WRITING

Journal

Use your journal to explore what the cartoon implies about race and assumptions.

Essay

In a sense, all of the essays and the cartoon in this chapter deal with implied or stated assumptions. Consider what those assumptions might be, what causes them and the effect they have, and choose two of the works to compare and contrast to determine which you find the more effective and why.

Argue

1   Compared with most of the issues that the venerable civil liberties lawyer Norman Siegel takes up, this one may seem like the ultimate in urban frivolity: Late last month, he joined hundreds of hip-hoppers, salsa dancers, Lindy Hoppers and techno-heads boogying along Fifth Avenue to protest New York City's 80-year-old restrictions on dancing in bars.

Barbara Ehrenreich begins her essay by setting a scene that both supplies information and implies a question: New York restricts dancing in bars, but what does dancing have to do with civil liberties? The essay then continues by setting out a historical context for public dancing, leading up to Ehrenreich's thesis.

In everyday speech, **argument** is so closely associated with *quarrel* or *fight* that it has a negative connotation, one that does not apply to essays. When you read the rest of Ehrenreich's essay, you will be analyzing it by examining its argument: the weight of the evidence and the assertion it leads to. When you write your own argumentative essays, you will want the reader to respond in one of several ways:

- adopt your view
- rethink his or her previous position
- take a particular action
- keep reading

Many argumentative essays focus on subjects readers already have an opinion about. But if someone who disagrees with you keeps on reading, you have constructed a successful argument.

Because an argumentative essay bases its thesis primarily on reason, the word *logic* may pop into your mind and raise images of mathematical models and seemingly tricky statements. Don't worry. The arguments you construct build on the kinds of essays you've written all along; your thesis is the heart of your argument, and examples, definitions, descriptions, and the like provide supporting evidence.

In this chapter you will discover how to write a short argumentative essay and how to use the various modes to support that aim. The essays that follow are examples of argument, though the subjects differ widely: banning dancing; DNA sampling; controlling illegal immigration; and drilling for gas.

How can you find a topic and support your argument?   Often the best topic for an argumentative essay is the one you come up with on your own, but at times you may be assigned a topic. If so, try to shape the topic so that you can connect to it. Because you already know something about the subject, you have done some thinking about it instead of starting from scratch or using secondhand opinions. Even abstract topics such as euthanasia can be made concrete and will be the better for it.

You may know little about mercy killing, but you may have had a member of your family who was terminally ill. Would euthanasia have been an appropriate alternative? Should it have been? In addition to using your own experience, research the topic. Newspaper accounts and editorials can help give form and focus to an abstract issue, as can book and periodical sources, all of which and more can be found on the Internet. The Web provides instant access to a huge and often unfiltered amount of information, so always check who or what is behind the information. Anyone can put anything on the Web. And does.

How can you shape your argument for your readers?   Audience plays a greater role in argument than in any other type of writing, and therein lies a problem: You must adapt both form and content to fit your audience, while at the same time maintaining your integrity. If you shape your position according to its probable acceptance by your readers rather than your own belief, the result is propaganda, not argument. Omitting evidence or distorting facts or resorting to illogical notions are dishonest.

Within honest bounds, however, you have much to draw on, and a sense of what your audience may or may not know and of what the audience believes about a topic can guide you. Even if your topic is familiar, what you have to say about it will be new.

What are logical fallacies and how can you avoid them?
Argumentative writing ranges from the personal to the abstract and draws on the various patterns that can be used to structure an essay. For instance, waiting tables in a restaurant may have convinced you that tips should be automatically included in the bill. To make the case that the present system is unfair to those in a service trade, you might draw primarily on your own experience and that of others, though you

need to make sure that your experience is representative. If you don't, your reader may discount your argument, thinking that one example isn't sufficient evidence. A quick check among others who are similarly employed and a look at government reports on employment statistics can support your example as typical and, therefore, to be trusted.

The technical term for an entire argument based on only one example is **hasty generalization,** one of many logical fallacies that can occur in argumentative writing. **Logical fallacies** are lapses in reasoning. If you argue that the reader should consider only the present system of tipping or the one you propose, you will be guilty of **either–or reasoning,** false because it permits no middle ground such as requiring a minimum tip of 12 percent. Quote LeBron James on the subject and you will be citing **false authority;** he knows basketball but not the restaurant industry. And obviously, if you call a 10-percent tipper a cheap idiot, you will be accused of name calling, the **ad hominem** (to the person) fallacy.

Say you noticed one evening that as closing time loomed, your tips got smaller. Is that because people who dine late tip minimally or because your customers felt rushed or because someone miscalculated the tip or some unknown reason? If you conclude that people who dine late are poor tippers, you may well be mistaking a temporal relationship for a causal one. Two events may occur at times close to each other (small tip, late hour) without implying a valid cause-and-effect relationship. To confuse the two is called **post hoc reasoning.**

Advertising and political campaigns are good places to spot logical fallacies. A flyer asks you to vote for a candidate for the school board because she is a Vietnam veteran with a successful law practice, but the logic doesn't follow (a literal translation of the Latin term **non sequitur**). What does being a veteran and an attorney have to do with the duties of a member of the school board? And if the flyer goes on to maintain that because the candidate is a mother with three children she can understand the problems of students in public schools when you know that all three go to private schools, then you've spotted a **false analogy**—a double one: Public and private schools are quite different, and three children from the family of a lawyer are not typical of the public school student population.

Such a flyer is also guilty of **begging the question.** The main question should be "What can this person contribute?" Being a Vietnam veteran and the mother of three children doesn't fit that question. **Shifting definition** is another form of begging the question. If this hypothetical candidate also claims to be a "good citizen" and then goes on to define that term by example, only citing service to her country and motherhood as proof, then as a voter you're left with a very narrow definition. Good citizenship involves much more.

Often when you read or hear about the holes in an argument, you may also hear the term **straw man.** With this technique (yet another form of begging the question), your attention is drawn away from the main point to focus on a minor one, with the hope that by demolishing it the main one will also suffer.

How can you appeal to reason, emotion, and persona? The **appeal to reason,** what the ancient Greeks called *logos,* is crucial. To present a logical pattern of thought, you will probably find yourself drawing on one or more modes, particularly definition, comparison, and cause and effect. If, for instance, you have a part-time job at a fast-food franchise, you may have noticed that most of the other employees are also part-time. The situation may strike you as exploitive, and you want to write about it.

You might start sketching out a first draft with the example of your job, then define what part-time means, using cause and effect to argue that franchise companies that depend primarily on part-time labor exploit their workers to create greater profits for the company. As you work, you will find that you are laying out a line of reasoning, the assertions— probably the topic sentences for paragraphs or paragraph clusters—that support your thesis. You will also have to do some research so that you place your example in a larger context, showing that it is clearly typical. Then, armed with some facts and figures, you can test your thesis and supporting sentences:

1. Am I making an assertion? Test the sentence by checking to see if it states an opinion.
   If yes, go to question 2.
   If no, review pages 5–6 and 17 and revise the sentence.
2. Is the assertion supported by evidence? List the evidence and sources.
   If yes, go to question 3.
   If no, research the topic to gather more evidence.
3. Is the evidence sufficient? Check it to make sure it's directly related to the assertion.
   If yes, the assertion checks out.
   If no, gather more evidence.

If your thesis and supporting sentences check out, then you know your argument rests on reason.

Logical thinking must undergird all argumentative essays, even those that use an **appeal to emotion,** or *pathos*—an appeal that often rests on example, description, and narration. Paint a picture of a part-time worker who has two other jobs in order to pay the medical expenses of an autistic child and you may find yourself substituting emotion for reason.

The ethical appeal, or *ethos,* rests on a credible **persona** and is more subtle than the others; the writer is not appealing directly to the reader's emotions or intellect but instead uses his or her persona to lend credence to the essay's major assertion. To understand how persona functions, think of the last time you took an essay test. What you were writing was a mini argument maintaining that your answer to the question is a correct one. Your persona, which you probably didn't even think about, was intended to create a sense of authority, that you knew what you were writing about. The tone you use for essay tests is more formal than informal, which means that your choice of words, your diction, is more elevated than conversational. And if a technical vocabulary is appropriate—the vocabulary of physics, sociology, the arts, and the like—you use it.

Successful essay answers also use evidence and are tightly organized so that the line of thought is clear and compelling, all of which comes under the appeal of reason, but don't underestimate the appeal of persona. If two test answers contain the exact same information, the one that is written in the more analytical style that implies a more thoughtful response is apt to receive the higher grade.

How can you structure your argument? The thesis of an argumentative essay should be readily identifiable: It is the conviction that you want an audience to adopt. Sometimes the thesis may be stated in the title, but more often you will state your position early on, then back it up with evidence in the body of your essay. If you organize your ideas by moving from the general (the thesis) to the particular (the evidence), you are using **deductive reasoning.** Most of the argumentative essays you run across will be using this kind of logical organization. As for the order in which you choose to present the evidence on which your thesis rests, you'll probably arrange it from the least important to the most important so that the essay has some dramatic tension. Putting the most important evidence first doesn't leave you anywhere to go.

Although sometimes you may want to put your thesis as your first sentence, usually you will want to lead up to it, *introduce* it in the literal sense. Often an argumentative essay will begin with a narrative or some explanation, ways of setting the scene so that when the thesis appears, it seems natural. As for the ending, you may want to return to the same narrative or information you started with, which is what Ehrenreich does, or call for action or point out what may happen unless your view is adopted.

Now and then, you'll find yourself reading an argument that is organized by moving from the particular to the general, from evidence to thesis. What you have then is called **inductive reasoning,** and it demands tight focus and control. Think of the essay's organization as a jigsaw puzzle. Your reader has to recognize each piece as a piece, and you have to build the evidence so that each one falls into a predetermined place. The completed picture is the thesis.

You'll find that the essays in this section represent both kinds of organization, so you'll have a chance to see how others have developed their ideas to argue a particular point.

Useful Terms

Ad hominem argument Name-calling, smearing the person instead of attacking the argument. A type of logical fallacy. Smearing the person's group instead of attacking the argument is the *ad populum* fallacy.

Appeal to emotion or *pathos* Playing or appealing to the reader's emotions.

Appeal to persona or *ethos* The appeal of the writer's character that creates the impression that the author can be trusted and, therefore, believed.

Appeal to reason or *logos* Presenting evidence that is logical, well thought out, so as to be believed.

Argument The writer's major assertion and the evidence on which it is based.

Begging the question Arguing off the point, changing direction. A type of logical fallacy.

Deductive reasoning Reasoning that moves from general to particular, from thesis to evidence.

Either–or reasoning Presenting choices as the only alternatives, excluding anything in between. A type of logical fallacy.

False analogy An analogy that does not stand up to logic. A type of logical fallacy.

False authority Citing an expert on one subject as an expert on another. A type of logical fallacy.

Hasty generalization Reasoning based on insufficient evidence, usually too few examples. A type of logical fallacy.

Inductive reasoning Reasoning that moves from particular to general, from evidence to thesis.

Logical fallacy An error in reasoning, a logical flaw that invalidates the argument.

Non sequitur Literally, it does not follow. No apparent link between points. A type of logical fallacy.

Persona The character of the writer that is created by the prose.

Post hoc reasoning Assuming a temporal relationship for a causal one. A type of logical fallacy.

Shifting definition Changing the definition of a key term, a form of begging the question. A type of logical fallacy.

Straw man Attacking and destroying an irrelevant point instead of the main subject.

POINTERS FOR USING ARGUMENT

Exploring the Topic

1. **What position do you want to take toward your subject?** Are you arguing to get your audience to adopt your thesis or to go further and take action? What is your thesis? What action is possible?

2. **How might your audience respond to your assertion if stated baldly?** How much background is necessary? What do you need to define? What arguments can be brought against your assertion?

3. **What examples can you think of to illustrate your topic?** Are all of them from your own experience? What other sources can you draw on?

4. **How can you appeal to your reader's emotions?** How can you use example, description, and narration to carry your emotional appeal?

5. **How can you appeal to your reader's reason?** How can you use example, cause and effect, process, comparison and contrast, analogy, or division and classification to strengthen your logic?

6. **What tone is most appropriate to the kind of appeal you want to emphasize?** Does your persona fit that tone? How can you use persona to support your argument?

Drafting the Paper

1. **Know your reader.** Estimate how familiar your reader is with your topic and how, if at all, the reader may react to it emotionally. Keeping those ideas in mind, review how the various patterns of development may help you contend with your audience's knowledge and attitudes, and decide whether your primary appeal should be to emotion or to reason.

Description, narration, and example lend themselves particularly well to emotional appeal; process, cause and effect, comparison and contrast, analogy, example, and division and classification are useful for rational appeal. Use definition to set the boundaries of your argument and its terms as well as to clear up anything the reader may not know.

2. **Know your purpose.** Depending on the predominant appeal you find most appropriate, your essay will argue a position using reason, though you may appeal to emotion to a lesser extent; you are trying to get your reader not only to understand your major assertion but also to adopt it and perhaps even to act on it. Short of that, a successful writer of argument must settle for the reader's "Well, I hadn't thought of it that way."

The greatest danger is to write to people who already agree with you. You need not think of your audience as actively hostile, but to stay on the argumentative track, it helps to reread constantly as you write, playing devil's advocate.

3. **Acknowledge the opposition.** Even though your reader may be the ideal—someone who holds no definite opposing view—you should bring out one or two of the strongest arguments against your position and demolish them. If you don't, the reader may, and there goes your essay.

4. **Avoid logical pitfalls.** One way to test for fallacies is to check your patterns of development. If you have used examples, does your generalization or assertion follow? Sometimes the examples are too few to support the assertion, leading to a hasty generalization; sometimes the examples don't fit, leading to begging the question or arguing off the point or misusing authority; and sometimes the assertion is stated as an absolute, in which case the reader may think of an example that is the exception, destroying your point.

If you have used analogy, double-check to see that the analogy can stand up to scrutiny by examining the pertinent aspects of the things compared. If you have used cause and effect, you need to be particularly careful. Check to see that the events you claim to have a causal relationship do not have a temporal one; otherwise, you fall into the post hoc fallacy. Also examine causal relationships to make sure that you have not merely assumed the cause in your statement of effect. If you claim "poor teaching is a major

(Continued)

---

cause of the high dropout rate during the freshman year in college," you must prove that the teaching is poor; if you don't, you are arguing in a circle or begging the question.

Non sequiturs can also obscure cause-and-effect relationships when an element in the relationship is missing or nonexistent. Definition also sets some traps. Make sure your definition is not only fully stated but also commonly shared and consistent throughout.

5. **Be aware of your persona.** The ethical appeal, the rational appeal, and the emotional appeal are fundamental concepts of argument, and it is the persona, together with tone, that provides the ethical appeal. To put it simply, you need to be credible.

If you are writing on an issue you feel strongly about and, for example, are depending primarily on an appeal to reason, you don't want to let your dispassionate, logical persona slip and resort to name-calling (formally known as arguing ad hominem or ad populem). That's obvious.

Not so obvious, however, is some slip in diction or tone that reveals the hothead behind the cool pen. Your reader may feel manipulated or use the slip to discount your entire argument, all because you lost sight of the ethical appeal. Tone should vary, yes, but never to the point of discord.

6. **Place your point where it does the most good.** Put each of your paragraphs on a separate piece of paper so that you can rearrange their order as you would a hand of cards. Try out your major assertion in different slots. If you have it at the beginning, try it at the end and vice versa. Or extend the introduction so that the thesis comes closer to the middle of the paper. See which placement carries greater impact.

You may want to organize your material starting with examples that lead up to the position you wish to attack and to the conviction you are arguing for; in that case your thesis may occur somewhere in the middle third or at the end of the paper. On the other hand, you may want to use deduction—starting with the opposition, stating your position, and then spending 90 percent of the remaining essay supporting your case. Remember that you want to win your reader over, so put your thesis where it will do the greatest good.

Dance, Dance, Revolution

Barbara Ehrenreich

Essayist, novelist, journalist, activist, Barbara Ehrenreich has written extensively on almost every imaginable subject, though politics and the media are her prime targets. At last count, she has written 15 books in addition to being a regular contributor to Time, Harpers, *and* The Nation *as well as numerous other magazines. She has her own blog, and her work also appears the* Huffington Post *and* The New York Times. *Her voice is often heard on* Today, Nightline, *and National Public Radio, among other radio and television shows and stations. Ehrenreich turned to writing after earning a PhD in cell biology from* The Rockefeller University. *About her career change, she says "Sure, I could have had more stability and financial security if I'd stuck to science or teaching. But I chose adventure and I've never for a moment regretted it" For a full account of her life and work, check out* http:// barbaraehrenreich.com/. *There you'll find her complete list of publications, but perhaps her best known book is* Nickel and Dimed: On (Not) Getting by in America *(2001). Her most recent books are the satiric commentary* This Land Is Their Land: Reports from a Divided Nation *(2008) and* Bright-sided: How Positive Thinking is Undermining America *(2009). The following essay is more closely related to her scholarly* Dancing in the Streets: A History of Collective Joy *(2007) and was published in* The New York Times *on June 3, 2007.*

What to Look For   Ehrenreich was bothered by what she thought was an unfair regulation, so in tackling it she places the activity the regulation is aimed at into a much larger historical context. As you read Ehrenreich's essay, keep track of the immediate and historical contexts for her argument so you can understand what they add to her credibility. Like Ehrenreich, you may want to set your personal opinion in a larger context so that it becomes a general stand, not a personal beef.

1   Compared with most of the issues that the venerable civil liberties lawyer Norman Siegel takes up, this one may seem like the ultimate in urban frivolity: Late last month, he joined hundreds of hip-hoppers, salsa dancers, Lindy Hoppers and techno-heads boogying along Fifth Avenue to protest New York City's 80-year-old restrictions on dancing in bars.

2   But disputes over who can dance, how and where, are at least as old as civilization, and arise from the longstanding conflict between the forces of order and hierarchy on the one hand, and the deep human craving for free-spirited joy on the other.

3   New York's cabaret laws limit dancing to licensed venues. They date back to the Harlem Renaissance, which had created the unsettling prospect of interracial dancing.

4   For decades, no one paid much attention to the laws until Mayor Rudolph Giuliani, bent on turning Manhattan into a giant mall/food court, decided to get tough. Today, the city far more famous for its night life than its Sunday services has only about 170 venues where it is legal to get up and dance—hence last month's danced protest, as well as an earlier one in February.

5   Dust-ups over dancing have become a regular feature of urban life. Dance clubs all over the country have faced the threat of shutdowns because the dancing sometimes spills over into the streets. While neighbors annoyed by sleepless nights or the suspicion of illegal drug use may be justified in their concerns, conflict over public dancing has a long history—one that goes all the way back to the ancient Mediterranean world.

6   The Greeks danced to worship their gods—especially Dionysus, the god of ecstasy. But then the far more strait-laced Romans cracked down viciously on Dionysian worship in 186 B.C., even going on to ban dancing schools for Roman children a few decades later. The early Christians incorporated dance into their liturgy, despite church leaders' worries about immodesty. But at the end of the fourth century, the archbishop of Constantinople issued the stern pronouncement: "For where there is a dance, there is also the Devil."

7   The Catholic Church did not succeed in prohibiting dancing within churches until the late Middle Ages, and in doing so perhaps inadvertently set off the dance "manias" that swept Belgium, Germany and Italy starting in the 14th century. Long attributed to some form of toxin—ergot or spider venom—the manias drove thousands of people to the streets day and night, mocking and menacing the priests who tried to stop them.

8   In northern Europe, Calvinism brought a hasty death to the old public forms of dancing, along with the costuming, masking and feasting that had usually accompanied them. All that survived, outside of vestiges of "folk dancing," were the elites' tame, indoor ballroom dances, fraught, as in today's "Dancing With the Stars,"

with anxiety over a possible misstep. When Europeans fanned out across the globe in the 18th and 19th centuries, the colonizers made it a priority to crush the danced rituals of indigenous people, which were seen as savagery, devil worship and prelude to rebellion.

9   To the secular opponents of public dancing, it is always a noxious source of disorder and, in New York's case, noise. But hardly anyone talks about what is lost when the music stops and the traditional venues close. Facing what he saw as an epidemic of melancholy, or what we would now call depression, the 17th-century English writer Robert Burton placed much of the blame on the Calvinist hostility to "dancing, singing, masking, mumming and stage plays." In fact, in some cultures, ecstatic dance has been routinely employed as a cure for emotional disorders. Banning dancing may not cause depression, but it removes an ancient cure for it.

10   The need for public, celebratory dance seems to be hardwired into us. Rock art from around the world depicts stick figures dancing in lines and circles at least as far back as 10,000 years ago. According to some anthropologists, dance helped bond prehistoric people together in the large groups that were necessary for collective defense against marauding predators, both animals and human. While language also serves to forge community, it doesn't come close to possessing the emotional urgency of dance. Without dance, we risk loneliness and anomie.

11   Dancing to music is not only mood-lifting and community-building; it's also a uniquely human capability. No other animals, not even chimpanzees, can keep together in time to music. Yes, we can live without it, as most of us do most of the time, but why not reclaim our distinctively human heritage as creatures who can generate our own communal pleasures out of music and dance?

12   This is why New Yorkers—as well as all Americans faced with anti-dance restrictions—should stand up and take action; and the best way to do so is by high stepping into the streets.

ORGANIZATION AND IDEAS

1. What paragraph or paragraphs introduce Ehrenreich's essay? How well does it relate to what follows? Given the rest of the essay, is the introduction too short or too long? How so?
2. Summarize the arguments—both religious and secular—Ehrenreich presents against dancing. Her historical accounts are based on general knowledge, which is why she sees no need to document them. Do any surprise you, and if so why? What would be the effect of documentation?

3. To what extent does cause and effect play a role in the essay? Where in the essay is it most prominent?
4. Consider the positive claims Ehrenreich makes for dancing. To what extent do you find them credible? Do you agree?
5. In paragraph 12, the essay concludes with a call to action. What do you think of it?

TECHNIQUE AND STYLE

1. To what extent does Ehrenreich take account of objections to her thesis?
2. Reread the essay with an eye out for Ehrenreich's diction. What words strike you as formal? Informal? What does her choice of words add to or detract from the essay?
3. Given your answers to the previous question, how would you describe Ehrenreich's tone? How serious is she?
4. It's possible to read the essay as a call for a Dionysian take-to-the-woods free-for-all. To what extent is that interpretation valid?
5. You can also read the essay as setting out two extremes—repression or anything goes. If it's possible that Ehrenreich also implies but does not state a middle ground, what then is her subject? Her thesis?

SUGGESTIONS FOR WRITING

Journal

1. How well do you think the title fits the essay? Explain your opinion.
2. To what extent does dance play a role in your life? If it plays no role at all, explain why.

Essay

1. Throughout history, as Ehrenreich explains, various forces have disapproved of dance, sometimes to the extent of banning it. The same is true of other forms of artistic expression. Use the Web to research a particular case of censorship, evaluating the strength of the arguments involved. Choose a particular example from one of the following categories or another of your own choosing.
   books
   paintings
   dances
   song lyrics
   plays
2. From the 1920s on (and probably before), various dances have become "the rage." You might think of the Charleston or any of the more recent ones of the 1960s on to the present. Some dances have regional popularity, such as western line dancing, and some have ethnic roots as in

the polka. Use the Web to research a particular kind of dance so you can analyze the positive and negative responses it generates. You may find yourself arguing for its greater acceptance or promoting its popularity or declaring it downright silly, and so on. You'll probably have no problem finding an argumentative position.

Freshman Specimen

Patricia J. Williams

Patricia J. Williams knows universities and the law. With a BA from Wellesley College and a JD from Harvard Law School, she has taught at Dartmouth College and the University of Wisconsin Law School. At present she is the James L. Dohr Professor of Law at Columbia University. In 2000, she was awarded a MacArthur Fellowship, a "genius grant" given by the John D. and Catherine T. MacArthur Foundation to "creative people and effective institutions committed to building a more just, verdant, and peaceful world." Williams' column "Diary of a Mad Law Professor" appears monthly in The Nation. *Her books range from the scholarly—*The Alchemy of Race and Rights: Diary of a Law Professor *(1991),* The Rooster's Egg: On the Persistence of Prejudice *(1995), and* Seeing a Color-Blind Future: The Paradox of Race *(1998)—to the more personal,* Open House: On Family Food, Friends, Piano Lessons and the Search for a Room of My Own *(2004). The essay reprinted here first appeared in* The Nation *in September 2010.*

What to Look For   Williams' essay shows how you can focus on an event, explore the questions its raises, and lead to a conclusion. It's one way to structure an argument that you may find useful.

1   The school year at the University of California, Berkeley, began with a swab. In a program called Bring Your Genes to Cal, 5,500 incoming freshmen were asked to provide samples of their saliva in an experiment designed to bring the student body together in the same manner that reading *To Kill a Mockingbird* might have in the past. The more than 700 students who responded had their DNA analyzed in Berkeley's (uncertified) labs, assessed for susceptibility

to alcoholism, lactose intolerance and relative metabolism of folic acid. The exercise provoked an international debate about the ethics of the assignment. Ultimately, the California Department of Public Health barred the university from dispensing individual profiles on the grounds that genetic analysis is correlative only and is neither necessarily predictive nor diagnostic at this point. A collective comparison of the class's genetic data was permitted, however, and circulated in "anonymized" form at orientation.

2   There are several reasons that Berkeley's undertaking should give us pause. The first and most obvious is that of privacy: this information reveals more than we can yet interpret at the singular, embodied level of human identity. DNA decoding will become infinitely more precise in the near future, and with that growing precision in familial tracking and biological identification, "anonymizing" results by removing names and Social Security numbers will mean less and less.

3   Second, Who owns, or ought to own, these data? Although the Berkeley experiment is framed as an exploration of a vast genetic commons, this information is the subject of intense commercial speculation. And the degree to which specific gene sequences may be patented is quite contested in the law. Should you, as the biological vessel of a particularly exploitable bit of genetic material, receive any remuneration? Are your genes to be valued, in purely pecuniary terms, as akin to a deposit of oil beneath your land? Once genes are patented, can rival researchers be barred from working on the same material?

4   Another problem with Berkeley's DNA swabbing is that it perpetuates the assumption that DNA analysis is as good as or the same as personalized medicine. Despite large gaps in understanding and the astonishing absence of standards, the results of genetic research are often held as being far more definitive than yet shown. The mere phrase "genetic correlation" is heard as a 100 percent infallible guarantee of whatever follows. This assumption is often implicit in the advertising of some direct-to-consumer companies like Navigenics and 23andMe. Indeed, both companies were hired to analyze the results of a medical school class's "spit party" at Stanford University recently.

5   On July 22, however, the Government Accountability Office issued a report that advised consumers of the scientific uncertainty of individual results, in which assessments of risk varied widely from company to company. The GAO also found "10 egregious examples of deceptive marketing, including claims made by four companies that a consumer's DNA could be used to create a personalized

supplement to cure diseases. Two of these companies further stated that their supplements could 'repair damaged DNA' or cure disease, even though experts confirmed there is no scientific basis for such claims.... Two other companies asserted that they could predict in which sports children would excel based on DNA analysis, claims that an expert characterized as 'complete garbage.' Further, two companies told GAO's fictitious consumer that she could secretly test her fiancé's DNA to 'surprise' him with test results—though this practice is restricted in 33 states. Perhaps most disturbing, one company told a donor that an above average risk prediction for breast cancer meant she was 'in the high risk of pretty much getting' the disease, a statement that experts found to be 'horrifying' because it implies the test is diagnostic."

6   This is not to say that genetic testing shows nothing at all, but the results inform only at the aggregate level or as a set of probabilities. This explicitly aggregate data collection has been the subject of yet another controversial program, called Gopher Kids, conducted by the University of Minnesota at the annual state fair. At a booth adorned with balloons and a cute animal mascot, researchers offered free T-shirts and amusement park rides to parents and children willing to submit saliva swabs and answer a lengthy questionnaire about lifestyle. The university advertises participation as altruistic, a contribution to public health and human knowledge. The problem with this is that, again, the law is not settled about whether our genetic makeup is more the property of the excavating mind of the scientist or the individual property of a particular identified body.

7   Finally, there is the question of motive. Spit parties are boosted as ways to get to know one another in the social realm—as though it were a collective séance or a big, slimy Ouija board. But the real reasons that so many companies market swabbing kits is not entirely altruistic: there is huge money to be made in expanding the data sets as broadly as possible. The predictive probabilities involved in reading genes for disease or physique or ancestry can become more precise only by sifting through data of whole populations and then correlating frequencies of particular conditions with particular genetic clustering. This, it is thought, will be very valuable in devising and marketing pharmaceuticals, as well as in forensic identification technologies.

8   As we enter the genomic era, we should be more thoughtful about the ends for which our bodies are being mined. The redemptive thrill of being co-creators of some medical miracle must be measured against the possibility that we are rendering fungible that

which most profoundly distinguishes us and, in the name of a gift, enabling a commodity exchange in which important aspects of our identities will be sold to the highest bidder.

ORGANIZATION AND IDEAS

1. Paragraph 1 introduces the essay. What points does it cover? How complete is it?
2. The lead sentence of paragraph 2 serves as a topic sentence for other paragraphs as well. What is the controlling idea? What paragraphs does it apply to?
3. In what way does paragraph 6 qualify Williams' objections? How does that qualification weaken or strengthen her argument?
4. Williams raises "the question of motive" in paragraph 7. To what extent do you think that's a legitimate issue?
5. Paragraph 8 concludes the essay. How well does it cap and summarize the earlier paragraphs?

TECHNIQUE AND STYLE

1. If you think of word choice on a sliding scale from slang all the way to most formal, where would you place the essay's level of diction and why?
2. Williams uses a number of unusual and technical words. Choose several examples and explain whether she makes their meaning clear.
3. Williams describes Berkeley's program as "an experiment designed to bring the student body together in the same manner that reading *To Kill a Mockingbird* might have in the past." Is she being serious, ironic, humorous, sardonic, what? Explain.
4. Paragraph 6 brings out another example of a "controversial program." What does the paragraph add to Williams' argument?
5. Take a hard look at the essay's last two paragraphs. The sentences vary in length from seven to fifty-two words, and the punctuation includes a dash, full colon, and multiple commas. Read the paragraphs out loud. What do those choices contribute to readability?

SUGGESTIONS FOR WRITING

Journal

1. Explain why you would or would not participate in a "spit party" or DNA testing program.
2. How appropriate is the essay's title? What others can you think of? Which is better and why?

Essay

1. Williams deals with questions of ownership and financial gain, and these questions become increasingly important as medicine and technology advance. Choose a subject where these issues arise and explore them, leading to your conclusion. Consider the sale of

   blood
   organs
   human eggs
   surrogate motherhood
   participation in an experiment

2. Your college or university has a privacy policy that applies to students. Often, you'll find it in the catalogue or on the Web site, but you can always get it from one of the offices in the institution's administration. Analyze the policy and write an essay in which you argue its validity. Is anything not covered? What rights do students have?

Guest Workers and the U.S. Heritage

Jay Bookman

Jay Bookman holds degrees in history and journalism from Pennsylvania State University. After writing for newspapers in Washington, Nevada, and Massachusetts, he joined the staff of The Atlanta Journal-Constitution *and is now that paper's deputy editorial page writer. His columns appear on the editorial page twice weekly and are carried by other papers as well. His interests range from national and state politics to technology and the environment, the latter leading to his book* Caught in the Current: Searching for Simplicity in the Technological Age *(2004). Bookman's work has earned him recognition from various environmental groups such as the Wilderness Society and the National Wildlife Federation, and he has also received the Aldo Leopold Award, as well as the Scripps Howard and National Headliner awards. Eight times Cox newspapers declared him the winner of the Best of Cox Newspapers Awards for his columns and editorials, work that also garnered him a Eugene Pulliam Fellowship from the Society of Professional Journalists. The essay below appeared in the Austin* American-Statesman *on April 4, 2006.*

What to Look For When you think about an issue that you want to take an argumentative stand on, you might try the approach that Bookman uses: analyzing the problem and the possible solutions. He discusses various solutions others have proposed, finds them unsatisfactory, and concludes with his own.

1   If the American people decide that 12 million illegal immigrants should be removed and sent back home, fine, we can try to do that.

2   The process would be hard and expensive and brutally inhumane at times, and it could never be entirely successful. But if we hardened our hearts and emptied our wallets, we could probably come somewhat close to achieving that goal.

3   Of course, banishing those millions from our borders would also mean that we would do without the labor they now provide in industries from construction to hotels and restaurants to agriculture to food processing. Some Americans—generally the most rabid and extremist among us—are ready to make that deal anyway, and there are politicians in Washington willing to pander to that crowd, at least in theory.

4   Others, however, are trying to find a way to retain the labor that illegal immigrants provide without offering them the right to live here permanently, let alone the right to pursue citizenship. It's an effort to solve a politically tough problem by cutting the baby in half, placating anti-immigrant fervor without denying American business the cheap, docile work force it relies upon.

5   That is in essence the proposal championed by President Bush, who advocates "legalizing" millions of immigrants now here illegally, but only on a temporary basis. After working several years, the temporary "guest workers" would be forced to return to their home countries to be replaced by new temporary workers.

6   That proposal has been condemned by extremists—most of them in Bush's own party—as offering "amnesty" to those who broke the law in coming here, as if punishment were more important than solving the problem. The more serious problem with that approach is practical; it assumes that workers will return home once their legal status has expired, and that's unlikely to happen.

7   It's also important to think about the guest worker approach in moral terms, in terms of the values that we claim to honor as Americans.

8   Under a guest worker policy, we will let the immigrants come here by the millions, but only temporarily. We will let them mangle their hands in our poultry plants and salt our farmlands with the sweat off their brows and break their backs at our construction sites and raise our children as nannies and clean our homes as maids, all at cut-rate wages.

9   But we will not allow them to dream—for themselves or their children—of sharing in the future they help to build here.

10   In other words, we are willing to let them serve us but not join us; they must by law be held apart and beneath us. We will import them to serve as a perpetually rotating servant class, and we will do so even while pretending to still honor that most American of principles, "that all men are created equal."

11   That system of second-class citizenship—far from slavery, but far from the full range of human rights as well—has precedent in American history. In colonial times, more than half of those who immigrated from Europe came here not as free people but as indentured servants.

12   In return for the cost of passage to the New World, they agreed to be legally bound to an employer for a number of years, unable to marry without permission and with no say over where they lived or how they worked. They could even be sold to another boss.

13   But even back then, when the period of bonded indenture ended—usually after seven years—the servant was freed and allowed to take his or her place as a full citizen.

14   In reality, there is nothing all that complicated about drafting a practical, humane policy on illegal immigration. It would have three basic components:

   • Tighter border security, to cut off as much as possible the supply of illegal workers coming into this country;
   • Much more effective enforcement against illegal employers, to reduce as much as possible the demand for illegal workers;
   • A way to deal effectively and humanely with the illegal immigrants already here.

15   Any proposed solution that does not include all three components is neither workable nor serious. But in a consideration that is just as important, any proposal that condemns millions to a permanent menial class, even while profiting from their labor, is beneath us as a country and a betrayal of all we are supposed to represent.

ORGANIZATION AND IDEAS

1. What paragraph or paragraphs introduce the essay? How effective is that introduction?
2. Paragraphs 8–10 discuss the drawbacks of a guest worker program. What are they? How are they related to American "values"?
3. Bookman draws an analogy between a guest worker program and indentured servitude. Explain the degree to which the analogy is accurate.
4. State Bookman's thesis in your own words. What words or sentences did you draw on in Bookman's essay to form your statement?
5. In paragraph 14, Bookman spells out three "basic components" of a "practical, humane policy on illegal immigration." To what extent is his overall argument weakened by his not fleshing out the third component?

TECHNIQUE AND STYLE

1. Take a good look at the verbs in paragraph 8. What effects do you think Bookman wants to achieve by choosing those verbs?
2. Where in the essay do you find examples of loaded language? What effect does it have on you?
3. Read the last paragraph out loud with your ear tuned to the way it sounds. What alliteration do you find? What purpose does it serve?
4. How would you characterize Bookman's persona? Given what he says in the essay and how he says it, what sort of person does he appear to be?
5. Reread the essay, marking the various places where Bookman appeals to emotion, reason, and his own persona. Which appeal is dominant? What evidence supports your view?

SUGGESTIONS FOR WRITING

Journal

1. Choose a sentence from the essay that strikes you as particularly effective and explain why you find it so.
2. What other titles can you think of for the essay? Which do you prefer and why?

Essay

1. Immigration is such a hot topic that it has spun off any number of related issues. Listed below are some of the questions raised in the course of the debate:
   Should American citizens be required to have and carry identity cards?
   Should English be the official language of the United States?

Should the official policy on asylum be modified?
Should we build a wall on the entire U.S./Mexican border?
Is deportation an effective solution for illegal immigration?
Choose one of the topics or a similar one of your own, research it, and gather enough evidence so that you can make your own argument.

2. In the heat of debate, *amnesty* can mean different things to different people. Use your library and other resources to discover how the word has been used in the past and how it is used in the current debate over immigration. Write an essay in which you argue for the "true" interpretation of the word.

We Don't Need 'Guest Workers'

Robert J. Samuelson

Any time you pick up Newsweek, *you will see Robert Samuelson's regular column on economics, but before joining the magazine in 1984, he was a reporter for* The Washington Post *and still contributes a column to that newspaper, one that also appears in the* Los Angeles Times *and* The Boston Globe. *There's hardly a journalism award that he hasn't won: the John Hancock Award for Best Business and Financial Columnist (1993), Gerald Loeb Award for Best Commentary (1993 and 1986), National Headliner Award for Feature Column on a Single Subject (1993 and 1992), as well as others. He is also the author of two books:* Untruth: Why the Conventional Wisdom is (Almost Always) Wrong *(2001) and* The Good Life and Its Discontents: The American Dream in the Age of Enlightenment *(1997). The following essay was published on March 22, 2006, in* The Washington Post.

What to Look For   Like Samuelson, you will be doing a lot of research to back up your argument, but research, particularly if it involves statistics, needs to be made interesting. One way to do that is by varying your tone and diction.

1   conomist Philip Martin of the University of California likes to tell a story about the state's tomato industry. In the early 1960s, growers relied on seasonal Mexican laborers, brought in under the government's "bracero" program. The Mexicans picked the tomatoes that were then processed into ketchup and other products. In 1964 Congress killed the program despite growers' warnings that its abolition would doom their industry. What happened? Well, plant scientists developed oblong tomatoes that could be harvested by machine. Since then, California's tomato output has risen fivefold.

2   It's a story worth remembering, because we're being warned again that we need huge numbers of "guest workers"—meaning unskilled laborers from Mexico and Central America—to relieve U.S. "labor shortages." Indeed, the shortages will supposedly worsen as baby boomers retire. President Bush wants an open-ended program. Sens. Edward M. Kennedy (D-Mass.) and John McCain (R-Ariz.) advocate initially admitting 400,000 guest workers annually. The Senate is considering these and other plans.

3   Gosh, they're all bad ideas.

4   Guest workers would mainly legalize today's vast inflows of illegal immigrants, with the same consequence: We'd be importing poverty. This isn't because these immigrants aren't hardworking; many are. Nor is it because they don't assimilate; many do. But they generally don't go home, assimilation is slow and the ranks of the poor are constantly replenished. Since 1980 the number of Hispanics with incomes below the government's poverty line (about $19,300 in 2004 for a family of four) has risen 162 percent. Over the same period, the number of non-Hispanic whites in poverty rose 3 percent and the number of blacks, 9.5 percent. What we have now—and would with guest workers—is a conscious policy of creating poverty in the United States while relieving it in Mexico. By and large, this is a bad bargain for the United States. It stresses local schools, hospitals and housing; it feeds social tensions (witness the Minutemen). To be sure, some Americans get cheap housecleaning or landscaping services. But if more mowed their own lawns or did their own laundry, it wouldn't be a tragedy.

5   The most lunatic notion is that admitting more poor Latino workers would ease the labor market strains of retiring baby boomers. The two aren't close substitutes for each other. Among immigrant Mexican and Central American workers in 2004, only 7 percent had a college degree and nearly 60 percent lacked a high school

diploma, according to the Congressional Budget Office. Among native-born U.S. workers, 32 percent had a college degree and only 6 percent did not have a high school diploma. Far from softening the social problems of an aging society, more poor immigrants might aggravate them by pitting older retirees against younger Hispanics for limited government benefits.

6   It's a myth that the U.S. economy "needs" more poor immigrants. The illegal immigrants already here represent only about 4.9 percent of the labor force, the Pew Hispanic Center reports. In no major occupation are they a majority. They're 36 percent of insulation workers, 28 percent of drywall installers and 20 percent of cooks. They're drawn here by wage differences, not labor "shortages." In 2004, the median hourly wage in Mexico was $1.86, compared with $9 for Mexicans working in the United States, said Rakesh Kochhar of Pew. With high labor turnover in the jobs they take, most new illegal immigrants can get work by accepting wages slightly below prevailing levels.

7   Hardly anyone thinks that most illegal immigrants will leave. But what would happen if new illegal immigration stopped and wasn't replaced by guest workers? Well, some employers would raise wages to attract U.S. workers. Facing greater labor costs, some industries would—like the tomato growers in the 1960s—find ways to minimize those costs. As to the rest, what's wrong with higher wages for the poorest workers? From 1994 to 2004, the wages of high school dropouts rose only 2.3 percent (after inflation) compared with 11.9 percent for college graduates.

8   President Bush says his guest worker program would "match willing foreign workers with willing American employers, when no Americans can be found to fill the jobs." But at some higher wage, there would be willing Americans. The number of native high school dropouts with jobs declined by 1.3 million from 2000 to 2005, estimates Steven Camarota of the Center for Immigration Studies, which favors less immigration. Some lost jobs to immigrants. Unemployment remains high for some groups (9.3 percent for African Americans, 12.7 percent for white teenagers).

9   Business organizations understandably support guest worker programs. They like cheap labor and ignore the social consequences. What's more perplexing is why liberals, staunch opponents of poverty and inequality, support a program that worsens poverty and inequality. Poor immigrant workers hurt the wages of unskilled Americans. The only question is how much. Studies suggest a range "from negligible to an earnings reduction of almost 10 percent," according to the CBO.

10   It's said that having guest workers is better than having poor illegal immigrants. With legal status, they'd have rights and protections. They'd have more peace of mind and face less exploitation by employers. This would be convincing if its premise were incontestable: that we can't control our southern border. But that's unproved. We've never tried a policy of real barriers and strict enforcement against companies that hire illegal immigrants. Until that's shown to be ineffective, we shouldn't adopt guest worker programs that don't solve serious social problems—but add to them.

ORGANIZATION AND IDEAS

1. Samuelson opens his essay with an example. How does it tie into the rest of the essay? How effective is it?
2. Reread paragraph 4, noting the causal relationships. What are the effects of poverty?
3. Where in the essay does Samuelson consider arguments that can be used against his points? How does he counter them?
4. Samuelson's argument rests on economic analysis. How effective is it?
5. Where in the essay is Samuelson's thesis? What effect does he achieve by that placement?

TECHNIQUE AND STYLE

1. How would you describe Samuelson's tone? What examples can you find to support your opinion?
2. Paragraph 3 consists of one sentence. What effect does it achieve?
3. The essay brims with facts and figures. How well does Samuelson judge his reader's tolerance for pure information? How clearly does he present it?
4. Reread the essay, marking examples of Samuelson's use of appeals. Which dominates? What evidence supports your opinion?
5. If Samuelson's essay were written for an academic audience instead of a popular one, all the information would be documented in notes. Opinion essays in newspapers, however, don't use notes but must present facts and figures credibly. How well does Samuelson do that?

SUGGESTIONS FOR WRITING

Journal

1. What fact or figure does Samuelson use that surprises you and why?
2. What do you associate with the word *immigrant*? After you've written a paragraph or two, reread what you've written and sum it up in one sentence. You then have a starting place for an essay.

Essay

1. Many arguments have been put forward as reasons to control illegal immigration:

>to protect national security
>to protect jobs and wages
>to prevent increased pressure on health services and public schools
>to prevent "back-door citizenship" (citizenship being granted automatically to children born in the United States)
>to preserve the English language

Choose one of these reasons and research it so that you can amass enough information to form an educated opinion you can then defend in an essay.

2. Samuelson's concluding paragraph suggests that illegal immigrants, lacking the "rights and protections" accorded to American citizens, are sometimes abused by their employers. Use research to explore the truth of that idea. You might start by picking a type of job that attracts illegal immigrants: house and garden work, restaurant jobs, construction, fruit and vegetable harvesting, and the like.

All These Illegals

Darrin Bell

You have met Darrin Bell in Chapter 7 with his cartoon that illustrates the interrelationship of cause and effect, and that's also where you'll find a short biographical sketch (198). The strip included here is also, appropriately, from Candorville *and like most of Bell's cartoons, one of the characters represents a minority, in this case Native-American. And, like most of Bell's cartoons, the drawing raises a number of questions and issues. The strip included here was published on April 10, 2006.*

For Discussion

1. Who are the characters in Bell's cartoon and what groups do they represent?
2. To what extent are Bell's characters typical? Stereotypical?
3. How does the drawing narrow the debate over immigration?
4. How does the drawing contribute a different perspective to the essays by Bookman and Samuelson?
5. Consider the cartoon as a political statement on the issue of immigration. What thesis would you give it and why?

Suggestions for Writing

Journal

Of the two, which frames do you prefer and why? Make specific reference to the drawings to support your point.

Essay

Perhaps a particular current issue interests you, or perhaps you're curious about how a certain political figure is portrayed, or maybe you want to know more about a political cartoonist. Can the cartoonist, for example, be labeled *liberal?* And if so, what sort of liberal and what positions does he or she take? Or think about how any prominent political figure is drawn by different artists. What is exaggerated? What is implied? Use a search engine to find cartoons or comic strips that deal with a current topic, political figure, or artist. More than likely, once you have brought up a site, you will be able to narrow a search so that you can explore the pertinent cartoons or comic strips. As you explore your topic, you will start to form a thesis that can be used for your essay, an essay that uses your description of the drawings and some examples of them to support your point.

When Cowboys Cry

Sandra Steingraber

If you run across a magazine article that brings together science, cancer, and the environment and is readable, you have probably met Sandra Steingraber. When she received the first annual Altman Award, it was for her "inspiring and poetic use of science to elucidate the causes of cancer." As a cancer survivor, that's a subject she knows well, both personally and professionally. Her book Living Downstream: An Ecologist's Personal Investigation of Cancer and the Environment *(1997) was the first study to examine data on toxic releases along side data from U.S. cancer registries and was later made into a documentary. The Sierra Club called Steingraber "the new Rachel Carson," and in 2006 she was given a Hero Award by the Breast Cancer Fund. Steingraber's other books about the relationship between cancer and the environment are* Having Faith: An Ecologist's Journey to Motherhood *(2001) and* Raising Elijah: Protecting Our Children in an Age of Environmental Crisis *(2011). At present, Steingraber is a scholar in residence in Ithaca College and a columnist for* Orion *magazine where the article below was published in the May/June 2011 issue.*

What to Look For   The essay's originally had a subtitle: "In Today's Wild West, energy corporations are the new outlaws." Steingraber picks up the old, classic images of the American West and applies them to the corporations extracting fossil fuels. As you read her essay, look for ways she weaves in that good guy/bad guy analogy.

1   LAST NOVEMBER, at the annual meeting of the Northern Plains Resource Council, which took place in the Crowne Plaza Hotel in Billings, Montana, I watched a cowboy cry.

2   As someone born east of the Mississippi, I'm aware that I may have my vocabulary words mixed up here. The crying man called himself a rancher, not a cowboy. But he had the hat. The legs in the blue jeans were bowed. And he said things like, *Sometimes you have to ride with the brand, and sometimes you have to speak your mind.*

3   Which sounded like cowboy talk to me.

4   What had him choked up was the ongoing ruination of the West caused by fossil fuel extraction. Coal mining. Coal-bed methane. Oil wells. Oil sands pipelines from Canada. And the newest atrocity: high volume, slickwater, horizontal hydrofracturing, which blows up deep layers of shale to get at natural gas bubbles. *Science* magazine describes fracking this way: under extreme pressure, large volumes of chemical-laced water are used to "create a football-shaped cloud of fractured shale 300 meters long."

5   The prospect of turning fresh water into a club to smash bedrock into footballish clouds had—along with coal mining— sunk a whole roomful of men into sorrow. They spoke about artesian springs that had stopped flowing. The difficult business of irrigating alfalfa. And something called subsidence—downward motion of the earth caused by collapsing tunnels or changes in pressure from gas extraction. Subsidence can roll boulders through people's front doors.

6   There was a panel called "Reflecting on the Importance of the Good Neighbor Agreement." There was a presentation about how to convince the state of Montana to study the environment before moving forward with destroying it (by permitting a coal mine at Otter Creek) and an update on the attempt to persuade TransCanada to withdraw its application for a waiver to use thinner-than-standard pipe for ferrying tar sands across the prairie.

7   The task force was pleased to report its success in this last effort.

8   Many conference participants looked like they had walked right out of central casting. And that created for me moments of cognitive dissonance. Their mild-mannered activities did not square, in my mind, with what cowboys do. I kept flashing on movie scenes. Gary Cooper as Marshal Will Kane in *High Noon* dispatching a gang of murderers. Woody Harrelson and Kiefer Sutherland in *The Cowboy Way* lassoing a thug to the end of a speeding train. Good riddance to you, bud.

9   From what I could see in Montana, the torch of Wild West lawlessness is now being carried by Wall Street–backed energy corporations, while the real-life cowboys are trying to find things in the law that will slow down the rate of plundering, raise the cost of plundering, or make the plundering marginally less accident-prone. And given that fossil fuel extraction in general—and fracking in particular—is exempt from many federal laws, the guys in the white hats are having a tough time of it. They're not exactly running the plunderers out of town.

10   Meanwhile, an entire way of life is disappearing so fast that the son of one rancher was interviewing for a job with the energy

company that had wrecked his father's land. I mean, you can't make a living on the range anymore.

11   The Crowne Plaza Hotel in Billings is the tallest brick building in the world. At the end of the day, my son and I rode the elevator up to the top—which is the kind of thing you do when traveling with a nine-year-old—and we found ourselves inside the Billings Petroleum Club. In no time at all, a security guard—or -somebody acting like one—steered us back to the elevator shaft. On the way down, we passed the field office for Stealth Energy. Its logo: a cartoon gusher.

12   But as soon as we were on the ground floor, I wanted to go back up in order to verify what I'd seen in the dimly lit chambers of the Petroleum Club while being hustled out of it: a March of Dimes poster. Of all the boldface names hanging on the walls up there, this one interested me most because, twenty-three stories below, I had just given a lecture about the evidence linking exposure to fossil fuel combustion products to shorter pregnancies. Preterm birth is the nation's leading cause of disability says the March of Dimes. So what was it doing inside the Petroleum Club? I found my answer in its newsletter, *Gusher*: in two days hence, the club was hosting a March of Dimes fundraiser.

13   Memo to Stealth Energy and the editorial staff of the Petroleum Club: Even my nine-year-old knows that gushers are the result of failed blowout preventers. They kill people. Memo to the March of Dimes: Take my name off your mailing list.

14   The desperate rush to force the earth's remaining fossil fuels out of their fossily graveyards—which requires ever more toxic methods of extraction—affects, of course, everyone everywhere, and crosses all cultural and party lines. Two weeks after the Montana meetings, I was standing in a forest next to a swarthy man carrying a gun. He, too, looked like a character actor—from a movie about the French Resistance. We were in the right place—the cave-riddled foothills of the Pyrenees that had served as a refuge for anti-Nazi partisans and, centuries before that, for the defiant Cathars facing the Pope's murderous army. (The man with the gun was hunting wild boar.)

15   Like Montana, southern France is also targeted for hydrofracking, along with the vales of England and the forests of Poland. And, a few days later, in the lobby outside the European Parliament in Brussels, I saw someone cry about it. That was the week that stories about fracking broke in the international press, and European environmentalists were scrambling to figure out what laws in the European Union might apply to this new technology. Like the sons and daughters of Montana's cowboys, the sons and daughters of the Allied Forces were having a hard time finding legal traction.

16   The British journal *The Ecologist* reached a similar conclusion in an investigative report about the European plans of Halliburton, Chevron, Exxon, and others. Although fracking in the United States is linked to toxic pollution and social conflict, notes *The Ecologist*, the technology is being rapidly exported. Fracking "exceeds the government regulatory process." It is "set to continue." It is, perhaps, "too powerful to oppose."

17   Really? *Drill, baby, drill* is more powerful than the *Wehrmacht*? So, now I'm looking for Marshal Kane and Winston Churchill, too. Meanwhile, in February, the un-legendary city of Buffalo, New York, quietly voted to ban fracking inside its borders. Pittsburgh, Pennsylvania, has done the same. And my town board in Ulysses, New York, is, at this writing, considering its own fracking ban, after more than a thousand residents (of the three thousand registered voters who live here) submitted a petition. All such communities who take this step are inviting a host of legal challenges. So we are told. *Vive la résistance.*

ORGANIZATION AND IDEAS

1. What differing geographical places does Steingraber use in her concluding analogy? How does their mention relate to her argument?
2. Where in the essay does Steingraber use outside sources. How reliable are they? Does she use them fairly?
3. How does Steingraber shape the readers' responses to the "cowboys"? To the energy corporations? What words does she use and how effective are they?
4. How much of the essay focuses on the example of fossil fuels in general? On fracking? Why might Steingraber have presented them in the order she does?
5. Exactly what is Steingraber against? State her thesis in your own words.

TECHNIQUE AND STYLE

1. What examples of irony can you find in the essay? How effective are they? Does irony characterize her overall tone? If not, what does?
2. Where in the essay can you pinpoint loaded or biased choices of words? To what extent do they have a negative effect on the reader?
3. Steingraber brings in her personal experience in paragraphs 11 and 14. Where else does she use the first person *I*? What does she achieve by doing so?
4. Paragraph 8 refers to two Westerns in which the "good guys" got rid of the "bad guys," roles she reverses in paragraph 9. Where else does she use this sort of reversal?

5. Steingraber ends her essay with references to World War II, setting "Drill, baby, drill" against the *Wehrmacht* (the German armed forces), blending High Noon's Marshal Kane with Winston Churchill, and comparing those who oppose fracking to the French resistance. What, in your own words, is she calling for with *Vive la résistance?*

SUGGESTIONS FOR WRITING

Journal

1. How would you describe the Sandra Steingraber behind the words in the essay? What sort of person does her writing suggest?
2. You can take Steingraber's analogy (opposition to fracking and the French Resistance) and plug in almost any other parties. What can you think of? Choose one comparison and flesh it out in your journal.

Essay

1. Think of an action that was considered acceptable in the past but today is either questionable or unacceptable. Fifty years ago, for instance, no one thought much about the hazards of smoking, nor of cholesterol levels, nor of needing to inspect meat. Segregation was acceptable, as were other forms of racism. Choose a subject and think about the ethics involved and how present knowledge has changed how we live. Other suggestions:
   sale of cigarettes
   advertising of alcoholic beverages
   popularity of natural foods
   sale of diet products
2. The combination of economic downturn, global warming, and finite fossil fuels may well lead to a number of proposed regulations. Mandatory mileage limits for cars are already on the books, and there's been some discussion of a mandatory—and lower—national speed limit. Consider a problem that we may face in the next five to ten years and think about possible regulations that could be proposed to lessen or solve that problem. The possible regulations you come up with may be as realistic or far-fetched as you like. Once you have some ideas to work with, choose one and research it so you can construct an argument in favor of it or against it. If you like, you could write a satiric essay.

Protecting the Environment

Pennsylvania Independent Oil and Gas Association (PIOGA)

> *PIOGA is an oil and gas trade association that represents over 800 members who are involved in all aspects of the industry: "oil and natural gas producers, drilling contractors, service companies, manufacturers, distributors, professional firms and consultants, [and] royalty owners"* (www.pioga.org).
>
> *The organization's mission statement says that "as the leading Appalachian oil and gas trade association," its aim is "promoting an environment favorable to the growth of the industry and developing Pennsylvania as an attractive state for oil and gas investment." To that end, PIOGA's Web site provides general information about the industry, industry news and events, and current oil and gas prices, along with separate headings for topics such as Marcellus Shale, Environment & Safety, Careers, and Resources. The information below comes from PIOGA's Web site under the heading Environment & Safety. The copyright is 2011.*

What to Look For   You will find a lot of information in the piece that follows but it is also an argument with an implied thesis. As you read, look for key words that help shape the implied argument.

1   Developing natural gas from the Marcellus Shale is a process regulated by both state and federal agencies responsible for the protection of the environment and the sound use of water resources. In fact, between 30–35 individual permits, depending on a well's specific location, are required to drill a natural gas well in Pennsylvania. The industry is committed to planning, drilling and operating its wells in compliance with the regulations that govern natural gas development, and operators typically go beyond what is required by these agencies.

Site Preparation

2   Protecting the environment begins with constructing roads and grading the drill pad location, through the use of controls to prevent soil erosion and sedimentation. Roads are often improved prior to starting the drilling process to accommodate additional

truck traffic, with culverts placed along road berms to reduce sedimentation. Filter socks and erosion control blankets are installed and maintained at the pad throughout the drilling process to prevent storm water runoff, and tons of gravel are spread and leveled across the pad to allow precipitation to drain properly. The result of this preliminary work is a drilling pad that is safe and does not cause soil erosion or the sedimentation of streams.

Drilling

3   The drilling process involves driving several increasingly smaller diameter steel pipes, called casing strings, into the wellbore, with the injection of cement into the pipe and up the sides of the wellbore at the completion of each casing string. This isolates the wellbore with two durable materials—steel and cement–from the earth, including groundwater aquifers. Each successive steel casing string is cemented into place as the well is drilled, extending to the end of the horizontal portion of the wellbore that will produce natural gas. The casing and cementing process is tested as the well is drilled to ensure its integrity. These steel and cement liners remain in place throughout the well's years of production

4   Material called drilling mud, which is also used to drill drinking water wells, is used to lubricate the drill bit and to aid in bringing rock cuttings to surface. The cuttings are then processed through a shaker and allowed to settle, with the rock fragments held at the drilling location, either for permitted disposal in a lined on-site facility, or for transportation to a permitted landfill. Drilling mud is processed in an on-site treatment facility and recycled for continued use in the drilling process.

Completion and Production

5   Environmental protection during hydraulic fracturing turns to the careful use of water and the additives required to fracture the Marcellus Shale formation, along with the proper management and recycling of flow back water that returns to the surface. Water allocation permits are required to withdraw water from streams for hydraulic fracturing; the state Department of Environmental Protection and federal interstate river basin commissions monitor withdrawals to ensure the protection of waterways. Permits must also be obtained to purchase water from municipal water suppliers. Water is stored in tanks or lined, secure impoundments at the drilling location.

6   Approximately 3 to 5 million gallons of water is used to fracture a horizontal well. Of this, about 20 percent of the water flowback is returned to the surface shortly after drilling. More and more of this flowback water is being recycled for use in subsequent fracturing operations, significantly reducing consumptive water use. Many drilling companies have been successful in recycling 100 percent of flowback water.

7   The additives used in the fracturing process are transported and managed at the drilling location according to state and federal regulations. Typically, only three to five additives are used in the hydraulic fracturing process, and those materials can be found in products in the home. These include a surfactant (or soap) to reduce the friction of the water, a biocide (similar to an anti-bacterial hand cleaner) to keep the wellbore free of bacteria, a scale inhibitor (comparable to a household product used to keep wastewater pipes free of scale) to prevent the buildup of scale, and a lubricant (similar to vegetable oil) to make the water heavier and reduce friction. The well stimulation process has not been identified as the source of groundwater contamination, as it takes place at depths between 5,000—8,000 feet below ground surface. Most groundwater aquifers are found between 100—200 feet below the surface, typically more than a mile above the shale being fractured.

8   After the drilling and hydraulic fracturing processes are completed, the drilling pad is restored, commonly as requested by the property owner. A completed and secure producing well only requires a surface footprint the size of a large garage, and includes the well head, water storage tanks and a small amount of production equipment.

9   Horizontal drilling allows for multiple wells to be drilled on each pad, resulting in fewer pad sites, access roads and equipment, along with less trucking and greatly reduced surface disruption. Producing wells are monitored and the pad site maintained throughout the life of the well by a well tender. Some water slowly returns to the surface over time, which is stored and pumped as needed into trucks for treatment at permitted facilities.

Shut in and Abandon/Reclamation

10   When a well is no longer capable of production, concrete is pumped down the wellbore to seal it from the earth, and production equipment is removed from site. The entire pad is then re-vegetated and fully restored.

ORGANIZATION AND IDEAS

1. What information is contained in paragraph 1? How well does it set up the sections that follow?
2. Headings begin paragraphs 2, 3, 5, and 10. How complete are the headings? Are any steps omitted and if so, what?
3. Check the Web site at *http://www.pioga.org/environment-safety/ protecting-environment/*. What is added by the photo? The explanation? How necessary are they?
4. How well does the title fit the article? What, in your own words, is the implied thesis?
5. The article seems to stop, not end. Based on the information in paragraph 1 and what you infer, what is the thesis, what would you put in a concluding paragraph, and why?

TECHNIQUE AND STYLE

1. If you were the author of this article, how would you describe its audience? What examples support your idea?
2. What concerns might that audience have? List them. Choose one and explain whether the article deals with it effectively?
3. Paragraphs 2 and 3 rely on cause and effect. Outline the causal relationships. How clear are they? How well do they work?
4. What sources provide the information in the article? To what extent are they reliable?
5. The article uses description, definition, comparison, process analysis, and causal analysis within its structure and its aim covers both explanation and argument. Which aim predominates? Which is more closely tied to the implied thesis?

SUGGESTIONS FOR WRITING

Journal

1. What does the article omit that you would like to know and why?
2. If you were a farmer, explain why you would or would not allow drilling on your land.

Essay

1. Federal and state regulation has become a hot topic in the news and on the political scene, and there's no question there's a lot of it. How necessary and how effective, however, are up for debate. Regulations are applied to:
   car emissions
   air quality
   meat
   cigarettes
   water quality

Choose one of these subjects or your own and research either state or federal regulations that apply to it. Evaluate what you find and build your own argument based on it.

2. Pick apart the article according to your own opinions and the evidence you turn up by research. No matter what you think about fracking, you will learn a lot and find much to write about. Quote from the article as well as your own research to support your thesis.

Drilling Down Deep

Mindy Lubber

> *Mindy Lubber has channeled her early interest in protecting the environment into a career in finance. When she was in her teens, she solved the problem of her town's lack of a recycling plan by starting her own, now so successful that each year it recycles many tons. She went on to earn a MBA and JD, becoming the executive director of the Massachusetts Public Interest Research Group, starting the National Environmental Law Center, and founding Green Century Capital Management, a mutual fund company. With publications in* Forbes *and the* Huffington Post, *she is now president of Ceres, a non-profit coalition of "investors, environmental organizations and other public interest groups working with companies to address sustainability challenges such as global climate change and water scarcity." It's obvious that Lubber would be concerned about drilling. Her essay was published as an opinion piece in the Lima, Ohio, newspaper* The Lima News, *on June 18, 2011.*

What to Look For   One useful way to organize an argumentative essay is to adopt a problem/solution structure. That's what Mindy Lubber does in her essay, and it's a pattern that may work well in your own essays.

1   Right now natural gas is the new big thing when it comes to solving our nation's energy challenges.

2   With gasoline hitting $4 a gallon and coal- and nuclear-based power reeling from environmental and safety concerns, many see

cheap, plentiful supplies of homegrown natural gas as the latest answer to our energy dreams, especially as hydraulic fracturing technology opens up vast new reserves. And most of it is being used to replace increasingly unattractive coal-based power's higher price tag and bigger carbon footprint.

3   Natural gas wells are popping up like spring dandelions. Once-empty landscapes in Colorado, Texas, Pennsylvania and Wyoming are now dotted with thousands of wells.

4   But it's time to calm the frenzy. We need a more balanced look at what's to be gained—and lost—if we embrace natural gas too heartily. Despite its many positives, natural gas is no panacea for a country with a long history of over-dependence on fossil fuels that still hasn't come to grips with climate change.

5   While many espouse "drill baby drill," investors, utility CEOs and industry analysts caution about moving too hard and fast on an industry that's just now getting close regulatory scrutiny—after numerous episodes of water contamination and blow-outs from poorly-constructed wells. Even where rules have been strength-ened, inadequate funding and staffing levels make compliance a challenge.

6   "We have to find ways to give the public confidence," said Robin West, chairman of PFC Energy, an industry consulting firm. "If shale is going to be a game changer, these (safety) issues have to be resolved." Investors made a similar point last month when they strongly supported shareholder resolutions with ExxonMobil, Chevron and Ultra Petroleum asking for better disclosure of the fracking chemicals they're using and steps being taken to reduce environmental and safety risks.

7   Some safety progress is being made. While comprehensive fed-eral action seems unlikely in the short term, states like Wyoming, Arkansas and Texas have passed new rules requiring better disclo-sure of the chemicals drillers use, and several more have proposals under consideration.

8   The disclosure rules all have shortcomings, however; the new Texas law, for example, exempts chemical mixtures deemed trade secrets and actually provides less disclosure than was originally sought by a collaboration of Southwestern Energy, five other com-panies and the Environmental Defense Fund.

9   Wyoming and Pennsylvania have also enacted tougher well integ-rity rules—poorly constructed wells can leak dangerous amounts of the potent greenhouse gas methane, which can also cause explosions.

10   Some companies are also taking steps to reduce safety risks and environmental impacts. Williams Co., a major producer in Colorado, has been a leader in curbing methane emissions while Range Resources has gained attention for strong wastewater recycling, which is cutting water use and operating costs. These incremental improvements are not a long-term answer, however, and the entire industry needs to come together on clean performance goals for chemicals and water use, wastewater management, well construction and emergency response.

11   Even if these environmental and safety issues can be addressed, investors, business leaders and electric utilities are leery of hitching much of the nation's energy future to a single fossil fuel historically prone to price spikes.

12   "The market left to its own devices will build only natural gas plants, and that's an enormously bad outcome," said David Crane, CEO of NRG Energy, a power company that's generating nearly 40 percent of its power from natural gas. "The best thing the American electric industry has going for it right now is that it is fuel-diverse."

13   Crane also recognizes that solar and other forms of renewable energy, which are cleaner than natural gas, must have far bigger roles as the U.S. gets more serious about reducing pollution causing climate change. He and others see natural gas mostly as a critical "bridge fuel" to that day.

14   The lesson in all this is simple: Rushing toward any single "savior" as our climate and energy challenges deepen would be a short sighted business, economic and environmental strategy. We need a wide array of low-carbon, clean energy solutions, including "safe" natural gas and exponentially more renewable energy.

ORGANIZATION AND IDEAS

1. What paragraphs introduce the essay? What reasons support your choice?
2. What problems does Lubber describe that are associated with drilling for natural gas? What solutions?
3. Lubber cites examples from Colorado, Texas, Pennsylvania, and Wyoming. How do these choices support her point about the negative side of drilling?
4. What companies does Lubber mention and why? How reliable are the sources?

5. In paragraph 14, start the second to last sentence (after the colon) with *Because,* change the *R* to lower case, put a comma after *strategy,* and change the *W* to lower case. The result is a full statement of Lubber's thesis. How convincing is she?

TECHNIQUE AND STYLE

1. In paragraph 3 Lubber adopts the term "bridge fuel" for natural gas. In what ways is the term appropriate? How does it tie into Lubber's thesis?
2. Lubber makes a number of assumptions in paragraph 4. What are they? Choose one and explain whether it's valid.
3. Reread the essay from the perspective of someone in favor of fracking. To what extent is Lubber fair to the natural gas industry? What examples support your opinion?
4. Lubber states, "rushing" into drilling for natural gas "would be a short sighted business, economic and environmental strategy." Where in the essay do you find evidence for her claim about business, the economy, the environment?
5. To describe the Mindy Lubber behind the words in the essay is to analyze her persona. What sort of person does she appear to be? What tentative conclusions can you reach about her level of education? Age? Reasonableness?

SUGGESTIONS FOR WRITING

Journal

1. Look again at the title of Lubber's essay. What other meanings are possible in addition to the literal one?
2. If you reread Lubber's essay, you'll see that the people mentioned are all men. What if anything does that say about the corporations cited?

Essay

1. Identifying problems and solutions is not easy, particularly when the problems are not readily identifiable as is often the case with disasters. More than likely, your state has had a recent event that can easily be labeled a disaster. Perhaps a:

   forest fire
   tornado
   sand or dust storm
   hurricane
   flood

While the disaster is obvious, the causes and solutions can be subtle, confusing, or even multiple. Choose a subject from the list or your own, narrow it down to a particular event, research it, and work up an essay identifying the problem and possible solutions. Argue for the solution you find best.

2. Lubber's essay mentions a number of problems that have been reported and attributed to fracking. Examine the problems Lubber brings out, choose one, and then use the Web to research it, narrowing down to one particular complaint or charge that you can investigate. Once you have accumulated information on both sides, you can draw a conclusion you can use as a thesis.

"Would Madam Care for Water?" (editorial cartoon)

Signe Wilkinson

In her appropriately entertaining profile (editorialcartoonists.com), *Wilkinson claims that after graduating from college with a BA in English she "found a job in the only profession that would have her—journalism." She worked part-time for a number of papers before signing up for a mission abroad "to bring peace to the island of Cyprus. Nine months later, war broke out." Back in the United States and in Philadelphia, she attended the Academy of Fine Art, did graphic design for the Academy of Natural Sciences, then got a full time job in California at the* San Jose Mercury News, *finally returning to Philadelphia and landing at the* Philadelphia Daily News. *She has been there ever since drawing editorial cartoons. It's a rare year that goes by without at least one of her drawings included in a* Best Editorial Cartoons of the Year *collection. One Nation, Under Surveillance, her own collection, was published in 2005. Wilkinson was the first woman to win the Pulitzer Prize for Editorial Cartooning (1992), and since then she has won the Overseas Press Club's Thomas Nast Award three times (1996, 2000, 2006) and the Robert F. Kennedy Journalism Award twice (2002 and 2008). The cartoon below appeared on August 18, 2010, in the* Philadelphia Daily News.

For Discussion

1. How would you describe the waiter? What sort of restaurant has a "water steward"?
2. Take a good look at the couple and the table. What do their expressions tell you? What does the setting of the table suggest?
3. If you add together your answers to the two previous questions, what does the cartoon imply about economic status? How might that tie into the subject of fracking?
4. If you had to supply a thesis for the cartoon, what would it be?
5. Reconsider the cartoon in relation to the three essays on drilling for natural gas. How is it related to each? Which is it closer to and why?

Suggestions for Writing

Journal

Revise the cartoon to make your own point about drilling for natural gas. Think about changing the setting, characters, bottles, labels, dialogue, anything you wish. You can make a copy of the cartoon and then edit it or draw your own version.

Essay

Make a short list of subjects that interest you, choose one or two, and then bring up *http://www.cartoonistgroup.com*. On both sides of the Web page, you'll see search engines. On the left, all you need to do is type in the cartoonist or topic you're interested in; on the right, you'll see ways to search the catalogue. For each of the categories—Who, What, When, Where, Why—you'll see a list that concludes with "and more." Click that to see the complete file of headings in the group. Once you've brought up the cartoons that relate to your topic, look around to see what appeals to you. Perhaps you like the work of a particular cartoonist or maybe a subject draws you in. At that point you'll probably be able to come up with a working thesis and chase down the drawings to support your point.

Multiple Modes

Two Topics, Six Views

ON A SENSE OF PLACE

"Where are you from?" is one of the first questions many people ask, but it can be confusing. It can mean where do you live or where were you born, but to many it is "Where are your roots?" Many Americans may find that a difficult question because we are a somewhat itinerant nation. According to the 1998 census, the average person over 15 years old moves every 5.2 years and only 15% have lived in the same house 20 or more years. No matter what the reasons for moving, one's roots often remain planted in a specific place. For the three authors included here, that place is where each one grew up. For John Wideman, it's Pittsburgh, Pennsylvania; for Stuart Overlin, it's Paducah, Kentucky; and for Mario Suarez, it's Tuscon, Arizona. The three writers represent different parts of the country, different times, and different backgrounds and environments, yet all have a strong sense of place.

John Wideman, the second African American to be named a Rhodes Scholar, now is teaching at Brown University where he is the Asa Messer Professor and Professor of Africana Studies. If you were to do a Google search for his name, you would be amazed by the quality of his works and quantity of his awards. Many of his novels and memoirs, particularly the *Homewood Trilogy* (1985) (*Damballah*, *Hiding Place*, and *Sent for You Yesterday*), examine the Black experience and his own family history. He explores a bit of that family history in his essay that follows, one that he read on NPR on April 18, 2008.

Unlike John Wideman, Stuart Overlin is just starting his career. A graduate of the U.S. Naval Academy, Overlin continued his studies at DePaul University where he earned an MA in Writing and Publishing, a degree that came with the honor of "Distinction." At the time his essay was written, Overlin lived in Chicago but now he and his wife live in San Diego,

California. Paducah, Kentucky, however is still "home." His piece about that town was published in *Brevity 35*, the January 2011 issue.

Son of immigrants and the oldest of five children, Mario Suárez grew up in Tucson, Arizona, in the neighborhood known as "El Hoyo." Shortly after graduating from high school, Suárez joined the Navy and served his tour of duty during World War II. When he returned home, he enrolled at the University of Arizona and found himself taking freshman English. The essay below was written for that class and so impressed his teacher, Ruth Keenan, that she not only encouraged him to take other writing courses but also to submit "El Hoyo" to the *Arizona Quarterly*, where it was published. That was a long time ago (1947), but it started Suárez on a successful writing career; it's rare for any anthology of Chicano literature to not include at least one of Suárez's works. Hailed as a "key figure in the foundation of Chicano literature," Suárez's stories have recently been collected and reissued as *Chicano Sketches*, published by the University of Arizona Press in 2004.

Life in 'My Town'

John Wideman

1   If you have to grow up poor, Pittsburgh in the 1940s and 1950s, not a bad place to do it. The blight of poverty didn't feel inborn, permanent; more like you'd arrived late and didn't quite fit in yet.

2   Pittsburgh immigrant territory, a promised land for colored refugees from the American South, immigrants from Eastern and Southern Europe, at the dawning of the 20th century, when one of my grandfathers came up from Virginia, the other from South Carolina, and married Pittsburgh girls.

3   Distant from both coasts, Pittsburgh, since its colonial beginnings as British fort and trading post at the edge of unexplored wilderness, has been a sign pointing beyond itself, a settlement for people who decline more alluring, perhaps, but riskier options.

4   An unadventurous image the town never quite forgets or sheds, Pittsburghers have developed a grumpy pessimism laced with stoic affection for the region's intemperate weather, rough work, lack of glamour, its destiny to be a polyglot patchwork town, never a smooth, swaggering big city. Lots of churches, lots of bars, plenty of Iron City beer at home in the fridge.

5   In Pittsburgh streets, I heard foreign accents, saw signs bearing strange alphabets. Riding a trolley in any direction 10 or 15 blocks from home, I would pass through a kaleidoscope of various nationalities, colors, religions, neighborhoods, rich and poor.

6   But Pittsburgh, also balkanized by three rivers and abrupt, steep hills, an abundance of tunnels and bridges divided as much as connected the city's diverse inhabitants. Detente, rather than interpenetration, except in the still of the night, characterized relationships among its cultures.

7   We tiptoed around each other in Pittsburgh, more aware of our differences and similarities than we were willing to admit; proud, maybe, not to make a public fuss about such stuff. But notions of difference, not consciously examined, not viewed as instruments of power, mutated into stereotypes and myths, the shorthand of prejudice.

8   Even if not maliciously intended, the instant, unthinking judgments passed on other groups stunt those who habitually deploy them. We squandered possibilities for cultural elaboration and enrichment. We

245

didn't learn from the city's near-fatal mistake, how Pittsburgh almost destroyed itself in the 1950s by narrowing its ambitions and adopting a monolithic identity: Steel Town, USA.

9   Though I haven't resided in Pittsburgh for over 40 years, my knowledge of it comes from regular visits, from writing fiction and essays that bear witness to what I absorb vicariously, viscerally, as son, brother, uncle, cousin of those who never left.

10   Pittsburgh matters deeply to me, like the intimate circle of my earliest friends, like the songs I grew up dancing to, making love to. My Pittsburgh fixed in a slice of time, but also transcends that time, because other cities, other friends, and other music I acquire are measured against the original. Pittsburgh's inside me, like your city or village or rural turf is inside you, a terrain you can't help reconstituting wherever you move on.

Paducah, Kentucky

Stuart Overlin

1   It's one of those places weathermen love saying, like *Kalamazoo* or *Tuscaloosa*. The name comes from Chief Paduke, a Chickasaw who welcomed the whites when they began arriving in the early nineteenth century. My hometown is situated near the end of the Ohio River's thousand-mile drift into the Mississippi, and during the steamboat age this prime real estate made it a bustling trade center. A handful of Paducahans have found fame since then. John Scopes was tried for teaching evolution down in Tennessee, in the Monkey Trial of 1925. Alben Barkley, best remembered for saying the vice presidency wasn't worth a bucket of warm piss, held the office under Truman.

2   Another favorite son was Charles "Speedy" Atkins, nicknamed for his skill as a tobacco picker. After Speedy drowned while fishing in 1928, the mortician at Paducah's black funeral parlor tried a special embalming fluid on him. He was so pleased with the results that he dressed the corpse in a suit and put it on display, where it remained for more than sixty years. Overlooked in life, Speedy became a tourist attraction and appeared on "That's Incredible!" and other TV shows until he was laid to rest in 1994.

3   Paducah was churchy, but for every house of worship there were two places of shame. Craps games were held at night behind Happy's Chili Parlor. The south side had adult cinemas and nude dancers at Regina's House of Dolls. Within eyeshot of the county courthouse stood a two-block hub of drugs and prostitution known as The Set. And in a wet town surrounded by dry counties, there was no shortage of twangy bars and drive-thru liquor stores.

4   Dad worked at Park Vue Liquors one summer when I was eight or nine years old. When Mom had the late shift at the hospital, I'd hang out at the store. A couple of times I even got to sip peach brandy and Sprite. There'd be a St. Louis Cardinals game on the radio, with Jack Buck calling the play-by-play in his Beechwood-aged growl. The store's shabby green carpet would become the Astroturf of Busch Stadium and I'd drop into my batting stance, belting imaginary home runs before a sellout crowd of liquor bottles. Years later, Dad told me about the night the carnies came in from the county fair. They spread out and combed the aisles while their leader, a little guy, approached the counter. He smiled and made small talk, making sure my dad saw the pistol tucked under his jacket, and a minute later they went clinking out the door.

5   Besides a steady dose of local crime, there was always the tingle of long-range danger. Paducah lies inside the radius of the New Madrid fault, where a massive earthquake is waiting to happen. It's also home to a uranium enrichment plant that was built in the 1950s. In the last years of the Cold War, I took a perverse civic pride in knowing our little community was a strategic target for Soviet nukes. Get your kicks where you can find them in Paducah.

6   By the time I reached high school in the mid-1980s, downtown was deader than Speedy, and the only action for teenagers was at the sprawling Kentucky Oaks Mall, where millions of purchases have been sealed with a down-home *Thay-en kyeew!* On Friday and Saturday nights, my friends and I would play video games and roam the mall's concourses until closing time. After that, there wasn't much to do but grind down the clock and the fuel gauge, looking for girls and alcohol.

7   I left after high school, about twenty years ago, and the census says I've had plenty of company. But even with a dwindling population, Paducah shows signs of life. Each year the country's largest quilt show draws 35,000 visitors, doubling the population for a week. Others come to browse the art galleries or to pull slots at the riverboat casino.

8   I go back a few times a year to visit my family. The drive from Chicago is flat and featureless, six hours of classic rock blocks and mental time-and-distance problems until I cross the Ohio River and the sign luminesces in my headlights, welcoming me back to the commonwealth of Kentucky. I pull off Interstate 24 at the second exit, a cluster of chain restaurants and cheap tobacco outlets. One more song and I'll be home.

El Hoyo

Mario Suárez

1   From the center of downtown Tucson the ground slopes gently away to Main Street, drops a few feet, and then rolls to the banks of the Santa Cruz River. Here lies the section of the city known as El Hoyo. Why it is called El Hoyo is not very clear. In no sense is it a hole as its name would imply; it is simply the river's immediate valley. Its inhabitants are chicanos who raise hell on Saturday night and listen to Padre Estanislao on Sunday morning. While the term chicano is the short way of saying Mexicano, it is not restricted to the paisanos who came from old Mexico with the territory or the last famine to work for the railroad, labor, sing, and go on relief. Chicano is the easy way of referring to everybody. Pablo Gutíerrez married the Chinese grocer's daughter and now runs a meat department; his sons are chicanos. So are the sons of Killer Jones who threw a fight in Harlem and fled to El Hoyo to marry Cristina Mendez. And so are all of them. However, it is doubtful that all these spiritual sons of Mexico live in El Hoyo because they love each other—many fight and bicker constantly. It is doubtful they live in El Hoyo because of its scenic beauty—it is everything but beautiful. Its houses are simple affairs of unplastered adobe, wood, and abandoned car parts. Its narrow streets are mostly clearings which have, in time, acquired names. Except for some tall trees which nobody has ever cared to identify, nurse, or destroy, the main things known to grow in the general area are weeds, garbage piles, dark-eyed chavalos, and dogs. And it is doubtful that the chicanos live in El Hoyo because it is safe—many times the Santa Cruz has risen and inundated the area.

2   In other respects living in El Hoyo has its advantages. If one is born with weakness for acquiring bills, El Hoyo is where the collectors are less likely to find you. If one has acquired the habit of listening to Octavio Perea's Mexican Hour in the wee hours of the morning with the radio on at full blast, El Hoyo is where you are less likely to be reported to the authorities. Besides, Perea is very popular and sooner or later to everyone "Smoke in the Eyes" is dedicated between the pinto beans and white flour commercials. If one, for any reason whatever, comes on an extended period of hard times, where, if not in El Hoyo, are the neighbors more willing to offer solace? When Teofila Malacara's house burned to the ground with all her belongings and two children, a benevolent gentleman carried through the gesture that made tolerable her burden. He made a list of 500 names and solicited from each a dollar. At the end of a month he turned over to the tearful but grateful señora $100 in cold cash and then accompanied her on a short vacation. When the new manager of a local store decided that no more chicanas were to work behind the counters, it was the chicanos of El Hoyo who, on taking their individually small but collectively great buying power elsewhere, drove the manager out and the girls returned to their jobs. When the Mexican Army was en route to Baja California and the chicanos found out that the enlisted men ate only at infrequent intervals, it was El Hoyo's chicanos who crusaded across town with pots of beans and trays of tortillas to meet the train. When someone gets married, celebrating is not restricted to the immediate friends of the couple. Everybody is invited. Anything calls for a celebration and a celebration calls for anything. On Memorial Day there are no less than half a dozen good fights at the Riverside Dance Hall. On Mexican Independence Day more than one flag is sworn allegiance to amid cheers for the queen.

3   And El Hoyo is something more. It is this something more which brought Felipe Suárez back from the wars after having killed a score of Japanese with his body resembling a patchwork quilt to marry Julia Armijo. It brought Joe Zepeda, a gunner,…back to compose boleros. He has a metal plate for a skull. Perhaps El Hoyo is proof that those people exist, and perhaps exist best, who have as yet failed to observe the more popular modes of human conduct. Perhaps the humble appearance of El Hoyo justifies the indifferent shrug of those made aware of its existence. Perhaps El Hoyo's simplicity motivates an occasional chicano to move away from its narrow streets, babbling comadres and shrieking children to deny

the bloodwell from which he springs and to claim the blood of a conquistador while his hair is straight and his face beardless. Yet El Hoyo is not an outpost of a few families against the world. It fights for no causes except those which soothe its immediate angers. It laughs and cries with the same amount of passion in times of plenty and of want.

4   Perhaps El Hoyo, its inhabitants, and its essence can best be explained by telling a bit about a dish called capirotada. Its origin is uncertain. But, according to the time and the circumstance, it is made of old, new or hard bread. It is softened with water and then cooked with peanuts, raisins, onions, cheese, and panocha. It is fired with sherry wine. Then it is served hot, cold, or just "on the weather" as they say in El Hoyo. The Sermeños like it one way, the Garcias another, and the Ortegas still another. While it might differ greatly from one home to another, nevertheless it is still capirotada. And so it is with El Hoyo's chicanos. While being divided from within and from without, like the capirotada, they remain chicanos.

ON FREEDOM, CENSORSHIP, AND EDUCATION ● ● ● ●

For the past 27 years, the last week in September has been declared Banned Books Week, an event sponsored by the American Library Association along with a host of other organizations including the American Booksellers Association, American Society of Journalists and Authors, and National Association of College Stores among them. To look at the Library Association's list of top 100 books banned or challenged is to see a lot of famous names. But censorship doesn't stop there. At a time when the Columbine and Virginia Tech shootings are still fresh memories, school and university authorities are understandably wary, a wariness that carries over to the rights of students, faculty members, and writers: Who or what might be "dangerous"? What may offend? The three essays included here present some answers and together provide varied perspectives on different aspects of censorship: Ursula Le Guin writes about a proposed banning of her book, Anna Quindlen tells of the mangling of her prose, and Michael Chabon speaks out on behalf of students.

Ursula Le Guin's name is familiar to anyone who reads science fiction—notably *The Left Hand of Darkness* (1969), the six *Earthsea* novels—though she also writes poetry, children's books, short stories, screenplays, fantasy, young adult novels, and essays. Put all those genres together, and the result is over 50 books. She has been awarded almost as many prizes and honors, among them the National Book Award, five Hugo Awards for science fiction, five Nebula Awards for science fiction/fantasy, and many, many more. Her most recent novel takes the reader to Virgil's Italy before the founding of Rome and into the mind and times of Lavinia, Aeneas' second wife whose name is the title of the novel (2008). But it's the reception of Le Guin's novel *The Lathe of Heaven* (1971) that prompted her to write the essay that follows. It was written originally for the "Forum" section of the newspaper *The Oregonian* in May 1984 and has been reprinted in her collection *Dancing at the Edge of the World* (1989).

Anna Quindlen started her career as a journalist, first as a reporter for *The New York Times,* moving on to become the *Times'* deputy metropolitan editor and then columnist, winning a Pulitzer Prize for her commentary in 1992. Since that time, essays from the column she wrote for *Newsweek* have been collected and published and she has concentrated on writing novels. Quindlen has written more than 14 books, including two for children, and is perhaps the only person to hit the *Times'* best-seller list in three categories—fiction, nonfiction, and self-help. Her essay "With a No. 2 Pencil, Delete" first appeared in June 2002 and is reprinted in her collection *Loud and Clear* (2005).

Like Ursula Le Guin, Michael Chabon has been honored with a Hugo Award and Nebula Award, both for his most recent novel *The Yiddish Policeman's Union* (2007), an imaginative comic noir mystery/thriller. Chabon's first novel *The Mysteries of Pittsburgh* (1988) was written for his master's degree in creative writing at the University of California at Irvine, and his list of publications suggests he hasn't stopped writing since. All told, he has published seven novels, two short story collections, and *Maps and Legends* (2008), a compilation of essays. His novel *The Amazing Adventures of Kavalier & Clay* (2000) received a Pulitzer Prize and reflects his off-beat interest in comic books, a subject he knows something about—he has written for DC Comics and coauthored the story for *Spider-Man 2*. He is also involved in the screen version of *The Amazing Adventures of Kavalier & Clay,* that came out in 2009. The piece that follows appeared as an op-ed in the April 13, 2004, *New York Times.*

Whose Lathe?

Ursula Le Guin

1   In a small town near Portland late this spring, a novel, *The Lathe of Heaven,* was the subject of a hearing concerning its suitability for use in a senior-high-school literature class. I took a lively interest in the outcome, because I wrote the novel.

2   The case against the book was presented first. The man who was asking that it be withdrawn stated his objections to the following elements in the book: fuzzy thinking and poor sentence structure; a mention of homosexuality; a character who keeps a flask of brandy in her purse, and who remarks that her mother did not love her. (It seemed curious to me that he did not mention the fact that this same character is a Black woman whose lover/husband is a White man. I had the feeling that this was really what he hated in the book, and that he was afraid to say so; but that was only my feeling.)

3   He also took exception to what he described as the author's advocacy of non-Christian religions and/or of non-separation of Church and State (his arguments on this point, or these points, were not clear to me).

4   Finally, during discussion, he compared the book to junk food, apparently because it was science fiction.

5   The English Department of the school then presented a carefully prepared, spirited defense of the book, including statements by students who had read it. Some liked it, some didn't like it, most objected to having it, or any other book, banned.

6   In discussion, teachers pointed out that since it is the policy of the Washougal School District to assign an alternative book to any student who objects on any grounds to reading an assigned one, the attempt to prevent a whole class from reading a book was an attempt to change policy, replacing free choice by censorship.

7   When the Instructional Materials Committee of the district voted on the motion to ban the book, the motion was defeated twenty votes to five. The hearing was public and was conducted in the most open and democratic fashion. I did not speak, as I felt the teachers and students had spoken eloquently for me.

8   Crankish attacks on the freedom to read are common at present. When backed and coordinated by organized groups, they become sinister. In this case, I saw something going on that worried me a

good deal because it did not seem to be coming from an outside pressure group, but from elements of the educational establishment itself: this was the movement to change policy radically by instituting, or "clarifying," guidelines or criteria for the selection/ elimination of books used in the schools. The motion on which this committee of the school district voted was actually that the book be withdrawn *"while guidelines and policies for the district are worked out."* Those guidelines and policies were the real goal, I think, of the motion.

9   Guidelines? That sounds dull. Innocent. Useful. Of course we have to be sure about the kinds of books we want our kids to read in school. Don't we?

10   Well, do we? The dangerous vagueness of the term "guidelines and policies for the district" slides right past such questions as: Who are "we"? Who decides what the children read? Does "we" include you? Me? Teachers? Librarians? Students? Are fifteen-to-eighteen-year-olds ever "we," or are they always "they"?

11   And what are the guidelines to be? On what criteria or doctrines are they to be based?

12   The people concerned with schools in Oregon try, with ever decreasing budgets, to provide good, sound food in the school cafeterias, knowing that for some students that's the only real meal they get. They try, with ever decreasing budgets, to provide beautiful, intelligent books in classes and school libraries, knowing that for many students those are the only books they read. To provide the best: everyone agrees on that (even the people who vote against school levies). But we don't and we can't agree on what books are the best. And therefore what is vital is that we provide variety, abundance, plenty—not books that reflect one body of opinion or doctrine, not books that one group or sect thinks good, but the broadest, richest range of intellectual and artistic material possible.

13   Nobody is forced to read any of it. There is that very important right to refuse and choose an alternative.

14   When a bad apple turns up, it can be taken out of the barrel on a case-by-case, book-by-book basis—investigated, defended, prosecuted, and judged, as in the hearing on my *Lathe of Heaven.** But

---

*Currently (1987) a textbook written for Oregon schools called *Let's Oregonize* is going through this process on the state level. The arguments against it were brought by environmentalists and others who found it tendentious and biased towards certain industries and interests. From my point of view it certainly sounds like a rather bad apple. But it is getting a scrupulously fair hearing.

this can't be done wholesale by using "guidelines," instructions for censorship. There is no such thing as a moral filter that lets good books through and keeps bad books out. Such criteria of "goodness" and "badness" are a moralist's dream but a democrat's nightmare.

15   Censorship, here or in Russia or wherever, is absolutely anti-democratic and elitist. The censor says: You don't know enough to choose, but we do, so you will read what we choose for you and nothing else. The democrat says: The process of learning is that of learning how to choose. Freedom isn't given, it's earned. Read, learn, and earn it.

16   I fear censorship in this Uriah Heepish guise of "protecting our children," "stricter criteria," "moral guidance," "a more definite policy," and so on. I hope administrators, teachers, librarians, parents, and students will resist it. Its advocates are people willing to treat others not only as if they were not free but were not even worthy of freedom.

With a No. 2 Pencil, Delete

Anna Quindlen

1   You can imagine how honored I was to learn that my work was going to be mangled for the sake of standardized testing. I got the word just after a vigilant parent had discovered that state-wide English tests in New York had included excerpts from literary writers edited so heavily and so nonsensically that the work had essentially lost all meaning. Isaac Bashevis Singer, Annie Dillard, even Chekhov—the pool of those singled out for red-penciling by bureaucrats was a distinguished one, and I found myself a little disappointed that I had not been turned into reading comp pablum.

2   But the State of Georgia was more accommodating. The folks at the Educational Testing Service, one of America's most powerful monopolies and the entity responsible for the SATs, were preparing something called the Georgia End-of-Course Tests and wanted to use an excerpt from a book I'd written called *How Reading Changed My Life*.

3   In the sentence that read "The Sumerians first used the written word to make laundry lists, to keep track of cows and slaves and household goods," the words "and slaves" had been deleted.

4   And in the sentence "And soon publishers had the means, and the will, to publish anything—cookbooks, broadsides, newspapers, novels, poetry, pornography, picture books for children" someone had drawn a black line through the word "pornography" and written "EDIT!" in the margin.

5   I got off easy. In the Singer excerpt on the Regents exam, which was about growing up a Jew in prewar Poland, all references to Jews and Poles were excised. Annie Dillard's essay about being the only white child in a library in the black section of town became almost unintelligible after all references to race were obliterated. The New York State Education Department's overheated guidelines are written so broadly that only the words "the" and "but" seem safe. "Does the material require the parent, teacher or examinee to support a position that is contrary to their religious beliefs or teaching?" the guidelines ask. "Does the material assume that the examinee has experience with a certain type of family structure?" As Jeanne Heifetz, an opponent of the required Regents exams who uncovered the editing, wrote, "Almost no piece of writing emerges from this process unscathed." Nor could any except the most homogenized piece of pap about Cape Cod tide pools.

6   "The words 'slave' and 'pornography' deal with controversial issues that could cause an emotional reaction in some students that could distract them from the test and affect their performance," wrote the ETS supernumerary snipping at my sentences.

7   This was in a week when students likely heard of another suicide bomber in Israel, the gunpoint abduction of a teenager in Utah, and the arrest of a rap star for appearing on videotape having sex with underage girls. And they're going to be distracted by the words "slaves" and "pornography"?

8   That's the saddest thing here: not the betrayal of writers by bureaucrats, but the betrayal of kids by educators. Everyone complains that teenagers don't read enough good stuff; the lists of banned books in school libraries are thick with quality, with Steinbeck and Margaret Atwood. Everyone complains that students are not intellectually engaged; controversial issues are excised from classroom discussions and those staggeringly boring textbooks. Everyone complains that kids are not excited about school; the point of school increasingly seems to be mindless and incessant testing that doesn't even have the grace to be mildly interesting. By the standards of the Regents tests, *The Catcher in the Rye* is unacceptable. ("Does the material require a student to take a position that challenges parental authority?") So is *To Kill a Mockingbird* and *The Merchant of Venice*.

9   Here is the most shocking question among the New York State Education Department guidelines: "Does the material assume values not shared by all test takers?" There is no book worth reading, no poem worth writing, no essay worth analyzing, that assumes the same values for all. That sentence is the death of intellectual engagement.

10   The education officials in New York have now backed down from their cut-and-paste-without-permission position, faced with an angry mob of distinguished writers. But what do the kids learn from this? That the written word doesn't really matter much, that it can be weakened at will. That no one trusts a student to understand that variations in opinion and background are both objectively interesting and intellectually challenging. That some of the most powerful people involved in their education have reduced them to the lowest common denominator.

11   I like kids, have a brace of them around here, and I'm damned (EDIT!) if I'm going to abet some skewed adult vision of their febrile emotional state. Unlike those in New York, the people preparing tests for the State of Georgia at least had the common courtesy to ask permission to mess with my stuff. I declined. It's not that one or two words are particularly precious; I have hacked away at my own sentences to get them to fit tidily in this space. But not to make pablum for students who deserve something tastier.

Solitude and the Fortresses of Youth

Michael Chabon

1   Earlier this month my local paper, the *San Francisco Chronicle,* reported that a college student had been expelled from art school here for submitting a story "rife with gruesome details about sexual torture, dismemberment and bloodlust" to his creative writing class. The instructor, a poet named Jan Richman, subsequently found herself out of a job. The university chose not to explain its failure to renew Ms. Richman's contract, but she intimated that she was being punished for having set the tone for the class by assigning a well-regarded if disturbing short story by the MacArthur-winning novelist David Foster Wallace, "Girl with Curious Hair." Ms. Richman had been troubled enough by the student's work to report it to her superiors in the first place, in spite of the fact that it was not, according to the *Chronicle,* "the first serial-killer story she had read in her six semesters on the faculty at the Academy of Art University."

2   Homicide inspectors were called in; a criminal profiler went to work on the student. The officers found no evidence of wrongdoing. The unnamed student had made no threat; his behavior was not considered suspicious. In the end, no criminal charges were brought.

3   In this regard, the San Francisco case differs from other incidents in California, and around the country, in which students, unlucky enough to have as literary precursor the Columbine mass-murderer Dylan Klebold, have found themselves expelled, even prosecuted and convicted on criminal charges, because of the violence depicted in their stories and poems. The threat posed by these prosecutions to civil liberties, to the First Amendment rights of our young people, is grave enough. But as a writer, a parent and a former teenager, I see the workings of something more iniquitous: not merely the denial of teenagers' rights in the name of their own protection, but the denial of their humanity in the name of preserving their innocence.

4   It is in the nature of a teenager to want to destroy. The destructive impulse is universal among children of all ages, rises to a peak of vividness, ingenuity and fascination in adolescence, and thereafter

never entirely goes away. Violence and hatred, and the fear of our own inability to control them in ourselves, are a fundamental part of our birthright, along with altruism, creativity, tenderness, pity and love. It therefore requires an immense act of hypocrisy to stigmatize our young adults and teenagers as agents of deviance and disorder. It requires a policy of dishonesty about and blindness to our own histories, as a species, as a nation, and as individuals who were troubled as teenagers, and who will always be troubled, by the same dark impulses. It also requires that favorite tool of the hypocritical, dishonest and fearful: the suppression of constitutional rights.

5   We justly celebrate the ideals enshrined in the Bill of Rights, but it is also a profoundly disillusioned document, in the best sense of that adjective. It stipulates all the worst impulses of humanity: toward repression, brutality, intolerance and fear. It couples an unbridled faith in the individual human being, redeemed time and again by his or her singular capacity for tenderness, pity and all the rest, with a profound disenchantment about groups of human beings acting as governments, court systems, armies, state religions and bureaucracies, unchecked by the sting of individual conscience and only belatedly if ever capable of anything resembling redemption.

6   In this light the Bill of Rights can be read as a classic expression of the teenage spirit: a powerful imagination reacting to a history of overwhelming institutional repression, hypocrisy, chicanery and weakness. It is a document written by men who, like teenagers, knew their enemy intimately, and saw in themselves all the potential they possessed to one day become him. We tend to view idealism and cynicism as opposites, when in fact neither possesses any merit or power unless tempered by, fused with, the other. The Bill of Rights is the fruit of that kind of fusion; so is the teenage imagination.

7   The imagination of teenagers is often—I'm tempted to say always—the only sure capital they possess apart from the love of their parents, which is a force far beyond their capacity to comprehend or control. During my own adolescence, my imagination, the kingdom inside my own skull, was my sole source of refuge, my fortress of solitude, at times my prison. But a fortress requires a constant line of supply; those who take refuge in attics and cellars require the unceasing aid of confederates; prisoners need advocates, escape plans, or simply a window that gives onto the sky.

8   Like all teenagers, I provisioned my garrison with art: books, movies, music, comic books, television, role-playing games. My secret

confederates were the works of Monty Python, H. P. Lovecraft, the cartoonist Vaughan Bodé, and the Ramones, among many others; they kept me watered and fed. They baked files into cakes and, on occasion, for a wondrous moment, made the walls of my prison disappear. Given their nature as human creations, as artifacts and devices of human nature, some of the provisions I consumed were bound to be of a dark, violent, even bloody and horrifying nature; otherwise I would not have cared for them. Tales and displays of violence, blood and horror rang true, answered a need, on some deep, angry level that maybe only those with scant power or capital, regardless of their age, can understand.

9   It was not long before I began to write: stories, poems, snatches of autobiographical jazz. Often I imitated the work of my confederates: stories of human beings in the most extreme situations and states of emotion—horror stories; accounts of madness and despair. In part—let's say in large part, if that's what it takes to entitle the writings of teenagers to unqualified protection under the First Amendment—this was about expression. I was writing what I felt, what I believed, wished for, raged against, hoped and dreaded. But the main reason I wrote stories—and the reason that I keep on writing them today—was not to express myself. I started to write because once it had been nourished, stoked and liberated by those secret confederates, I could not hold back the force of my imagination. I had been freed, and I felt that it was now up to me to do the same for somebody else, somewhere, trapped in his or her own lonely tower.

10   We don't want teenagers to write violent poems, horrifying stories, explicit lyrics and rhymes; they're ugly, in precisely the way that we are ugly, and out of protectiveness and hypocrisy, even out of pity and love and tenderness, we try to force young people to be innocent of everything but the effects of that ugliness. And so we censor the art they consume and produce, and prosecute and suspend and expel them, and when, once in a great while, a teenager reaches for an easy gun and shoots somebody or himself, we tell ourselves that if we had only censored his journals and curtailed his music and video games, that awful burst of final ugliness could surely have been prevented. As if art caused the ugliness, when of course all it can ever do is reflect and, perhaps, attempt to explain it.

11   Let teenagers languish, therefore, in their sense of isolation, without outlet or nourishment, bereft of the only thing that makes it all

bearable: knowing that somebody else has felt the way that you feel, has faced it, run from it, rued it, lamented it and transformed it into art; has been there, and returned, and lived, for the only good reason we have: to tell the tale. How confident we shall be, once we have done this, of never encountering the ugliness again! How happy our children will be, and how brave, and how safe!

CREDITS

262   *Credits*

Page 106: "Baby Blues" used with the permission of the Baby Blues Partnership, King Features Syndicate and the Cartoonist Group. All rights reserved.

Page 115: "Living on Tokyo Time" by Lynnika Butler, originally published in the *Salt Journal*, Fall 2001. Used by permission of the author.

Page 118: "Who's Watching? Reality TV and Sports" (originally titled "Commentary: Reality TV Affecting Sports Viewership") by Frank Deford on National Public Radio, June 2, 2004. Used by permission of the author.

Page 121: "Playing House" by Denise Leight Comeau from *Becoming Writers*, Spring 2001. Used by permission of the author.

Page 125: "5 Reasons Why E-Books Aren't There Yet" by John C. Abell from *WIRED*, June 2011. Used by permission of Conde Nast.

Page 130: "Dustin" used with the permission of the Steve Kelley and Jeff Parker, King Features Syndicate and the Cartoonist Group. All rights reserved.

Page 136: "Watching the Clock: A Sport All Its Own" by Frank Deford on National Public Radio, March 4, 2009. Used by permission of the author.

Page 139: "What Are the Different Types of Social Network Applications?" by G. Wiesen from *WISEGEEK*. Used by permission.

Page 142: "The Plot Against the People" by Russell Baker from the *New York Times*, June 18, 1968, ©1968 The New York Times. All rights reserved. Used by permission.

Page 146: "Desert Religions" by Richard Rodriguez. Copyright © 2002 by Richard Rodriguez. Originally aired on the NewsHour with Jim Lehrer (PBS) on July 8, 2002. Reprinted by permission of Georges Borchardt, Inc., on behalf of the author.

Page 150: @2003 M Twohy

Page 157: "A Woman's Place" by Naomi Wolf from the *New York Times*, May 31, 1992. Copyright © 1992 by Naomi Wolf. Reprinted by permission of the author.

Page 162: "Runner" by Laura McLaurin. Used by permission of the author.

Page 165: "Independence Day", copyright © 2000 by Dave Barry, from *Dave Barry Is Not Taking This Sitting Down* by Dave Barry. Used by permission of Crown Publishers, a division of Random House, Inc.

Page 169: "Becoming a Sanvicentena: Five Stages" by Kate Hopper. Originally appeared in *Brevity*, Issue 32. Reprinted by permission of the author.

Page 179: "Black Men and Public Spaces" by Brent Staples. Reprinted by permission of the author

Page 184: "Forget A's, B's and C's—What Students Need Is More Zzzz's" by Mary Carskadon from the *Chronicle of Higher Education*, November 20, 2011. Copyright © 2011 by Mary Carskadon. Reprinted by permission of the author.

Page 188: "When Music Heals Body and Soul," originally published in *Parade*, March 31, 2002, by Oliver Sacks, M.D. Copyright ©2002 by Oliver Sacks, M.D., used by permission of The Wylie Agency.

Page 193: "Retreat into the iWorld (originally titled" Society Is Dead: We Have Retreated into the iWorld") by Andrew Sullivan from the *Sunday Times of London*, February 20, 2005. Used by permission of NI Syndication Ltd.

Page 198: "Candorville" used with the permission of the Darrin Bell, the Washington Post Writers Group and the Cartoonist Group. All rights reserved.

Page 209: "Dance, Dance, Revolution" by Barbara Ehrenreich from the *New York Times*, June 3, 2007, ©2007 The New York Times. Used by permission.

Page 213: "Freshman Specimen" by Patricia Williams reprinted with permission from *The Nation*, September 9, 2010. *www.thenation.com*

Page 217: "On Guest Workers and the U.S. Heritage" (originally titled "Guest worker idea threatens U.S. heritage") by Jay Bookman from the *Atlanta Journal Constitution*, May 19, 2003. Reproduced with permission of *Atlanta Journal-Constitution* conveyed through Copyright Clearance Center, Inc.

Page 221: "We Don't Need 'Guest Workers'" by Robert J. Samuelson from *The Washington Post*, March 22, 2006, copyright © 2006 The Washington Post. Used by permission.

Page 225: "Candorville" used with the permission of the Darrin Bell, the Washington Post Writers Group and the Cartoonist Group. All rights reserved.

Page 227: "When Cowboys Cry" by Sandra Steingraber from *Orion Magazine*, May/June 2011. Copyright © 2011 by Sandra Steingraber. Used by permission of the author.

Page 232: "Protecting the Environment" Used by permission of Pennsylvania Independent Oil and Gas Association (PIOGA).

Page 236: "Drilling Down Deep" Reprinted by permission of Mindy S. Lubber.

Page 240: Signe Wilkinson Editorial Cartoon used with the permission of Signe Wilkinson, the Washington Post Writers Group and the Cartoonist Group. All rights reserved.

Page 245: "Life in 'My Town'" by John Wideman from PBS NewsHour April 18, 2008. Reprinted by permission of the author.

Page 246: "Paducah Kentucky" by Stuart Overlin, originally published in *Brevity*, Issue 35. Used by permission of the author.

Page 248: "El Hoyo" by Mario Suarez from *Arizona Quarterly*, 3.2 (1947). Reprinted by permission of the Regents of the University of Arizona.

Page 253: "Whose Lathe?" from *Dancing at the Edge of The World* by Ursula LeGuin. Copyright © 1989 by Ursula K. LeGuin. Used by permission of Grove/Atlantic, Inc.

Page 254: "With a No. 2 Pencil, Delete" from *Loud and Clear* by Anna Quindlen. Copyright © 2005 by Anna Quindlen. Reprinted by permission of International Creative Management, Inc.

Page 257: "Solitude and the Fortress of Youth" by Michael Chabon from the *New York Times*, April 13, 2004, ©2004 The New York Times. All rights reserved. Used by permission and protected by the Copyright Laws of the United States. The printing, copying, redistribution, or retransmission of this Content without express written permission is prohibited.

INDEX